SHARIAH
THE THREAT TO AMERICA

AN EXERCISE IN COMPETITIVE ANALYSIS
REPORT OF TEAM B II

SHARIAHTHETHREAT.COM

Copyright © 2010 Center for Security Policy
October 2010 Edition

Shariah: The Threat to America
An Exercise in Competitive Analysis—Report of Team B II
is published in the United States by the Center for Security Policy
Press, a division of the Center for Security Policy.

THE CENTER FOR SECURITY POLICY
1901 Pennsylvania Avenue, Suite 201
Washington, DC 20006
Phone: (202) 835-9077
Email: info@securefreedom.org
For more information, please see securefreedom.org

ISBN 978-0-9822947-6-5

Book design by David Reaboi.

PREFACE

This study is the result of months of analysis, discussion and drafting by a group of top security policy experts concerned with the preeminent totalitarian threat of our time: the legal-political-military doctrine known within Islam as *shariah*. It is designed to provide a comprehensive and articulate "second opinion" on the official characterizations and assessments of this threat as put forth by the United States government.

The authors, under the sponsorship of the Center for Security Policy, have modeled this work on an earlier "exercise in competitive analysis" which came to be known as the "Team B" Report. That 1976 document challenged the then-prevailing official U.S. government intelligence ("Team A") estimates of the intentions and offensive capabilities of the Soviet Union and the policy known as *détente* that such estimates ostensibly justified.

Unlike its predecessor, which a group of independent security policy professionals conducted at the request and under the sponsorship of the Director of Central Intelligence, George H.W. Bush, the present Team B II report is based entirely on unclassified, readily available sources. As with the original Team B analysis, however, this study challenges the assumptions underpinning the official line in the conflict with today's totalitarian threat, which is currently euphemistically described as "violent extremism," and the policies of co-existence, accommodation and submission that are rooted in those assumptions.

Special thanks are due Clare Lopez, whose efforts to transform the Team B II members' various individual contributions into a seamless and powerful report are deeply appreciated.

MEMBERS OF TEAM B II

Team Leaders

LIEUTENANT GENERAL WILLIAM G. "JERRY" BOYKIN
*US Army (Ret.), former Deputy Undersecretary of
Defense for Intelligence*

LIEUTENANT GENERAL HARRY EDWARD SOYSTER
US Army (Ret.), former Director, Defense Intelligence Agency

Associates

CHRISTINE BRIM
Chief Operating Officer, Center for Security Policy

AMBASSADOR HENRY COOPER
*former Chief Negotiator, Defense and Space Talks, former Director,
Strategic Defense Initiative*

STEPHEN C. COUGHLIN, ESQ.
*Major (Res.) USA, former Senior Consultant, Office of the Joint Chiefs
of Staff*

MICHAEL DEL ROSSO
Senior Fellow, Claremont Institute and Center for Security Policy

FRANK J. GAFFNEY, JR.
*former Assistant Secretary of Defense for International Security Policy
(Acting), President, Center for Security Policy*

JOHN GUANDOLO
*former Special Agent, Counter-Terrorism Division, Federal Bureau of
Investigation*

BRIAN KENNEDY
President, Claremont Institute

CLARE M. LOPEZ
Senior Fellow, Center for Security Policy

ADMIRAL JAMES A. "ACE" LYONS
US Navy (Ret.), former Commander-in-Chief, Pacific Fleet

ANDREW C. MCCARTHY
former Chief Assistant U.S. Attorney; Senior Fellow, National Review Institute; Contributing Editor, National Review

PATRICK POOLE
Consultant to the military and law enforcement on anti-terrorism issues

JOSEPH E. SCHMITZ
former Inspector General, Department of Defense

TOM TRENTO
Executive Director, Florida Security Council

J. MICHAEL WALLER
Annenberg Professor of International Communication, Institute of World Politics, and Vice President for Information Operations, Center for Security Policy

DIANA WEST
author and columnist

R. JAMES WOOLSEY
former Director of Central Intelligence

DAVID YERUSHALMI, ESQ.
General Counsel to the Center for Security Policy

CONTENTS

PART I :
THE THREAT POSED BY SHARIAH

PART II :
THE UNITED STATES AND SHARIAH

INTRODUCTION

In 1976, the then-Director of Central Intelligence, George H. W. Bush, commissioned an "Experiment in Competitive Analysis." Its purpose was to expose to critical scrutiny the assumptions and factual basis underpinning the official assessment of the totalitarian ideology that confronted America at the time: Soviet Communism. That official assessment was rooted in the belief that, through a policy of engagement known as *détente*, the United States and the USSR could not only avoid horrifically destructive conflicts, but could peacefully coexist permanently.

DCI Bush invited a group of known skeptics about *détente* to review the classified National Intelligence Estimates and other data concerning Soviet objectives, intentions and present and future military capabilities. The object was to provide an informed second opinion on the U.S. policy toward the Kremlin that was, ostensibly, warranted in light of such information. The conclusions of this experimental initiative – which came to be known popularly as the "Team B" study – differed sharply from those of "Team A": the Ford Administration and the intelligence community.

Team B found that the Soviet Union was, pursuant to its ideology, determined to secure the defeat of the United States and its allies and the realization of the worldwide triumph of Soviet Communism. As a result Team B found that not only was *détente* unlikely to succeed the way the U.S. government had envisioned, but the U.S. national security posture and policies undertaken in its pursuit were exposing the nation to grave danger.

The effect of this authoritative alternative view was profound. Among others, former California Governor Ronald Reagan used the thrust of its findings to challenge *détente* and those in public office who supported this doctrine. Drawing on the thinking of Team B with regard to national security issues, Reagan nearly defeated President Gerald Ford's bid for reelection in the 1976 primaries. Four years later, Reagan successfully opposed President Jimmy Carter, with their disagreement over the latter's *détentist* foreign and defense policies towards Moscow featuring prominently in the former's victory.

Most importantly, as President, Ronald Reagan drew on the work of Team B as an intellectual foundation for his strategy for destroying the Soviet Union and discrediting its ideology – a feat begun during his tenure and finally accomplished, thanks to his implementation of that strategy, several years after he left office.

THE CONTEMPORARY THREAT

Today, the United States faces what is, if anything, an even more insidious ideological threat: the totalitarian socio-political doctrine that Islam calls shariah. Translated as "the path," shariah is a comprehensive legal and political framework. Though it certainly has spiritual elements, it would be a mistake to think of shariah as a "religious" code in the Western sense because it seeks to regulate all manner of behavior in the secular sphere – economic, social, military, legal and political.

Shariah is the crucial fault line of Islam's internecine struggle. On one side of the divide are Muslim reformers and authentic moderates – figures like Abdurrahman Wahid, the late president of Indonesia and leader of the world's largest libertarian

2

Muslim organization, *Nahdlatul Ulama* – whose members espouse the Enlightenment's embrace of reason and, in particular, its separation of the spiritual and secular realms. On this side of the divide, shariah is a reference point for a Muslim's personal conduct, not a corpus to be imposed on the life of a pluralistic society.

By contrast, the other side of the divide is dominated by Muslim supremacists, often called Islamists. Like erstwhile proponents of Communism and Nazism, these supremacists – some terrorists, others employing stealthier means – seek to impose a totalitarian regime: a global totalitarian system cloaked as an Islamic State and called a caliphate. On that side of the divide, which is the focus of the present study, shariah is an immutable, compulsory system that Muslims are obliged to install and the world required to adopt, the failure to do so being deemed a damnable offence against Allah. For these ideologues, shariah is not a private matter. Adherents see the West as an obstacle to be overcome, not a culture and civilization to be embraced, or at least tolerated. It is impossible, they maintain, for alternative legal systems and forms of governments peacefully to coexist with the end-state they seek.

THE TEAM B II CONSENSUS

It is not within the scope of this study to solve the widely divergent estimates of the strength of these respective camps. The imperative driving this study is America's national security and, by extension, the security of its friends and allies.

Like their counterparts a generation ago, the members of Team B II collectively bring to this task decades of hands-on experience as security policy practitioners and analysts, much of it involving shariah's proponents of both the violent jihadist and pre-violent *dawa* stripes. They have distinguished backgrounds in national defense policy-making, military, intelligence, homeland security and law enforcement communities, in academia and in the war of ideas. Thanks to their expertise and dedication, this new report represents an authoritative, valuable and timely critique of the U.S. government's present policy towards shariah and its adherents, an assessment of the threat it entails and a call for a long-overdue course-correction. This report reflects consensus on the following significant points:

First, the shariah adherents who comprise the supremacist camp constitute a mainstream and dynamic movement in Islam. Importantly, that characterization does not speak to the question of whether this camp is or is not representative of the "true Islam." There are over a billion Muslims in the world, and their understandings about their belief system, as well as their practices with respect to it, vary. In light of this, there may not be a single "true Islam." If there is one, we do not presume to pronounce what it holds.

What cannot credibly be denied, however, is that:

  a. shariah is firmly rooted in Islam's doctrinal texts, and it is favored by influential Islamic commentators, institutions, and academic centers (for example, the faculty at al-Azhar University in Cairo, for centuries the seat of Sunni learning and jurisprudence);

  b. shariah has been, for over a half-century, lavishly financed and propagated by Islamic regimes (particularly Saudi Arabia and Iran), through the offices of disciplined international organizations (particularly the Muslim Brotherhood and the Organization of the Islamic Conference); and

  c. due to the fact that Islam lacks a central, universally recognized hierarchical authority (in contrast to, say, the Roman Catholic papacy), authentic Islamic moderates and reformers have an incredibly difficult task in endeavoring to delegitimize shariah in the community where it matters most: the world's Muslims.

Consequently, regardless of what percentage of the global Islamic population adheres or otherwise defers to shariah (and some persuasive polling indicates that percentage is high in many Islamic countries[1]), that segment is punching well above its weight. For that reason, proponents of an expansionist shariah present a serious threat to the United States even if we assume, for argument's sake, that hopeful pundits are correct in claiming that shariah adherent Islam is not the preponderant Muslim ideology.

A second point follows that it is vital to the national security of the United States, and to Western civilization at large, that we do what we can to empower Islam's *authentic* moderates and reformers. That cannot be done by following the failed strategy of fictionalizing the state of Islam in the vain hope that reality will, at some point, catch up to the benign fable. Empowering the condign elements of Islam requires a candid assessment, which acknowledges the strength of shariah – just as defeat of Twentieth Century totalitarian ideologies required an acknowledgment of, and respect for, their malevolent capabilities.

To do this, we must no longer allow those who mean to destroy our society by sabotaging it from within to camouflage themselves as "moderates."[2] The definition of *moderation* needs to be reset, to bore in on the shariah fault-line. Only by identifying those Muslims who wish to impose shariah can we succeed in marginalizing them.

As this study manifests, the shariah system is totalitarian. It imposes itself on all aspects of civil society and human life, both public and private. Anyone obliged actually to defend the proposition that shariah should be adopted here will find few takers and be properly seen for what they are – marginal and extremist fig-

5

ures. That, and only that, will strengthen true proponents of a moderate or reformist Islam that embraces freedom and equality.

Third, we have an obligation to protect our nation and our way of life regardless of the ultimate resolution of Islam's internal strife. We can do a far better job of empowering non-shariah-adherent Muslims, who are our natural allies, but we cannot win for them. They have to do that for themselves. Irrespective of whether they succeed in the formidable task of delegitimizing shariah globally, we must face it down in the United States, throughout the West and wherever on earth it launches violent or ideological offensives against us.

SHARIAH IS ANTI-CONSTITUTIONAL

If we are to face down shariah, we must understand what we are up against, not simply hope that dialogue and "engagement" will make the challenge go away. Those who today support shariah and the establishment of a global Islamic State (caliphate) are perforce supporting objectives that are incompatible with the U.S. Constitution, the civil rights the Constitution guarantees and the representative, accountable government it authorizes. In fact, shariah's pursuit in the United States is tantamount to sedition.

Whether pursued through the violent form of jihad (holy war) or stealthier practices that shariah Islamists often refer to as "*dawa*" (the "call to Islam"), shariah rejects fundamental premises of American society and values:

    a. the bedrock proposition that the governed have a right to make law for themselves;

    b. the republican democracy governed by the Constitution;

    c. freedom of conscience; individual liberty (including in matters of personal privacy and sexual preference);

d.   freedom of expression (including the liberty to analyze and criticize shariah);

e.   economic liberty (including private property);

f.   equal treatment under the law (including that of men and women, and of Muslims and non-Muslims);

g.   freedom from cruel and unusual punishments; an unequivocal condemnation of terrorism (i.e., one that is based on a common sense meaning of the term and does not rationalize barbarity as legitimate "resistance"); and

h.   an abiding commitment to deflate and resolve political controversies by the ordinary mechanisms of federalism and democracy, not wanton violence.

The subversion campaign known as "civilization jihad" must not be confused with, or tolerated as, a constitutionally protected form of religious practice. Its ambitions transcend what American law recognizes as the sacrosanct realm of private conscience and belief. It seeks to supplant our Constitution with its own totalitarian framework. In fact, we get this concept of civilization jihad from, among other sources, a document that was entered into evidence in the 2008 *United States v. Holy Land Foundation* terrorist finance trial titled the *An Explanatory Memorandum: On the General Strategic Goal for the Group*.[3]

The *Explanatory Memorandum* was written in 1991 by Mohamed Akram, a senior Hamas leader in the U.S. and a member of the Board of Directors for the Muslim Brotherhood in North America (MB, also known as the Ikhwan).[The Memorandum is reproduced in full as Appendix II of this report]

The document makes plain that the Islamic Movement is a MB effort, led by the Ikhwan in America.[4]   The *Explanatory Memorandum* goes on to explain that the "Movement" is a "settlement process" to establish itself inside the United States and, once established, to undertake a "grand jihad" characterized as a "civilization jihadist" mission that is likewise led by the Muslim Brotherhood.[5] Specifically, the document describes the "settlement process" as a "grand jihad in eliminating and destroying the Western civilization from within and 'sabotaging' its miserable house by their hands and the hands of the believers so that it is eliminated...."[6]

To put it simply, according to the Muslim Brotherhood, the civilization jihad is the "Settlement Process" and the "Settlement Process" is the mission of the "Islamic Movement." And that mission entails "eliminating and destroying" our way of life. Author Robert Spencer has popularized this concept with a term that captures both the character and deadly purpose of the Ikhwan's efforts in America: "stealth jihad."

LESSONS FROM THE COLD WAR

There is a loose analogy to the distinctions we made in the Cold War. America and its allies enjoyed a general unanimity that we needed to deal effectively with any potential violent aggression by the chief communist power, the Soviet Union, and we readily maintained a sizeable military force and alliances to that end. But we had more difficulty as a nation deciding how to deal with non-violent domestic communists under foreign control, such as the Communist Party USA (CPUSA) and the constellation of domestic and international front organizations under party control or Soviet ideological discipline. These tactically non-violent or pre-violent forces, like their violent comrades-in-arms, had as their objective the establishment of a world-wide dictatorship of the proletariat.

Congress, taking note of this objective even before the Cold War, at first tried to force agents of foreign powers to register as such with the Department of Justice, with the Foreign Agents Registration Act (FARA) of 1938. Later, in 1940, Congress attempted to make it illegal to be a communist in the U.S. by passing the Smith Act, which President Franklin D. Roosevelt signed into law. Congress enacted the McCarran-Walter Act (the 1952 Immigration and Nationality

Act), signed by President Harry S Truman, which authorized the exclusion and deportation of aliens on such ideological grounds as support for overthrowing the United States government. The government took a number of other steps with regard to domestic non-violent supporters of the proposition that our Constitution should be replaced by a dictatorship, including: being required to register with the government and forgo government service. In addition, their organization, the Communist Party of the United States of America was penetrated by the FBI. As a nation we made some mistakes in this process, but in the end it worked reasonably well to protect American democracy against Nazi and Soviet ideological penetration.

Beginning in the 1960s, however, the Supreme Court drastically reinterpreted the First Amendment, gradually extending the original guarantee of American citizens' right to engage in political speech, to include a constitutional protection to (a) subversive speech that could be construed as "advocacy," rather than incitement to imminent lawlessness, and (b) the speech of non-Americans. Bowing to elite opinion, which scoffed at fears of communist penetration of our government and institutions, Congress (in such legislation as the 1965 Immigration Act, the 1978 McGovern Amendment, the 1989 Moynihan-Frank Amendment, and the 1990 Immigration Act) gutted the statutory basis for excluding and deporting individuals based on ideological beliefs, regardless of their subversive tendencies – at least in the absence of demonstrable ties to terrorism, espionage or sabotage.

Let us assume, again for argument's sake, that there was some validity in the opinion elite's critique that anti-communism went too far – and set aside the fact that such an assumption requires overlooking post-Soviet revelations that have confirmed communist infiltrations. The prior experience would not mean the security precautions that sufficed to protect our nation from communism are sufficient to shield us from a totalitarian ideology cloaked in religious garb.

Such precautions are wholly inadequate for navigating a threat environment in which secretive foreign-sponsored international networks undermine our nation from within. That is especially the case where such networks can exploit the atmosphere of intimidation created by the tactics of their terrorist counterparts (including individual assassinations and mass-murder attacks on our homeland, and the mere threat of violence) in a modern technological age of instantaneous cross-continental communications and the increasing availability of mass-destruction weapons that allow ever fewer people to project ever more power.

MISSTEPS HAVE COMPOUNDED THE DANGER

As this report will demonstrate, there is plenty of blame to go around. The fact is that, under both political parties, the U.S. government has comprehensively failed to grasp the true nature of this enemy – an adversary that fights to reinstate the totalitarian Islamic caliphate and impose shariah globally. Indeed, under successive Democratic and Republican administrations, America's civilian and military leaders have too often focused single-mindedly on the kinetic terror tactics deployed by al Qaeda and its affiliates to the exclusion of the overarching supremacist ideology of shariah that animates them.

Our leadership generally has also failed to appreciate the complementary subversion campaigns posed by groups like the Muslim Brotherhood – groups that fully share the objectives of the violent jihadists but believe that, for the moment at least, more stealthy, "pre-violent" means of jihad are likely to prove more effective in achieving those goals. It must always be kept in mind, of course, that stealthy jihad tactics are just that: tactics to prepare the U.S. battlefield for the inevitable violence to come. Former House Speaker Newt Gingrich has issued several salutary warnings along these lines, including a major address at the American Enterprise Institute on July 26, 2010.[7]

By neglecting their professional duty to understand the doctrinal and legal basis of jihad, policymakers commit national resources in blood and treasure to foreign battlefields without ever realizing that what we must fight for is not just security from Islamist suicide bombers. Rather, we must also preserve here at home the system of government, laws, and freedoms guaranteed by our Constitution. Our national leaders and military and intelligence officers took oaths to "support and defend" the Constitution that is now being targeted by those foreign and domestic enemies who seek our submission to shariah.

THE BOTTOM LINE

Absent such an understanding, and the policy and operational adjustments it necessitates, we risk winning on the battlefield but losing the war. While the U.S. launches intelligence assets and the finest military the world has ever seen with devastating tactical effect, our shariah-adherent foes deploy their forces strategically across the full battlespace of 21st Century warfare, including here in North America.

Team B II believes that the role played in this regard by shariah's most sophisticated jihadists, the Muslim Brotherhood, is of particular concern. Steeped in Islamic doctrine, and already embedded deep inside both the United States and our allies, the Brotherhood has become highly skilled in exploiting the civil liberties and multicultural proclivities of Western societies for the purpose of destroying the latter from within. As America's top national security leadership continues to be guided by its post-modernist, scientific, and high-tech world-view, it neglects the reality that 7th Century impulses, enshrined in shariah, have reemerged as the most critical existential threat to constitutional governance and the freedom-loving, reason-driven principles that undergird Western civilization. Worse yet, as this report documents powerfully, our leaders have failed to perceive – let alone respond effectively to – the real progress being made by the Muslim Brotherhood in insinuating shariah into the very heartland of America through stealthy means. Team B II believes that the defeat of the enemy's stealth jihad requires that the American people and their leaders be aroused to the high stakes in this war, as well as to the very real possibility that we could lose, absent a determined and vigorous program to keep America shariah-free. To that end, Team B II sets forth in plain language who this enemy is, what the ideology is that motivates and justifies their war against us, what are the various forms of warfare the enemy employs to achieve their ends and the United States' vulnerability to them, and what we must do to emerge victorious.

Andrew C. McCarthy

Harry Edward Soyster

R. James Woolsey

EXECUTIVE SUMMARY

Sun Tzu stressed the imperative of warriors understanding both themselves and their enemy: "If you know the enemy and know yourself, you need not fear the results of a hundred battles." The U.S. military has carefully followed Sun Tzu's guidance in the training and education of its warriors.

Yet, today, America is engaged in existential conflict with foes that have succeeded brilliantly in concealing their true identity and very dangerous capabilities. In this, they have been helped by our own willful blindness – a practice in which, given the real, present and growing danger, we simply can no longer afford to indulge. This report is a contribution toward knowing the enemy.

THE THREAT IS SHARIAH

The enemy adheres to an all-encompassing Islamic political-military-legal doctrine known as shariah. Shariah obliges them to engage in jihad to achieve the triumph of Islam worldwide through the establishment of a global Islamic State governed exclusively by shariah, under a restored caliphate.

The good news is that millions of Muslims around the world – including many in America – do not follow the directives of shariah, let alone engage in jihad. The bad news is that this reality reflects the fact that the imposition of strict shariah doctrine is at different stages across Muslim-majority and -minority countries.

The appearance is thus created that there is variation in sha-riah. Of late, representatives of Muslim- and Arab-American groups[8] and their apologists[9] have been claiming that there is no single sha-riah, that it is subject to interpretation and no one interpretation is any more legitimate than any other.

In fact, for especially the Sunni and with regard to non-Muslims, there is ultimately but one shariah. It is totalitarian in character, incompatible with our Constitution and a threat to freedom here and around the world. Shariah's adherents are mak-ing a determined, sustained, and well-financed effort to impose it on all Muslims and non-Muslims, alike.

That effort is abetted enormously by several factors. Too many Muslims, to borrow a metaphor from Mao, provide the sea in which the jihadis swim. By offering little meaningful opposition to the jihadist agenda and by meekly submitting to it, a large number of Muslim communities and nations generally project a tacit agreement with jihadis' ends, if not with their means. At the very least, they exhibit an unwillingness to face the consequences of standing up to shariah's enforcers within Islam. Such conse-quences include the distinct possibility of being denounced as an apostate, a capital offense under shariah.

There are, moreover, Muslims around the world – includ-ing some in Europe, Canada, Australia and the United States – who *do* support shariah by various means. These include: (1) by contributing to "charity" (*zakat*), even though, according to sha-riah, those engaged in jihad are among the authorized recipient categories for what amounts to a mandatory tax;[10] (2) by inculcat-ing their children with shariah at mosques or *madrassas*; and (3) by participating in, or simply failing to report, abhorrent behavior condoned or commanded by shariah (e.g., underage and forced marriage,[11] honor killing,[12] female genital mutilation,[13] polyg-amy,[14] and domestic abuse,[15] including marital rape[16]).

Evidence of the extent to which shariah is being insinuated into the fabric of American society abounds, if one is willing to see it. A particularly egregious example was the 2009 case of a Muslim woman whose request for a restraining order against her Moroccan husband who had serially tortured and raped her was denied by New Jersey family court Judge Joseph Charles. The judge ruled on the grounds that the abusive husband had acted according to his Muslim (shariah) beliefs, and thus not with criminal intent.

In this instance, a New Jersey appellate court overturned the ruling in July 2010, making clear that in the United States, the laws of the land derive from the Constitution and the alien dictates of shariah have no place in a U.S. courtroom.[17] Still, the fact that such a reversal was necessary is instructive.

MISPERCEIVING THE THREAT

Few Americans are aware of the diversity and success to date of such efforts to insinuate shariah into the United States – let alone the full implications of the mortal threat this totalitarian doctrine represents to our freedoms, society and government. Fewer still understand the nature of the jihad being waged to impose it here.

To be sure, since 9/11, most in this country have come to appreciate that America is put at risk by violent jihadis who launch military assaults and plot destructive attacks against our friends and allies, our armed forces and our homeland. Far less recognizable, however, is the menace posed by jihadist enemies who operate by deceit and stealth from inside the gates. The latter threat is, arguably, a far more serious one to open, tolerant societies like ours. This report is substantially devoted to laying bare the danger posed by so-called "non-violent" jihadists, exposing their organizational infrastructure and modus operandi and recommending actions that must be taken to prevent their success.

The first thing to understand about the jihadis who operate by stealth is that they have precisely the same dual objectives as the openly violent jihadists (including al Qaeda, Hezbollah, Hamas and the Taliban): global imposition of shariah and re-establishment of the Islamic caliphate to rule in accordance with it. They differ only with respect to timing and tactics. In fact, the seemingly innocuous outreach tactics of *dawa* are merely part of the initial stages of what the U.S. military would call "intelligence preparation of the battlefield" that is calculated favorably to sculpt the terrain over the long term, preceding the ultimate, violent seizure of the U.S. government and replacement of the U.S. Constitution with shariah.[18]

U.S. national security leaders, academia, the media and society as a whole have been rendered all but incapable of recognizing this dimension as part of the enemy jihad. A number of factors have contributed to that lack of situational awareness. For one, it follows decades during which pride in American heritage, traditions and values steadily has eroded and pro-shariah sheikhs have poured millions into U.S. Middle East studies and inter-religious dialogue programs.

At the same time, a massive propaganda operation has targeted Western society. Its immediate goal is to obscure the fact that jihadist violence and more stealthy supremacism is rooted in the Islamic texts, teachings, and interpretations that constitute shariah.

The net result of these combined forces is that the United States has been infiltrated and deeply influenced by an enemy within that is openly determined to replace the U.S. Constitution with shariah.

THE MUSLIM BROTHERHOOD

The most important entity promoting Islamic suprema-cism, shariah, and the caliphate through – at least for the moment

– non-violent means is the Muslim Brotherhood (MB, or in Arabic, the Ikhwan). The MB defined this form of warfare as "civilization jihad" in its strategic document for North America, entitled the *Explanatory Memorandum: On the General Strategic Goal for the Group,* which was entered into evidence in the 2008 *United States v. Holy Land Foundation* trial.[19]

Written in 1991 by Mohamed Akram, a senior Hamas leader in the United States and a member of the Board of Directors of the Muslim Brotherhood in North America, the *Explanatory Memorandum* declared that the Islamic Movement is an MB effort led by the Ikhwan in America.[20] It went on to explain that the "Movement" is a "settlement" process to establish itself inside the United States and, once rooted, to undertake a "grand jihad" characterized as a "civilization jihadist" mission that is likewise led by the Muslim Brotherhood.[21]

Specifically, the document explained that the civilization jihadist process involves a "grand jihad in eliminating and destroying the Western civilization from within and 'sabotaging' its miserable house by their hands and the hands of the believers so that it is eliminated…."[22] Author Robert Spencer has popularized the term "stealth jihad"[23] to describe this part of the shariah adherents' civilization jihad. The two terms are used interchangeably in this report.

This commitment to employ whatever tactics are most expedient was expressed in 1966 by one of the Brotherhood's seminal ideologues, Sayyid Qutb, in his influential book, *Milestones:* "Wherever an Islamic community exists which is a concrete example of the Divinely-ordained system of life, it has a God-given right to step forward and take control of the political authority….When Allah restrained Muslims from jihad for a certain period, it was a question of strategy rather than of principle…:"[24]

Other, more contemporary affirmations of the Brotherhood's commitment to stealth jihad can be found in the words of some of the Ikhwan's most prominent operatives in America today. For example, Louay Safi, a leader of two Brotherhood fronts – the International Institute of Islamic Thought (IIIT) and the Islamic Society of North America (ISNA), has declared that, "The principle of jihad obligates the Muslims to maintain and achieve these objectives [i.e., the triumph of Islam and the institution of the caliphate]. The best way to achieve these objectives and most appropriate method upholding the principle of jihad is, however, a question of leadership and strategy." [25]

A particularly telling indication of the stealth jihad agenda comes from Omar Ahmad, one of the founders of the Brotherhood's Council on American Islamic Relations (CAIR) and an unindicted co-conspirator in the Holy Land Foundation trial for funding international terrorism from the United States.[26] Ahmad made a reference to the MB's dual-messaging, a form of esoteric communication in which words seem innocuous to the uninitiated, but which have definite meaning to those duly indoctrinated: "I believe that our problem is that we stopped working underground. We will recognize the source of any message which comes out of us. I mean, if a message is publicized, we will know… the media person among us will recognize that you send two messages: one to the Americans and one to the Muslims."[27]

Note the Muslim Brotherhood operative's differentiation between "Americans" and "Muslims," as if presuming that Muslims are not or should not be good Americans. This differentiation is clear in CAIR's own name. In short, it is the enemy among us, working out in the open but disguised by deceit, that poses the greater long-term threat to our legal system and way of life.

As this report demonstrates, many of the most prominent Muslim organizations in America are front groups for, or derivatives of, the Muslim Brotherhood.[28] New Brotherhood entities are added each year. That so hostile an entity enjoys such a large footprint and dominant position within our society speaks volumes about the Ikhwan's organizational and financial reach.[29] No other *Muslim* group in the United States has been able even remotely to rival the Ikhwan's resource base, organizational skill or financial resources.

Multiculturalism, political correctness, misguided notions of tolerance and sheer willful blindness have combined to create an atmosphere of confusion and denial in America about the current threat confronting the nation. Of particular concern is the fact that political and military leaders in the United States find it difficult and/or distasteful to explain the true nature of the enemy to the public, and even to discuss it among themselves. Even when presented with detailed factual briefings and voluminous information about the essential linkage between shariah and violent acts of terrorism, most simply refuse to speak candidly about that connection.

To the contrary, U.S. national intelligence, law enforcement and security leadership seems determined to hide the Islamic origins of jihadist terrorism from the public. Through internal policy as well as public statements, U.S. officials have devised and seek to impose purposefully obscure and counterfactual language, evidently selected to divert American attention away from the Arab/Muslim origins of shariah and the Islamic doctrine of jihad.[30]

Particularly worrying is the fact that, as counterterrorism expert Patrick Poole has put it: "Senior Pentagon commanders have labored to define the threat out of existence."[31] Despite the rapidly expanding incidence of jihadist attacks and plots inside this country – whose perpetrators readily explain their Muslim identity and motivation – officials persist doggedly (and implausibly) in insisting on "lone wolf," "homegrown radical," or "isolated extremist" descriptions of our foes. The most recent example of this phenomenon was the Pentagon's final after-action report on the Fort Hood massacre of November, 2009.[32]

Why would those sworn to support and defend the Constitution behave in a manner so detrimental to national security? Perhaps it is out of fear and perhaps out of recognition that they have abdicated their professional duty to develop an appropriate national security response. Perhaps, as Poole says, "Pretending that the threat is random and unknowable gives them license to do nothing."[33] Ikhwan pushback and allegations of racism and bigotry make it professionally difficult to challenge the Muslim Brotherhood's propaganda and operations.

THE WELLSPRING OF JIHAD

The truth is that today's enemy is completely comprehensible and can be professionally analyzed and factually understood in precise and specific detail. When analysis is so conducted, it is clear that conformance to shariah in America constitutes as great a threat as any enemy the nation has ever confronted.

The Obama administration has nonetheless built upon the willful blindness-induced failures of previous administrations with respect to shariah. The incumbent president and his team have not only declared that there is no "War on Terror" for the United States. They insist – *reductio ad absurdum* and in conformance with the policy dictates of the Organization of the Islamic Conference (OIC), the second-largest multinational entity (after the United Nations) made up of 56 predominantly Muslim nations and the Palestine Authority – that Islam has nothing to do with terrorism. Such a statement can only be made because, as will be shown below, the OIC and others who adhere to and promote shariah do not define acts of jihad as "terrorism."

The U.S. government line remains unchanged even as our enemies make plain the connection between their aggressive behavior and shariah-adherent jihad. To cite but one example, Iran's President Mahmoud Ahmadinejad publicly describes the ongoing "historic war between the oppressor and the world of Islam."[34]

Yet, Obama's top counterterrorism advisor, John Brennan, insists that the President does not accept that there is a "global war" with Islamic terrorists.

Brennan further announced that the term "jihadists" will no longer be used to describe our enemies. According to Mr. Brennan, to use the term "jihadists" in describing Islamic terrorists is a mistake because it is "a legitimate term, 'jihad' meaning to purify oneself or to wage a holy struggle for a moral goal." He maintains that this use of the term to describe al Qaeda's ruthless operatives "risks giving these murderers the religious legitimacy they desperately seek, but in no way deserve."[35] The problem with this formulation is that jihad as a "holy struggle for a moral goal" may not be in conflict with al Qaeda's "ruthless" operations.

At a speech in late May 2010 at the Center for Strategic and International Studies (CSIS), Brennan expanded on the theme: "Nor do we describe our enemy as 'jihadists' or 'Islamists' because jihad is a holy struggle, a legitimate tenet of Islam, meaning to purify oneself or one's community, and there is nothing holy or legitimate or Islamic about murdering innocent men, women and children."[36] Left unresolved by Brennan is whether shariah classifies non-Muslims as innocent.

A NEEDED REALITY CHECK

Brennan's statements reflect a common lack of understanding of the fundamentals of shariah, including the doctrinal basis of the Quran, *hadiths*, the role of abrogation, and that status of consensus in which shariah is rooted. In fact, Brennan's assertions directly contradict the teachings of leading Islamic scholars.

For example, even a cursory review of the writings of Islamic authorities shows that "jihad" is warfare against non-Muslims.[37] The top counterterrorism adviser to the President of the United States has a professional responsibility to know these facts.

Brennan is correct in one respect: America is not in a "war on terror." Terrorism is indeed merely a tactic, like aerial or naval bombardment, ambush, maneuver and other similar activities. But America is at war with a determined enemy who has yet to be honestly identified by anyone in a position of authority in the United States.

It is also accurate to label jihad as a "legitimate tenet of Islam." But neither shariah nor its practitioners, our enemy, define it in terms that are even close to what Brennan used at CSIS. The shariah definition of jihad and that of the jihadis are the same.

This is not a partisan critique of behavior uniquely exhibited by the incumbent administration, or by Democrats alone. For example, President George W. Bush noted on September 20, 2001 that "terrorists are traitors to their own faith" that "hijacked their own religion."[38] Regrettably, this and similar statements subsequently issued by various Bush administration officials set the stage for the misleading comments being uttered by their successors today.

Notably, these include President Obama's statement made on January 7, 2010, that, "We are at war; we are at war with al Qaeda."[39] The President was discussing the results of an investigation into the attempted Christmas Day bombing of a Northwest Airlines flight over Detroit by a young Muslim from Nigeria named Umar Farouk Abdulmutallab. Even some of the President's critics expressed relief that the Chief Executive was finally recognizing that the nation was indeed facing a genuine enemy (albeit one comprised of many elements besides al Qaeda).

Since shariah emerged as a real threat, Obama, like Brennan and most of the U.S. national security leadership, has failed to define or explain accurately the nature of an enemy that explicitly threatens the American way of life; indeed, this threat imperils the constitutional framework that drives the exceptionalism that way of life sustains.

In fact, the forces of shariah have been at war with non-Muslims for 1,400 years and with the United States of America for 200 years.[40] While the most recent campaign to impose this totalitarian code began in the late 20th Century, it is but the latest in a historical record of offensive warfare that stretches back to the origins of Islam itself.

When Army Major Nidal Hasan murdered thirteen people at Fort Hood, Texas on November 5, 2009, the media, as well as the FBI, searched for answers as to why this American-born military officer would commit such an unconscionable act – the worst terrorist attack on U.S. soil since September 11, 2001. While myriad theories and opinions were offered, few in the Administration, the media, academia or the rest of the elite seemed capable of comprehending the killer's motives – even as he expressly stated them for years leading up to the event.

In fact, Hasan fully articulated his intentions to senior officers in the U.S. Army Medical Corps years before his rampage, and the warnings were ignored when brought to higher ranks. In a fifty-slide briefing given to his medical school class in 2007, entitled "Koranic View as it Relates to Muslims in the U.S Military,"[41] Hasan explained the requirement that Muslims under Islamic law conduct jihad against non-Muslims, and he specifically defined the parameters within which Muslims must act. For Hasan, the relevant parameter was being deployed to the Middle East as this would put him in a status where he could be required to "kill without right." As can be demonstrated in detail, Hasan's presentation tracks exactly with Islamic law[42] – and he should know since, at the time of the massacre, he was the acting imam for Fort Hood.

Had anyone in the audience been taught the enemy threat doctrine (i.e., shariah on jihad), Hasan's amazingly candid presentation, which thoroughly explained his concerns given the fundamental concepts of shariah, would have alerted authorities in time to prevent his attack. Furthermore, the briefing contained an explicit declaration of Hasan's allegiance as a Muslim soldier in the Army of Allah. And yet, seemingly, none of the audience of senior medical officers recognized the threat that Hasan posed to his fellow soldiers. Hasan announced himself an enemy combatant and no one was either able or willing to process that information properly.

THE ENEMY WITHIN

Instinctively, even Americans who are unfamiliar with the term "shariah" understand that it poses a threat. For example, focus groups have shown that, when asked about "the law of Saudi Arabia," there is a considerable awareness about its brutal repression of those subjected to it and its aggressive designs on the rest of humanity.

Most of the public believes that it is the terrorists who seek to advance shariah via violence who pose the greatest threat. While this may be an understandable conclusion, it also points to how uninformed the public actually is.

Our intelligence community and law enforcement entities have disrupted roughly thirty terrorist attacks since September 11, 2001, and demonstrated laudable vigilance in pursuit of terrorists. Still, the community's failures – Major Hasan; the Christmas Day bomber, Umar Farouk Abdulmutallab; and the Times Square bomber, Faisal Shahzad – highlight serious flaws that remain in our intelligence collection and understanding of the true nature of the threat we face. In the Christmas Day case, U.S. intelligence failed to act even when warned specifically in advance by Abdulmutallab's own father.

Yet, al Qaeda and other Islamist groups who perpetrate terrorist acts are *not* the most dangerous threat. These threats, regardless of their brutality, cannot bring America to submit to shariah – at least were they to act alone. While the terrorists can and will inflict great pain on the nation, the ultimate goal of shariah-adherent Islam cannot be achieved by these groups solely through acts of terrorism, without a more subtle, well-organized component operating in tandem with them.

That component takes the form of "civilization jihad." This form of warfare includes multi-layered cultural subversion, the co-opting of senior leaders, influence operations and propaganda and other means of insinuating shariah into Western societies. These are the sorts of techniques alluded to by Yusuf al-Qaradawi, the spiritual leader of the Muslim Brotherhood, when he told a Toledo, Ohio Muslim Arab Youth Association convention in 1995: 'We will conquer Europe, we will conquer America! Not through the sword, but through *dawa*."[43]

The prime practitioners of this stealthy form of jihad are the ostensibly "non-violent" Muslim Brothers and their front groups and affiliates. It must always be kept in mind that such tactics are "non-violent" not because the Brotherhood eschews violence out of principle, but rather because it has decided that this phase of battlefield preparation is better accomplished through stealthy means. The violence is always implicit in the overall strategy, albeit held in reserve for the final stages of the offensive. It is the combined effect of the violent and pre-violent strains of jihad that constitutes the most serious threat to America and its free people.

As the pages that follow document in detail, the Muslim Brotherhood has been in this country for decades and is an existential threat to American society and the fundamental liberties ordained and established by the Founding Fathers in the U.S. Constitution. Its own mission statement asserts that "the Ikhwan must understand that their work in America is a kind of grand Jihad in eliminating and destroying the Western civilization from within and 'sabotaging' its miserable house by their hands and the hands of the believers so that it is eliminated and God's religion is made victorious over all other religions."[44]

This carefully articulated mission flows ineluctably from shariah, which holds that only Allah can make laws and that democratic rule whereby people legislate is impermissible. Therefore, the destruction of Western-style governments and subjugation of free societies to the Ikhwan's view of Allah's will is obligatory for the Muslim Brotherhood, as for other adherents to shariah. Since America is the world's preeminent exponent of individual liberties and the most powerful democratic country, those who are fighting to establish the Islamic caliphate have targeted this nation for destruction – not necessarily in the military or physical sense of the word, but in the destruction of American society as we know it.

Ultimately, the Muslim Brotherhood intends for America to live under shariah. This ambition was explicitly stated in 1996 by Abdurahman Alamoudi, at the time one of the top agents of the Muslim Brotherhood operation in the United States. Back then, Alamoudi enjoyed access to the Clinton White House since, as the founder of the American Muslim Council and a director of numerous other Brotherhood fronts, he was considered a leading spokesman for the Muslim community in America. (He is currently serving a twenty-three year federal prison term on terrorism-related charges.)

At the Islamic Association of Palestine's annual convention in Illinois in 1996, Alamoudi declared: "I have no doubt in my mind, Muslims sooner or later will be the moral leadership of America. It depends on me and you, either we do it now or we do it after a hundred years, but this country will become a Muslim country."[45]

THE TACIT SUPPORTERS OF CIVILIZATION JIHAD

The Team B II Report details the Muslim Brotherhood's multi-phased plan of operations for the destruction of Western civilization. The successful execution of this plan depends on at least tacit support or submission from the Muslim population at large.

At the very least, popular Muslim passivity signals an unwillingness to face the consequences of standing up to the Muslim Brothers and other enforcers within Islam. Those consequences can be quite severe, starting with social ostracism and sometimes ending with death. Since the Ikhwan's instrument of discipline and control over their fellow Muslims is the fact that any criticism of shariah or the Quran can be considered to be apostasy, for which the penalty is death, enforcement through social pressure is simple and unseen. This is particularly true among Muslim immigrant communities that have fled such brutality in their native countries and come to America for shelter, only to find the threat emerge in their new homeland.

There are, moreover, Muslims in Europe and the United States who *do* support shariah by various means. As we have seen, these include mandatory *zakat* contributions to certain "charities" even when the "donor" knows that, under shariah, jihad is one of the authorized recipient categories[46]; indoctrinating children with shariah at mosques and madrassas; and by participating in or failing to report abhorrent behavior including child abuse[47], wife abuse[48], female genital mutilation[49], polygamy[50], underage[51] and forced marriage[52], marital rape[53] and "honor killing."[54] One appalling example offers an insight into the extent to which shariah is being insinuated into the fabric of American society: The 2009 case of a Muslim woman whose request for a legal restraining order against her Moroccan husband who had serially abused and raped her was denied by New Jersey family court Judge Joseph

Charles. The judge ruled that the abusive husband had acted according to his Muslim (shariah) beliefs[55] and thus not with criminal intent.

Fortunately, a New Jersey appellate court overturned the ruling in July 2010, making clear that in the United States, the laws of the land derive from the Constitution and the alien dictates of shariah have no place in a U.S. courtroom.[56] Still, the fact that such a reversal was necessary is frighteningly instructive.

According to shariah, the Quran and *hadiths* (accounts of the actions and sayings of Mohammed) comprise the authoritative roadmap for Muslims and, hence, the Muslim Brotherhood. In accordance with that roadmap, its members – like other adherents to shariah[57] – are engaged in a global war of conquest.[58] One can see this battle campaign being executed in every part of the world. Europe is in a tremendous struggle with an ever-increasing and influential Islamic threat. Many Europeans are perplexed by what they see happening in their countries as Islam infiltrates every sector of their society. Notably, after the London subway bombing in 2005, many in the United Kingdom were astonished that British-born Muslims identified first and foremost with Pakistan and shariah, rather than with the nation where they were born and raised and its traditional values.

Like most Americans, these Britons fail to understand that the shariah-adherent Muslims do not identify with any sovereign nation. They see themselves as Muslims first and part of the future caliphate. Nowhere has this world view been more clearly enunciated than in the words of the late Ayatollah Ruhollah Khomeini, spoken in 1980 about the country of his birth: "We do not worship Iran, we worship Allah....I say, let this land [Iran] burn. I say let this land go up in smoke, provided Islam emerges triumphant...."[59]

THE NEED FOR CORRECTIVE ACTION

Given the gravity of this threat, it is simply astounding that the United States has, to date, neither developed nor adopted a strategy for defeating shariah's designs, and the Muslim Brotherhood's efforts to realize them. This information is not even being taught at a basic level to FBI counterterrorism agents and analysts, nor is it taught at the Justice Department, Department of Homeland Security, the State or Defense Departments, or the CIA.

Amidst the increasingly heated assertion of First Amendment protections for the practice and promotion of shariah in America, almost entirely missing is any recognition of the fundamental incompatibility with Article VI's requirement that "this Constitution shall be...the supreme law of the land" inherent in efforts to insinuate Islamic law into the United States.

Such a deplorable state of affairs helps explain why there is no strategy to defeat the shariah movement: that movement and its agenda are simply not understood within the ranks of the organizations legally charged with protecting America and its Constitution from such threats.

It bears repeating: no such strategy can be put into place, let alone be successfully executed, as long as our national leadership refuses to define the enemy in realistic and comprehensive terms. If such ignorance is allowed to persist, the Muslim Brotherhood will continue infiltrating American society at every level and executing a very deliberate plan to manipulate the nation into piecemeal submission to shariah.

To discount the possibility that such a seemingly preposterous state of affairs will eventuate in America would be a serious mistake. It is one that many Europeans have been making for years. Experts like Bernard Lewis, the internationally acclaimed authority on Islam, are now saying that Europe will be an Islamic continent by the end of this century,[60] if not before. While the proportion of Muslims to non-Muslims in the United States is much smaller than in Europe, America's accelerating submission to shariah documented in the following pages suggests that this country, too, is at risk of being fundamentally and unacceptably altered.

Heretofore, the United States has confronted primarily external threats. Today, we are facing an internal threat that has masked itself as a religion and that uses the tolerance for religious practice guaranteed by the Constitution's First Amendment to parry efforts to restrict or prevent what amount to seditious activities. In the process, the First Amendment itself is being infringed upon, as Muslim Brothers and others demand that free speech be barred where it gives offense to them – effectively imposing shariah blasphemy laws in this country.

For these reasons, among others, it should be understood that shariah is fundamentally about power, namely the enforcement of a body of law, not faith. In the words of the Muslim Brotherhood's Sayyid Qutb: "Whenever an Islamic community exists which is a concrete example of the Divinely-ordained system of life, it has a God-given right to step forward and control the political authority so that it may establish the divine system on earth, while it leaves the matter of belief to individual conscience."[61]

Shariah dictates a comprehensive and totalitarian system of laws, an aggressive military doctrine, an all-encompassing socio-economic program and a ruthless enforcement mechanism. It is, in short, a complete way of life. It is against this backdrop that the obligation shariah demands of its followers – namely, to conduct a global campaign to replace non-Muslim governments with Islamic States governed by Islamic law, to conquer *Dar al-Harb* (the House of War) for *Dar al-Islam* (the House of Islam) – must be seen as an illegal effort to supplant our Constitution with another legal code, not a religious practice protected by that document. Islamic scholar Majid Khadduri put it this way:

"It follows that the existence of a *Dar al-Harb* is ultimately outlawed under the Islamic jural order; that the dar al-Islam is permanently under jihad obligation until the *Dar al-Harb* is reduced to nonexistence; and that any community accepting certain disabilities – must submit to Islamic rule and reside in the dar al-Islam or be bound as clients to the Muslim community. The universalism of Islam, in its all-embracing creed, is imposed on the believers as a continuous process of warfare, psychological and political if not strictly military."[62]

Yet, many in this country – particularly in governmental, academic, and media elites – have shown themselves susceptible to the Muslim Brotherhood's strategy for waging sabotage against the United States in order to destroy "its miserable house...by their own hand." They are enabling shariah's spread by enforcing a tolerance of that doctrine under the rubric of freedom of religion and diversity, instead of recognizing it for the seditious and anti-constitutional agenda it openly espouses.

In the words of Muslim scholar Shamim Siddiqi: "The movement may also seek legal protection from the court for fundamental human rights *to propagate what its adherents believe to be correct* and to profess the same through democratic, peaceful and constitutional means."[63] (Emphasis added.)

Recent research indicates that in many mosques across the country the overthrow of the U.S. Constitution is being encouraged in the printed material offered on-site or in the textbooks used in children's classes, if not directly from the Friday pulpit.[64]

In addition, the 2008 Holy Land Foundation trial in Dallas, Texas, provided evidence that the majority of Islamic organizations in America are affiliates of or associated with the Muslim Brotherhood in some way and many of them are raising funds for jihad.[65] The convictions of all defendants in that case make clear that such behavior is not protected by the First Amendment. And yet, American elites still deal with shariah as just a religious system, when in fact it is as totalitarian a political program as ever were those of communism, fascism, National Socialism, or Japanese imperialism.

Military historians and combat veterans understand that it is far easier to defend against an attack that comes from an enemy outside one's defensive perimeter. In that case, the defending army need only train its fire outwards and have no fear of fratricide. By contrast, the most difficult attack to defend against is the one that comes from *inside* the defensive perimeter, because distinguishing the enemy from friendly forces is problematic.

That is the situation in America today. *We have an enemy inside our perimeter.* But for this nation, the challenge is not just an inability to distinguish friend from foe. Rather, it is an unwillingness to do so.

As the succeeding pages establish in greater detail, accurate and highly relevant information is available concerning what the Muslim Brotherhood and other shariah-adherent Muslims are doing in America, their goals and strategy. Much of that information comes from the Brotherhood's own documents and leadership statements.

Other insights can be obtained from those who were at one time part of the Muslim Brotherhood, but have chosen a new direction for their lives. Three such individuals – Walid Shoebat (formerly with the Palestinian Liberation Organization or PLO),[66] Kamal Saleem (former Muslim Brotherhood),[67] and Mosab Yousef (former Hamas and author of *Son of Hamas*)[68] – are proclaiming to all who will hear them that the Muslim Brotherhood is in America to destroy our Constitution and replace it with shariah. These brave men are helping to define the enemy. Their testimony, taken together with that available from other sources, leaves us with no excuse for remaining ignorant of the truth.

Armed with that truth – as compiled and analyzed in the Team B II report – the American people and their leaders are in a position to comprehend fully the nature of the threat posed by shariah and by those who seek through violence or stealthy subversion to impose it upon us. This knowledge obligates one to take action.

RECOMMENDATIONS

While detailed recommendations for adopting a more prudential and effective strategy for surviving shariah's onslaught are beyond the scope of this study, several policy and programmatic changes are in order. These include:

- U.S. policymakers, financiers, businessmen, judges, journalists, community leaders and the public at large must be equipped with an accurate understanding of the nature of shariah and the necessity of keeping America shariah-free. At a minimum, this will entail resisting – rather than acquiescing to – the concerted efforts now being made to allow that alien legal code to become established in this country as an alternate, parallel system to the Constitution and the laws enacted pursuant to it. Arguably, this is already in effect for those who have taken an oath to "support and defend" the Constitution, because the requirement is subsumed in that oath.

- U.S. government agencies and organizations should cease their outreach to Muslim communities through Muslim Brotherhood fronts whose mission is to destroy our country from within, as such practices are both reckless and counterproductive. Indeed, these activities serve to legitimate, protect and expand the influence of our enemies. They conduce to no successful legal outcome that cannot be better advanced

33

via aggressive prosecution of terrorists, terror-funders and other lawbreakers. The practice also discourages patriotic Muslims from providing actual assistance to the U.S. government lest they be marked for ostracism or worse by the Ikhwan and other shariah-adherent members of their communities.

- In keeping with Article VI of the Constitution, extend bans currently in effect that bar members of hate groups such as the Ku Klux Klan, and endorsers of child abuse and other crimes, from holding positions of trust in federal, state, or local governments or the armed forces of the United States to those who espouse or support shariah. Instead, every effort should be made to identify and empower Muslims who are willing publicly to denounce shariah.

- Practices that promote shariah – notably, shariah-compliant finance and the establishment or promotion in public spaces or with public funds or facilities and activities that give preferential treatment to shariah's adherents – are incompatible with the Constitution and the freedoms it enshrines and must be proscribed.

- Sedition is prohibited by law in the United States. To the extent that imams and mosques are being used to advocate shariah in America, they are promoting seditious activity and should be warned that they will be subject to investigation and prosecution.

- Textbooks used in both secular educational systems and Islamic schools must not promote shariah, its tenets, or the notion that America must submit to its dictates. Schools that promote anti-constitutional teaching should be denied taxpayer funding and lose their charters, accreditation and charitable tax status.

- Compounds and communities that seek to segregate themselves on the basis of shariah law, apply it alongside or in lieu of the law of the land or otherwise establish themselves as "no-go" zones for law enforcement and other authorities must be thwarted in such efforts. In this connection, assertion of claims to territory around segregationist mosques should be proscribed.

- Immigration of those who adhere to shariah must be precluded, as was previously done with adherents to the seditious ideology of communism.

Such measures will, of course, be controversial in some quarters. They will certainly be contested by shariah-adherent Muslims committed to jihad and others who, in the name of exercising or protecting civil liberties, are enabling the destruction of those liberties in furtherance of shariah. Far from being dispositive, their opposition should be seen as an opportunity – a chance, at a minimum, for a long-overdue debate about the sorts of policies that have brought the West in general and the United States in particular to the present, parlous state of affairs. If this study catalyzes and usefully informs that debate, it will have succeeded.

KEY FINDINGS

- The United States is under attack by foes who are openly animated by what is known in Islam as shariah (Islamic law). According to shariah, every faithful Muslim is obligated to wage jihad, whether violent or not, against those who do not adhere to this comprehensive, totalitarian, political-military code. The enemy's explicit goal is to establish a global Islamic State, known as the caliphate, governed by shariah.

- Shariah is based on the Quran (held by all Muslims to be the "uncreated" word of Allah as dictated to Mohammed), *hadiths* (sayings of Mohammed) and agreed interpretations. It commands Muslims to carry out jihad (holy war) indefinitely until all of the *Dar al-Harb* (i.e., the House of War, where shariah is not enforced) is brought under the domination of *Dar al-Islam* (the House of Islam – or literally the House of Submission, where shariah *is* enforced).

- Shariah dictates that non-Muslims be given three choices: convert to Islam and conform to shariah; submit as second-class citizens (*dhimmis*); or be killed. Not all classes are given the second option.

- Both Islamic terrorism and pre-violent, "civilization jihad" (popularly referred to as "stealth jihad") are commanded by shariah. That is not only the view of "extremists" and "fringe" elements "hijacking the religion," but of many authorities of Islam widely recognized as mainstream and drawing upon orthodox texts, interpretations and practices of the faith.

- The Muslim Brotherhood is the font of modern Islamic jihad. It is dedicated to the same global supremacist objectives as those (like al Qaeda and the Taliban) who share its adherence to shariah but who believe that violent jihad is more likely to more quickly produce the common goal of a global caliphate.

- The Brotherhood's internal documents make clear that civilization jihad is subversion waged by stealth instead of violence only until such time as Muslims are powerful enough to progress to violent jihad for the final conquest.

- Those who work to insinuate shariah into the United States intend to subvert and replace the Constitution (itself a violation of Article VI) because, according to shariah, freedom of religion, other civil liberties enshrined in the Constitution, and the rule of man-made law are incompatible with Islam (which means "submission").

- The shariah-adherent enemy prioritizes information warfare, manifested in American society as propaganda, political warfare, psychological warfare, influence operations and subversion of our foundational institutions. Our government structure fails to recognize this strategy because it is focused so exclusively on kinetic attacks. As a result, the United States remains crippled in its inability to engage this enemy effectively *on his primary battlefield.*

- The Brotherhood exploits the atmosphere of intimidation created by Islamic terrorists, thus inculcating in the West a perceived need for "outreach" to the "Muslim community" which, in turn, opens up opportunities to pursue a campaign of stealthy infiltration into American and other Western societies. The combined effect of such "civilization jihad" and jihadism of the violent kind may prove to be considerably more dangerous for this country and other Western societies than violent jihad alone.

- The Brotherhood has succeeded in penetrating our educational, legal and political systems, as well as top levels of government, intelligence, the media, and U.S. military, virtually paralyzing our ability to plan or respond effectively.

- Muslim Brotherhood organizations conduct outreach to the government, law enforcement, media, religious community, and others for one reason: to *subvert* them in furtherance of their objective, which is implementation of Islamic law.

- An informed and determined counter-strategy to defend the Constitution from shariah can yet succeed – provided it is undertaken in the prompt, timely and comprehensive manner recommended by Team B II.

KEY TENETS OF SHARIAH

The following are some of the most important – and, particularly for Western non-Muslims, deeply problematic – tenets of shariah, arranged in alphabetical order. The citations drawn from the Quran, schools of Islam and other recognized sources are offered as illustrative examples of the basis for such practices under shariah.

1. **Abrogation** (*'Al-mansukh wa al-nasikh'* in Arabic—the abrogated and the abrogating): verses that come later in the Quran, chronologically, supersede, or abrogate, the earlier ones. In effect, this results in the more moderate verses of the Meccan period being abrogated by the later, violent, Medinan verses. "When we cancel a message, or throw it into oblivion, we replace it with one better or one similar. Do you not know that Allah has power over all things?" (Quran 2:106)

2. **Adultery** (*'Zina'* in Arabic): unlawful intercourse is a capital crime under shariah, punishable by lashing and stoning to death. "Nor come nigh to adultery: for it is a shameful deed and an evil, opening the road to other evils." (Q 17:32) "The woman and the man guilty of adultery or fornication, flog each of them with a hundred stripes; let not compassion move you in their case, in a matter prescribed by Allah, if ye believe in Allah

and the Last Day: and let a party of the Believers witness the punishment." (Q 24:2) "It is not lawful to shed the blood of a Muslim except for one of three sins: a married person committing fornication, and in just retribution for premeditated murder, and [for sin of treason involving] a person renouncing Islam, and thus leaving the community [to join the enemy camp in order to wage war against the faithful]." (Al-Bukhari, Muslim, Abu Dawud, Tirmidhi, and An-Nasa'i)

3. **Apostasy** (*'Irtidad'* or *'Ridda'* in Arabic): The established ruling of shariah is that apostates are to be killed wherever they may be found. "Anyone who, after accepting Faith in Allah, utters Unbelief, except under compulsion, his heart remaining firm in Faith—but such as open their heart to Unbelief—on them is Wrath from Allah, and theirs will be a dreadful Penalty." (Q 16:106)

"Some atheists were brought to Ali and he burnt them. The news of this event, reached Ibn Abbas who said, 'If I had been in his place, I would not have burnt them, as Allah's messenger forbade it, saying, 'Do not punish anybody with Allah's punishment (fire).' I would have killed them according to the statement of Allah's Messenger, 'Whoever changed his Islamic religion, then kill him.'" (Bukhari, Volume 9, #17)

"Leaving Islam is the ugliest form of unbelief (*kufr*) and the worst.....When a person who has reached puberty and is sane voluntarily apostasizes from Islam, he deserves to be killed... There is no indemnity for killing an apostate..." (*'Umdat al-Salik*, Reliance of the Traveler, Chapter o8.0-o8.4)

4. **Democracy & Islam:** Any system of man-made law is considered illicit under Islamic law, for whose adherents Allah already has provided the only law permitted, shariah. Islam and western-style democracy can never co-exist in harmony. "And if any fail to judge by the light of what Allah has revealed, they are no better than unbelievers." (Q 5:47) "Sovereignty in Islam is the prerogative of Almighty Allah alone. He is the absolute arbiter of values and it is His will that determines good and evil, right and wrong." (Mohammed Hashim Kamali, *Principles of Islamic Jurisprudence*, 3d rev. ed., (Cambridge, UK: The Islamic Text Society, 2003), 8.)

    "The shariah cannot be amended to conform to changing human values and standards. Rather, it is the absolute norm to which all human values and conduct must conform." (Muslim Brotherhood spiritual leader Yousef al-Qaradawi)

5. **Female Genital Mutilation:** "Circumcision is obligatory....for both men and women." (*'Umdat al-Salik*, e4.3)

6. **Gender Inequality:** Shariah explicitly relegates women to a status inferior to men.

    - Testimony of a woman before a judge is worth half that of a man: "And get two witnesses, not of your own men, and if there are not two men, then a man and two women, such as ye choose for witnesses." (Q 2:282)

    - Women are to receive just one half the inheritance of a male: "Allah thus directs you as regards your children's inheritance: to the male, a portion equal to that of two females...." (Q 4:11)

- Muslim men are given permission by Allah in the Quran to beat their wives: "As to those women on whose part ye fear disloyalty and ill conduct, admonish them first, next refuse to share their beds, and last, beat them." (Q 4:34)

- Muslim men are given permission by Allah to commit marital rape, as they please: "Your wives are as a tilth unto you, so approach your tilth when or how ye will...." (Q 2: 223)

- Muslim men are permitted to marry up to four wives and to keep concubines in any number: "...Marry women of your choice, two, or three, or four; but if ye fear that ye shall not be able to deal justly with them, then only one, or a captive that your right hands possess..." (Q 4:3)

- Muslim women may marry only one Muslim man and are forbidden to marry a non-Muslim: "And give not (your daughters) in marriage to Al-Mushrikun [non-Muslims] till they believe in Allah alone and verily a believing slave is better than a (free) Mushrik, even though he pleases you...." (Q 2:221)

- A woman may not travel outside the home without the permission of her male guardian and must be accompanied by a male family member if she does so: "A woman may not leave the city without her husband or a member of her unmarriageable kin....accompanying her, unless the journey is obligatory, like the hajj. It is unlawful for her to travel otherwise, and unlawful for her husband to allow her." (*'Umdat al-Salik*, m10.3)

- Under shariah, to bring a claim of rape, a Muslim woman must present four male Muslim witnesses in good standing. Islam thus places the burden of avoiding illicit sexual encounters entirely on the woman. In effect, under shariah, women who bring a claim of rape without being able to produce the requisite four male Muslim witnesses are admitting to having had illicit sex. If she or the man is married, this amounts to an admission of adultery. The following Quranic passages, while explicitly applying to men are cited by shariah authorities and judges in adjudicating rape cases: "And those who accuse free women then do not bring four witnesses (to adultery), flog them..." Q 24:4) "Why did they not bring four witnesses to prove it? When they have not brought the witnesses, such men, in the sight of Allah, stand forth themselves as liars!" (Q 24:13)

- A Muslim woman who divorces and remarries loses custody of children from a prior marriage: "A woman has no right to custody of her child from a previous marriage when she remarries because married life will occupy her with fulfilling the rights of her husband and prevent her from tending the child." (*'Umdat al-Salik*, m13.4)

7. **"Honor" Killing** (aka Muslim family executions): A Muslim parent faces no legal penalty under Islamic law for murdering his child or grandchild: " ...not subject to retaliation" is "a father or mother (or their fathers or

mothers) for killing their offspring, or offspring's off-spring." (*'Umdat al-Salik*, o1.1-2)

8. **Hudud Punishments:** The plural of *hadd*, is "a fixed penalty prescribed as a right of Allah. Because *hudud* penalties belong to Allah, Islamic law does not permit them to be waived or commuted."[69]

   - "Let not compassion move you in their case, in a matter prescribed by Allah, if you believe in Allah and the Last Day: and let a party of believers witness their punishment." (Q 24:2)

   - "On that account, We ordained for the Children of Israel that if any one slew a [Muslim] person – unless it be for murder or for spreading mischief in the land – it would be as if he slew the whole people....The punishment of those who wage war against Allah and his apostle, and strive with might and main for mischief through the land is execution, or crucifixion, or the cutting off of hands and feet from opposite sides, or exile from the land..." (Q 32-33)

   - From the *Kitab al-kaba'ir* (*Book of Enormities*) of Imam Dhahabi, who defines an *enormity* as any sin entailing either a threat of punishment in the hereafter explicitly mentioned by the Koran or hadith, a prescribed legal penalty (Hadd), or being accursed by Allah or His messenger (Allah bless him & give him peace). (*'Umdat al-Salik*, Book P "Enormities," at § p0.0)

   - "Shariah stipulates these punishments and methods of execution such as amputation, crucifixion, flogging, and stoning, for offenses such as adultery, homosexuality, killing without right, theft, and 'spreading mischief in the land' because these punishments were mandated by the Qur'an or Sunnah." (*Islamic Hudood Laws in Pakistan*, Edn 1996, 5.)

9. **Islamic Supremacism:** belief that Islam is superior to every other culture, faith, government, and society and that it is ordained by Allah to conquer and dominate them: "And whoever desires a religion other than Islam, it shall not be accepted from him, and in the hereafter he shall be one of the losers." (Q 3:85):

   - "Ye are the best of Peoples, evolved for mankind." (Q 3:110)

   - Non-Muslims are "the most vile of created beings" (Q 98:6)

   - Be "merciful to one another, but ruthless to the unbelievers" (Q 48:29)

   - "It is the nature of Islam to dominate, not to be dominated, to impose its law on all nations and to extend its power to the entire planet." (Hassan al-Banna, founder of the Muslim Brotherhood)

   - "Islam isn't in America to be equal to any other faith, but to become dominant. The Koran should be the highest authority in America, and Islam the only accepted religion on Earth." (Omar Ahmad, Council on American Islamic Relations co-founder/Board Chairman, 1998)

10. **Jew Hatred:** Antisemitism is intrinsic to shariah and is based on the genocidal behavior of Mohammed himself

in wiping out the entire Jewish population of the Arabian Peninsula.

- "And certainly you have known those among you who exceeded the limits of the Sabbath, as we said to them: Be as apes, despised and hated." (Q 2:65)

- "And you will most certainly find them [the Jews] the greediest of men for life, greedier than even those who are polytheists…" (Q 2:96)

- "O you who believe! Do not take the Jews and the Christians for friends; for they are friends but of each other; and whoever amongst you takes them for a friend, then surely he is one of them; surely Allah does not guide the unjust people." (Q 5:51)

- "Fight those who believe not in Allah nor the Last Day, nor hold that forbidden which hath been forbidden by Allah and his apostle, nor acknowledge the religion of truth, even if they be of the People of the Book [Christians and Jews], until they pay the *jizya* with willing submission and feel themselves subdued." (Q 9:29)

11. **Jihad:** Jihad is warfare to spread Islam:

- "Fight and kill the disbelievers wherever you find them, and seize them, beleaguer them and lie in wait for them in every stratagem of war…" (Q 9:5)

- "Fight those who believe not in Allah nor the Last Day, nor hold that forbidden by Allah and His Messenger, nor acknowledge the Religion of Truth, from among the People of the Book, until they pay the *jizya* with willing submission and feel themselves subdued." (Q 9:29)

- "So fight them until there is no more *fitna* and all submit to the religion of Allah alone." (Q 8:39)

- "I have been commanded to fight people until they testify that there is no god but Allah and that Mohammed is the Messenger of Allah, and perform the prayer, and pay the *zakat*. If they say it, they have saved their blood and possessions from me, except for the rights of Islam over them. And their final reckoning is with Allah" (Sahih Bukhari and Sahih Muslim – agreed upon – as cited in *'Umdat al-Salik* o9.1 Jihad)

- "Jihad means to wage war against non-Muslims and is etymologically derived from the word *mujahada*, signifying warfare to establish the religion." (*'Umdat al-Salik*, o9.0, Jihad)

- "Islam makes it incumbent on all adult males, provided they are not disabled or incapacitated, to prepare themselves for the conquest of [other] countries so that the writ of Islam is obeyed in every country in the world.... But those who study Islamic Holy War will understand why Islam wants to conquer the whole world.... Those who know nothing of Islam pretend that Islam counsels against war. Those [who say this] are witless. Islam says: Kill all the unbelievers just as they would kill you all!" (Ayatollah Khomeini as quoted by Amir Taheri.)

- "Does this mean that Muslims should sit back until they are devoured by [the unbelievers]? Islam says: Kill them [the non-Muslims], put them to the sword and scatter [their armies]. Does this mean sitting back until [non-Muslims] overcome us? Islam says: Kill in the service of Allah those who may want to kill you! Does this mean that we should surrender [to the enemy]? Islam says: Whatever good there is exists thanks to the sword and in the shadow of the sword! People cannot be made obedient except with the sword! The sword is the key to Paradise, which can be opened only for the Holy Warriors! There are hundreds of other [Quranic] psalms and *Hadiths* [sayings of the prophet] urging Muslims to value war and to fight. Does all this mean that Islam is a religion that prevents men from waging war? I spit upon those foolish souls who make such a claim." (Ayatollah Khomeini as quoted by Amir Taheri.[70])

12. **Lying/*Taqiyya*:** It is permissible for a Muslim to lie, especially to non-Muslims, to safeguard himself personally or to protect Islam.

  - "Let not the believers take the disbelievers as friends instead of the believers, and whoever does that, will never be helped by Allah in any way, *unless you indeed fear a danger from them.* And Allah warns you against Himself, and to Allah is the final return." (Q 3:28)

  - "*'Unless you indeed fear a danger from them'* meaning, except those believers who in some areas or times fear for their safety from the disbelievers. In this case, such believers are allowed to show friendship to the disbelievers outwardly, but never inwardly....'We smile in the face of some people although our hearts curse them.'" (*Tafsir Ibn Kathir*, vol. 2, 141)

- "Mohammed said, 'War is deceit.'" (Bukhari vol. 4:267 and 269)

- "He who makes peace between the people by inventing good information or saying good things, is not a liar." (Bukhari vol. 3:857 p.533)

13. **Slander/Blasphemy:** In shariah, slander means anything that might offend a Muslim, even if it is true: "... The reality of tale-bearing lies in divulging a secret, in revealing something confidential whose disclosure is resented. A person should not speak of anything he notices about people besides that which benefits a Muslim to relate or prevent disobedience." (*'Umdat al-Salik,* r3.1)

14. **Underage Marriage:** Islamic doctrine permits the marriage of pre-pubescent girls. There is no minimum age for a marriage contract and consummation may take place when the girl is age eight or nine.

- "And those of your women as have passed the age of monthly courses [periods], for them the *'Iddah* [prescribed period before divorce is final], if you have doubts (about their periods), is three months, *and for those who have no courses [(i.e. they are still immature) their 'Iddah (prescribed period) is three months likewise, except* in case of death]. And for those who are pregnant (whether they are divorced or their husbands are dead), their 'Iddah (prescribed period) is until they deliver (their burdens), and whosoever fears Allah and keeps his duty to Him, He will make his matter easy for him." (Q 65:4)

- "Aisha narrated: that the Prophet married her when she was six years old and he consummated his marriage when she was nine years old, and then she remained with him for nine years (i.e., till his death)." (*Sahih al-Bukhari*, vol. 7, Book 62, Number 64; see also Numbers 65 and 88)"They may not have menstruated as yet either because of young age, or delayed menstrual discharge as it happens in the case of some women, or because of no discharge at all throughout life which, though rare, may also be the case. In any case, the waiting-period of such a woman is the same as of the woman who has stopped menstruation, that is, three months from the time divorce was pronounced.

- "Here, one should bear in mind the fact that, according to the explanations given in the Qur'an, the question of the waiting period arises in respect of the women with whom marriage may have been consummated, for there is no waiting-period in case divorce is pronounced before the consummation of marriage. (Al-Ahzab: 49). Therefore, making mention of the waiting-period for girls who have not yet menstruated, clearly proves that it is not only permissible to give away the girl at this age but it is permissible for the husband to consummate marriage with her. Now, obviously no Muslim has the right to forbid a thing which the Qur'an has held as permissible." (Syed Abu-Ala' Maududi, *Towards Understanding the Qur'an*, volume 5, p. 620, note 13)

15. **Zakat**: the obligation for Muslims to pay *zakat* arises out of Quran Verse 9:60 and is one of the Five Pillars of Islam. *Zakat* may be given only to Muslims, never to non-Muslims.

   - *Zakat* is for the poor and the needy, and those employed to administer the (funds); for those whose hearts have been (recently) reconciled (to Truth); for those in bondage and in debt; in the cause of Allah; and for the wayfarer: (thus is it) ordained by Allah, and Allah is full of knowledge and wisdom. (Q 9:60) "Of their goods take alms so that thou mightiest purify and sanctify them...." (Q 9:103) "*Zakat* is obligatory: (a) for every free Muslim and (b) who has possessed a *zakat-payable amount* [the minimum that necessitates *zakat*] (*'Umdat al-Salik*, h1.1)

   - According to shariah, there are eight categories of recipients for *Zakat*: The poor; Those short of money; *Zakat* workers (those whose job it is to collect the *zakat*); Those whose hearts are to be reconciled; Those purchasing their freedom; Those in debt; Those fighting for Allah (Jihad); Travelers needing money (*'Umdat al-Salik*, h8.7-h8.18)

- "It is not permissible to give *Zakat* to a non-Muslim..." (*'Umdat al-Salik,* h8.24)

PART I

THE THREAT POSED BY SHARIAH

①

WHAT IS 'SHARIAH'?

The Arabic word "shariah," according to one modern English-language student textbook on Islam, "literally means a *straight path* (Quran 45:18) or *an endless supply of water*. It is the term used to describe the rules of the lifestyle (*Deen*) ordained for us by Allah. In more practical terms, shariah includes all the do's and don'ts of Islam."[71]

In other words, shariah is held by mainstream Islamic authorities – not to be confused with "radical," "extremist" or "political" elements said to operate at the fringes of Islam – to be the perfect expression of divine will and justice and thus is the supreme law that must comprehensively govern all aspects of Muslims' lives, irrespective of when or where they live. Shariah is characterized as a "complete way of life" (social, cultural, military, religious, and political), governed from cradle to grave by Islamic law.

While many, many millions of Muslims around the world do not practice their faith in a manner consistent with shariah, as this chapter makes clear, those who *do* practice shariah have grounds for arguing that their version of Islam is the authoritative one. And those who claim that there is no single shariah – a narrative that has recently emerged from representatives of Muslim- and Arab-American groups[72] and their non-Muslim apologists[73] – are either ignorant of the facts about shariah discussed below, or deliberately dissembling (see chapter three).

THE SOURCES OF SHARIAH

There are four sources for shariah that make it authoritative: the Quran, the *Sunna, ijma,* and *qiyas.* Deemed the "uncreated word of Allah," the Quran reflects direct divine revelation and is understood to be the primary source of Islamic law. After the Quran, Islamic jurists next turn to the *Sunna,* considered to be indirect divine revelation arising out of the *hadiths,* or sayings or acts of Mohammed. *Ijma* refers to the consensus of the grand *mujtahids* of the past, a historic process in which, once consensus attached, became a permanent part of the immutable body of Islamic law. Finally, the fourth source for shariah is *qiyas,* or reasoning by analogy, which applies an accepted principle or assumption to arrive at a legal ruling.[74]

In order fully to understand shariah, it is necessary to examine each of these sources and their contributions in turn.

The Quran: In Islamic parlance, the Quran is considered to be the uncreated word of Allah. According to Muslim belief, it has existed since the beginning of time and was revealed by the Archangel Gabriel in the 7th Century to the Prophet Mohammed in the Arabic language of his homeland.

It follows from the characterization of the Quran as the uncreated word of Allah that its points are timeless. Clearly, if it were possible to place the Quran in context within a certain historical period, it could be said that it has subsequently become obsolete – especially since so many of its tenets are unique to 7th Century Bedouin culture. That would be tantamount, however, to asserting that Allah's uncreated, and therefore eternal, word is actually time-limited. Thus, it is mandatory that the Quran be deemed as eternal and eternally applicable to *everyone*, not just Muslims.

The preeminence of the Quran in shariah is closed to debate. An Indian Islamic jurist, Asaf A.A. Fyzee, put it in his work *Outlines of Mohammedan Law*: "The Koran according to this theory is the first source of law. ... It is for this reason that the verse of the Koran (*ayat*), although only a few of them deal specifically with legal questions, are held to be of paramount authority." [75]

The Quran is comprised of 114 chapters (or *Suras*) that include some 6,236 *ayat* or verses, and is believed by Muslims to have been revealed over a period of 22 years (from 610 to 632 A.D., the year of Mohammed's death). Chronologically speaking, the first 86 of the 114 chapters were said to have been revealed to the Prophet in Mecca while the remaining 28 came after the *hijra* to Medina in 622.

Although the chronological order of these verses is known, the Quran itself is not laid out in order of reported revelation but by length of verses (longest to shortest). In the beginning, Quranic verses were memorized and recited orally, with some being jotted down in a haphazard manner on pieces of parchment, plant leaves, and even stones. It was not until about 650 that the third Caliph, Uthman, commissioned an official, standardized version of the Quran, after which a concerted effort was made to find and destroy any earlier remnants and versions.

It is important to appreciate that *the Quran was not compiled in the chronological order of revelations, but rather organized from longest to shortest verses*. This decision makes for difficult reading and even more difficult understanding of what was said and when.

In light of the Islamic *doctrine of "abrogation"* – which holds that the later verses supersede, or abrogate, the earlier ones – the actual chronological order of the Quranic verses makes a critical difference. This is because there are contradictions among the verses, a delicate situation that had to be dealt with by Mohammed himself. Thus arose the device known as *al-mansukh wa al-nasikh* ("that which is abrogated and that which abrogates"). The basis for this solution to an otherwise difficult conundrum in what is supposed to be a perfect book can be found in both the *hadiths* and the Quran itself, where verse 2:106 states: "When we cancel a message, or throw it into oblivion, we replace it with one better or one similar. Do you not know that God has power over all things?" A number of other verses convey the same understanding. All four schools of Sunni Islamic jurisprudence are in complete agreement on doctrine of abrogation and in general agreement on the abrogating and abrogated import of shariah doctrine regarding Quranic texts.[76] Seventy-five percent of Sunni Islamic law is recognized in common across all four schools. An Islamic jurist does not read Islamic law and decide for himself what is or is not abrogated as this has already been determined by the school of law to which the jurist belongs. These issues have already been decided. A Hanafi, Shafite, Maliki, and even Hanbali Islamic scholar will refer to their respective school's books on abrogating and abrogated texts. No one can become a shariah judge unless he knows these passages *by heart*; they are that important.

In practice, Quranic abrogation results in a known doctrinal footprint that subordinates the milder, more moderate verses of the Quran from the Meccan period of revelation, to the later and violent verses of the Medina period. *Islamic law is substantially derived from the Medinan period.* Where a conflict exists, anything said during the Medinan period overrules anything on the same subject in the Meccan. And anything said in the later part of the Medinan period either overrules or controls anything said in the earlier part.

To put a fine point on it: When our shariah-compliant enemies cite from the most violent verses of the Quran to justify their actions, they are completely aligned with Islamic law and doctrine.

As the noted scholar David Bukay wrote in a 2007 essay for the *Middle East Quarterly*, "Statements that there is no compulsion in religion and that jihad is primarily about internal struggle and not about holy war may receive applause in university lecture halls and diplomatic board rooms, but they misunderstand the importance of abrogation in Islamic theology."[77] The point also should be made here that, independent of abrogation, the forcible imposition of shariah is intended to set the pre-conditions within a society that will "open minds and hearts to Islam, and thereby encourage conversion." (We shall discuss below the implications for national security leaders whose professional responsibility includes understanding the motivations and claimed justifications of the jihadi enemy.)

Closely related to the doctrine of abrogation is the *concept of progressive revelation*, which means that the Quran's verses were revealed gradually over a lengthy period of some 20 years. As Sayyid Qutb, the Muslim Brotherhood strategist put it: "The Quran did not come down all at once; rather it came down according to the needs of the Islamic society in facing new problems…."[78]

According to Muslim belief, the gradual revelation of the Quranic verses tracked with the development of the early Muslim community itself under the Prophet Mohammed's leadership. Early on, when his followers were a small, reviled group in Mecca, the corresponding revelations from Allah commanded a protective low profile. Even in the face of harsh criticism, Mohammed instructed his followers to maintain a peaceful attitude and the Quranic verses of the period reflect that attitude.

Later on, after Mohammed's move to Medina (the *hijra*), circumstances for the early Muslims improved and their numbers, and strength, grew significantly. At this time, new revelations permitted them to fight back against those who attacked them. This is precisely the point made by Major Nidal Malik Hasan in his pre-Fort Hood massacre presentation at Walter Reed.[79] Hasan explained the "Jihad-rule of Abrogation" in Slide 35 of his presentation.[80]

Finally, after the signal Battle of Badr in the year 624, where a relatively small Muslim force overcame a much larger enemy force of non-Muslims for the first time, revelations emerged that permitted – and then commanded – Muslims to go on the offensive from that time onward, until all the world should be under shariah. Specifically, the chronologically last Sura to address jihad is Sura 9, the "Sura of the Sword." In accordance with the doctrine of abrogation, its passages represent the ultimate authority on the requirements of jihad:

> Fight and slay the unbelievers wherever ye find them, and lie in wait for them in every stratagem of war. But if they repent, and establish regular prayers and practice regular charity, then open the way for them; for Allah is Oft-forgiving, Most Merciful. (Q 9:5)

> Fight those who believe not in Allah nor the Last Day, nor hold that forbidden which hath been forbidden by Allah and His Apostle, nor acknowledge the religion of truth, even if they are of the people of the Book, until they pay the jizya with willing submission, and feel themselves subdued. (Q 9:29)

Instructions on Muslim relations with Christians and Jews were laid out in the late Medinan period as well. Those familiar with Islamic concerns with regard to terrorism are familiar with the Quranic injunction: "Let there be no compulsion in religion." (Q 5:99) This passage is a particular favorite of those Muslim Brotherhood operatives and others seeking to obscure the true character of shariah.

What most non-Muslims have not heard is Quran 3:85: *"Whoever seeks a religion other than Islam will never have it accepted of him, and he will be of those who have truly failed in the hereafter."* (Emphasis added.) Even more graphic is Sura 98:6 where it is asserted that non-Muslims are "the most vile of created beings."

These verses are interpreted under shariah to mean that anyone who does not accept Islam is unacceptable in the eyes of Allah and that he will send them to Hell. When it is said that shariah is a supremacist program, this is one of the bases for it.

And even more specifically, regarding the possibility of Muslim friendship with any but fellow Muslims: "Oh ye who believe! Take not the Jews and the Christians for your friends and protectors; they are but friends and protectors to each other. And he amongst you that turns to them for friendship is of them. Verily Allah guideth not the unjust."(Q 5:51)

This verse lays down the rule for Muslims that "the unjust" are not only the Christians and Jews: they are also Muslims who take Christians and Jews as friends.

And lastly, to quote just one of the Quranic verses that is used repeatedly by shariah-adherent Muslims to castigate Jews and Christians, and by extension, the West:

> "Shall I point out to you something much worse than this, (as judged) by the treatment it received from Allah? Those who incurred the curse of Allah and His wrath, those of whom some He transformed into apes and swine, those who worshipped evil...." (Quran 5:60)

So, according to Sura 5:60, Allah turned people who worshipped evil into apes and swine. The references refer, respectively, to the apes, who are the Jews (the people of the Sabbath), while the swine are Christians, the infidels who adhere to the communion of Jesus.

Apologists for shariah try to dismiss such citations as "cherry picking" from the Quran. However, *these Sura are selected precisely because they are operative according to shariah's doctrine of abrogation.* This stepped process of development through which the first Muslims moved forms the model for all Muslims to the current day.

Muslim children, and those studying to become converts to Islam, are typically taught first about the gentle "your religion for you, mine for me" verses of the Quran.

Instruction to Westerners, as it turns out, is strictly limited to understanding Islam in its early peaceful phases. In fact, it is a top priority of the Islamic Movement to discourage U.S. leaders from studying Islamic doctrine and law. As Edward Said famously argued in his 1978 book *Orientalism*, only those who can speak classical Arabic can understand the true meaning of Islam, so why read anything at all?

Muslims, however, are required to proceed on to eventual understanding of the complete sequence contained in the Quran and *hadiths*. This graduated progression to manage the Muslim community is what Ikhwan strategist Sayyid Qutb made as the object of his seminal jihadist monograph *Milestones*. The method of graduated progression is why it is impossible to understand the full import of Islam without mastering the doctrines of abrogation and its associated "progressive revelation."

Finally, progressive revelation along "milestones" tracks with the stepped-learning process that many national security and law enforcement officials have taken to calling "the self-radicalization process." Shariah itself calls for this evolution. The practice may or may not be properly described as "radical," but it certainly reflects the gradual revelation of Islam itself.

The *Sunna*: The second most authoritative source for shariah is the *Sunna*, commonly understood to be the actions and sayings of the Prophet. The *Sunna* includes the *ahadith* (plural of *hadith*), or collections by Mohammed's contemporaries of what he did and said during his lifetime. Also within the *Sunna* is the *Sira*, which are biographical accounts of the life of Mohammed. It should be noted that the *ahadith* (not the *Sira*) constitute the legally significant element of the *Sunna*.[81]

The many hundreds of thousands of *hadiths* have been recorded in a number of *hadith* collections, of which six collections are held to be the most authoritative (or "strong *hadiths*," meaning their chain of transmission is considered solid). The two most important collections of all are those by Sahih Al-Bukhari (collected and compiled by Mohammed bin Isma'il, known as Imam Bukhari, born 810, died 870) and Sahih Muslim (Muslim bin al-Hajjaj, known as Imam Muslim, born 817/818, died 874/875).

Ijma: In addition to the Quran and *Sunna*, there are also two accepted secondary sources for shariah: these are *ijma* (consensus of the scholars) and *qiyas* (analytical deduction). Consensus of the Islamic jurists refers to the achievement of agreement on particular legal issues and finds its justification in numerous verses of the Quran.[82] *Hadith* accounts also provide support with the words of Mohammed: "My followers will never agree upon an error or what is wrong." The early Muslim scholars turned to this device of *ijma* only when they could not find a specific legal ruling in either the Quran or the *Sunna*.

Qiyas: *Qiyas* make up the fourth most important source for shariah. The term means "to judge by comparing with a thing." Its methods of deductive reasoning derive from the previous three sources of authenticity, namely the Quran, the *Sunna*, and *ijma*. When a legal ruling was required but could not be found in the other sources, the Islamic jurists employed analogy, reasoning, and legal precedent to arrive at new case law. Although all four schools of Sunni jurisprudence (Hanafi, Shafi'i, Maliki, and Hanbali) accept *ijma* as a legitimate source of shariah, Shiite Muslims do not; however, they replace *ijma* with *aql* (or reason). Considering that Shiites do not accept the authority of the Sunni Caliphs after Imam Ali, it is understandable that they would reject a source of legal authority that arose under their authority. In any case, the Shia practice of *aql* is essentially identical to *ijma*.

THE APPLICATION OF SHARIAH

Shariah contains categories and subjects of Islamic law called the branches of *fiqh* (literally, "understanding"). They include Islamic worship, family relations, inheritance, commerce, property law, civil (tort) law, criminal law, administration, taxation, constitution, international relations, war and ethics, and other categories.

Four Sunni and two Shiite schools (*madhhab*) of jurisprudence address these legal issues. The Islamic scholars of the Sunni schools – Hanafi, Hanbali, Maliki, and Shafi'i – as well as the Ja'fari and Ismaili Fatimid Shiite schools, completed codification of Islamic law by the tenth century. From that time until the present, Islamic *fiqh* has remained reasonably fixed.

Despite a measure of variation on minor details, and a more flexible attitude about *ijtihad* by traditional Shiite scholars, all of the major schools of shariah are in agreement on more than 70 percent of substantive matters. In 1959, al-Azhar University (today the seat of Sunni jurisprudence although it was founded by the Shiite Fatimids) issued a fatwa that recognized Shia Islam as legitimate. Despite its own adherence to *fiqh* of the Ja'fari Twelver school, the Iranian constitution of 1989 likewise made a point of explicitly recognizing the validity of the four Sunni madhhabs.

According to shariah, all of Islam – its doctrines, practices, theology and adherents – are subordinate to that comprehensive code. The enemy fights jihad at the command of and in legal compliance with Shariah expressly to achieve the global imposition of shariah. Indeed, shariah is law of the land within the Dar al-Islam (Abode or House of Islam or those places where shariah is implemented) and its imposition within the *Dar al-Harb* (Abode or House of War or places where shariah is not implemented at all or not fully implemented) is the primary objective of jihad.

Much can be said about the brutally repressive, even totalitarian character of shariah with its harsh treatment of women, homosexuals, Jews and other "infidels," apostates and petty criminals, among others. Shariah is wholly at odds with U.S. national sovereignty, the U.S. Constitution, and the liberties it guarantees. (This subject is dealt with at greater length in chapter six).

To get a sense for the character of shariah, a brief sampling is in order of contemporary Islamic legal scholars who are generally considered "moderate." Representative is the commentary about the importance of shariah and its centrality to Islam of Abdur Rahman I. Doi. Doi, who died in 1999, was born in India but lived and taught Islamic law in Malaysia, Nigeria, and South Africa. In *Shariah: The Islamic Law,* he wrote:

> In the shariah, there is an explicit emphasis on the fact that Allah is the Lawgiver and the whole *ummah,* the nation of Islam, is merely His trustee. It is because of this principle that the *ummah* enjoys a derivative rule-making power and not an absolute law-creating prerogative. The Islamic State, like the whole of what one might call Islamic political psychology, views the Dar al-Islam (Abode of Islam) as one vast homogeneous commonwealth of people who have a common ideology in all matters both spiritual and temporal. The entire Muslim *ummah* lives under the shariah to which every member has to submit, with sovereignty belonging to Allah alone.
> 83

For Doi, shariah is incompatible with democracy: "It is because of this principle that the *Ummah* enjoys a *derivative rule-making power.*" Unfortunately, that is not a minority view. Rather, it is the position of the collective Islamic scholars speaking in consensus (*ijma*).

Take for example, the analysis of Muhammad Hashim Kamali, who was born in Afghanistan in 1944 and is a professor of Islamic law at the International Islamic University of Malaysia. As he put it in his *Principles of Islamic Jurisprudence*: "Sovereignty in Islam is the prerogative of Almighty Allah alone. He is the absolute arbiter of values and it is His will that determines good and evil, right and wrong."[84] Kamali added: "It is neither the will of the ruler nor of any assembly of men, nor even the community as a whole, that determines the values and the laws which uphold those values....The sovereignty of the people, if the use of the word 'sovereignty' is appropriate at all, is a delegated, or executive, sovereignty...only.[85]

Yet another confirmation of the expressed inherent incompatibility of shariah with democratic principles can be found in *Theories of Islamic Law: The Methodology of Ijtihad*[86] by Imran Ahsan Khan Nyazee, a Pakistani professor of Islamic law in the Faculty of shariah and Law of Islamabad: "Islam, it is generally acknowledged, is a 'complete way of life' and at the core of this code is the law of Islam." It follows that:

> No other sovereign or authority is acceptable to the Muslim, unless it guarantees the application of these laws [shariah] in their entirety. Any other legal system, howsoever attractive it may appear on the surface, is alien for Muslims and is not likely to succeed in the solution of their problems; it would be doomed from the start....A comprehensive application of these laws, which flow directly or indirectly from the decrees (*ahkam*) of Allah, would mean that they should regulate every area of life, from politics to private transactions, from criminal justice to the laws of traffic, from ritual to international law, and from the laws of taxation and finance to embezzlement and white collar crimes.[87]

For those who hold out hope that a more moderate form of shariah might exist or be developed that would be more compatible with Western mores, principles, and rights, Doi makes the point that shariah is absolutely immutable:

> The shariah was not revealed for limited application for a specific age. It will suit every age and time. It will remain valid and shall continue to be, till the end of this life on earth. Its injunctions were coined in such a manner that they are not affected by the lapse of time. They do not become obsolete, nor do their general principles and basic theories need to be changed or renovated. [88]

In fact, as was noted above, doctrinal Islam holds that within the first two centuries after the death of Mohammed, the *Mujtaheed* (the recognized Islamic scholars of the day)[89] came to consensus (*ijma*) regarding various aspects of shariah. Once the *Mujtaheed* completed this process, once agreement among the scholars was established on an issue, that element of Islamic law became permanently established as an element of sacred law.[90]

Yousuf al-Qaradawi, spiritual leader of the Muslim Brotherhood, affirmed this reality in that shariah-promoting organization's online forum: "The shariah cannot be amended to conform to changing human values and standards. Rather, it is the absolute norm to which all human values and conduct must conform."[91]

Abdur Rahman Doi cites the Quran directly[92] in describing the fate of those who fail to conform to shariah:

> "And if any fail to judge by the light of what Allah has revealed, they are not better than those who rebel." (5:50)

> "And if any fail to judge by the light of what Allah has revealed, they are no better than wrong-doers." (5:48)

> "And if any fail to judge by the light of what Allah has revealed, they are no better than unbelievers." (5:47)

Even a mass-market, English-language seventh-grade text-book entitled, *What Islam Is All About*, by Yahiya Emerick – one of the most popular texts used in Islamic schools in America today – makes plain that shariah is a program wholly at odds with the American form of government and way of life: "Muslims know that Allah is the Supreme Being in the universe, therefore, His laws and commandments must form the basis for all human affairs."[93] The textbook also notes that, "The basis of the legal and political system is the shariah of Allah. Its main sources are the Quran and *Sunnah*. Muslims dream of establishing the power of Islam in the world."[94] In short, "The law of the land is the shariah of Allah."[95] (This book is also used in connection with Islamic proselytizing in U.S. federal penitentiaries.)

It bears repeating: The foregoing quotes are from Islamic legal texts which were written by so-called "non-radicalized" Muslim legal scholars, yet they proclaim that Islamic law is categorically and unquestionably a monopoly, the absolute and sole law of the land. As will be discussed further below, this reality creates an unavoidable legal problem with respect to shariah in America because Article VI of the U.S. Constitution established that, in this country, the Constitution is "the supreme law of the land."

SHARIAH AND JIHAD

Shariah – derived from Islam's foundational documents – defines Islamic doctrine, including the universal obligation to jihad against non-believers. The question is: What is meant by "jihad"? Is jihad merely a personal struggle to be the best possible Muslim? Or does jihad mean holy war, the pursuit of a global Islamic State (caliphate) that rules in accordance with shariah?

THE QURAN AND JIHAD

The answer is readily accessible to those willing to seek it. Islamic jurisprudence, fiqh in Arabic, forms the legal context for shariah and its rulings. As such, it relies first and foremost on the Quran and cites its verses to support the caliphate and jihad. Simple citation of the verses themselves, without the context provided by how the shariah scholars interpreted these verses, provides an incomplete and incorrect understanding.

Shariah scholars typically cite as authority for jihad from the Quran any of the 164 verses that specifically refer to jihad against non-Muslims in terms that include military expeditions, fighting enemies, or distributing the spoils of war. Among these are: "Fighting is prescribed for you" (Q 2:216); "Slay them wherever you find them" (Q 4:89); and "Fight the idolaters utterly" (Q 9:36).

Among the most categorical of such Quranic entries and the most often cited as authoritative by the shariah scholars is the "Verse of the Sword": "So when the sacred months have passed, then fight and slay the pagans wherever you find them, and seize them, beleaguer them, and lie in wait for them in every stratagem of war; but if they repent and establish regular prayers, and practice regular charity, then leave their way free to them; for surely Allah is Forgiving, Merciful." (Q 9:5)

As regards pagans (or polytheists), therefore, the doctrine is clear: Convert or die. The treatment for "People of the Book," Christians and Jews, is controlled by a Sura 9: "Fight those who believe not in God nor the Last Day, nor hold that forbidden which hath been forbidden by God and His Apostle, nor acknowledge the Religion of truth, even if they be People of the book [Christians and Jews] until they pay the *Jizya* with willing submission and feel themselves subdued." (Q 9:29)

Thus, Christians and Jews are afforded a third choice not available to polytheists: convert, die or submit to Islam as *dhimmis*.[96]

In the Quran and in later Muslim usage, the word jihad is commonly followed by the expression *fi sabil Allah*, "in the path of Allah."[97] By describing the warfare of jihad as something sanctioned by Allah himself, Islamic authorities set it apart from the common tribal warfare of the time and elevated it to a superior status as something sacred.

THE HADITHS AND JIHAD

The *hadiths* are the second source of shariah. Throughout those *hadiths* considered authoritative, jihad means warfare. The hadith collections of Sahih al-Bukhari and Sahih Muslim are accorded the highest level of authenticity by Islamic scholars and both include hundreds of references to jihad. Each and every one of these citations leaves no room for doubt that jihad means warfare.[98]

For example, one of the most oft-cited Sahih al-Bukhari *hadiths* about jihad says:

> Narrated abu Huraira: Allah's Apostle said, "I have been ordered to fight with the people till they say, 'None has the right to be worshipped but Allah,' and whoever says, 'None has the right to be worshipped but Allah,' his life and property will be saved by me except for Islamic laws and his accounts will be with Allah, (either to punish him or to forgive him)." [99]

The wording of this *"sahih" hadith* (meaning that its authoritative status has already been determined) not only states unequivocally that it is Allah himself who has ordered Muslims to war against non-Muslims, but also states the command in completely open-ended terms; i.e., Muslims are to fight "the people" who do not worship Allah until "they" all submit to Islam. This is not a command to convert non-believers but to subjugate them to "Islamic laws."

THE CLASSICAL SOURCES ON JIHAD

There are, moreover, a number of recognized compilations that systematize and codify Islamic law. They spell out the duty of jihad as holy war, which all Muslims, so the shariah states, must advance in one or more carefully delineated ways.

Excerpts from several of these texts are illustrative. The first is from the Shafite school's *Reliance of the Traveller: The Clas-*

sic *Manual of Islamic Sacred Law (Umdat Al-Salik)* by Ahmad ibn Naqib al-Misri. An English-language edition of *Reliance* was published in 1994, with Nu Ha Mim Keller as the translator and chief commentator. Readers are advised at the outset that this version of the 14th Century classic is an officially approved translation, complete with testimonials to that effect in English and Arabic from the governments of Syria, Jordan, Egypt and Saudi Arabia.[100]

In Chapter O, o9.0, *Reliance of the Traveler* states: "Jihad means to wage war against non-Muslims, and is etymologically derived from the word *mujahada,* signifying warfare to establish the religion. And it is the lesser Jihad."[101] Al-Misri goes on to explain that the "greater" jihad is the struggle for the spiritual self. Importantly, he adds that *the hadith upon which that distinction is based is weak or false,* depending on which authority is referenced, *and so is not authoritative.*[102]

Consequently, when *Reliance* refers to the greater and lesser jihad, it indicates that this differentiation is not a part of the law of jihad – leaving us with no alternative but to understand that, under shariah, the meaning of 'jihad' connotes force and violence.

Al-Misri also cites at o9.0:

> ... Such *hadiths* as the one related by Bukhari and Muslim that the Prophet ... said: "I have been commanded to fight the people until they testify that there is no god but Allah and that Mohammed is the Messenger of Allah, and perform the prayer, and pay the *zakat.* If they say it, they have saved their blood and possessions from me, except for the rights of Islam over them."[103]

Other confirmations of this interpretation can be found in the *Al-Hidayah,* which came out in the 12th century and is a classic from the Hanafi Islamic school of law.[104] Then, there is *The Distinguished Jurist's Primer* by Ibn Rushd, which was published in the 12th century, and is a classic Maliki text.[105] It is worth noting that

Ibn Rushd was a *qhadi,* an Islamic law judge, in the court of Cordoba in Andalus. He is best known as "Averroës" in the West.

Each of these texts contains similar treatments on the subject of "jihad." In Ibn Rushd's work, Book Ten is entitled, "Jihad." In the *Hidayah,* Book Thirteen entitled "The Siyar," deals with jihad and relations with non-Muslims. It maps almost exactly with the book *Shaybani Siyar,* or, as translated by a Professor Majid Khadduri – *The Islamic Law of Nations* – which is the oldest, most completely extant text of Islamic law on warfare.[106]

CONTEMPORARY ADVOCATES OF JIHAD

Moving to modern times, Abu al-A'la Mawdudi (1903-79), the Indian-born (and later, Pakistani) thinker, paved the way for Muslim Brotherhood ideologues such as Hasan al-Banna (1906-49) and Sayyid Qutb (1906-56). Those Ikhwan ideologues recast modern jihad in the fiery language of revolution and anti-colonialism of the times and not just strictly warfare to expand Islamic legal and political dominance. Their war was directed against oppressive colonialist forces or Muslim rulers ("the near enemy") who were judged apostates because of their failure to uphold shariah.[107] Mawdudi's approach harkened back to the 13th century Islamic jurist, Taqi ad-Din Ahmed ibn Tamiyya (1263-1328), who declared the overthrow of unjust governments to be lawful.

In his capstone book, *Milestones,* Muslim Brotherhood chief theoretician Qutb[108] declared:

> The reasons for Jihad which have been described in...verses [from cited sacred texts] are these: to establish God's authority in the earth; to arrange human affairs according to the true guidance provided by God; to abolish all the Satanic forces and Satanic systems of life; to end the lordship of one man over others since all men are creatures of God and no one has the authority to make them his servants or to make arbitrary laws for them. These reasons are sufficient for proclaiming Jihad.[109]

By "Satanic systems of life," Qutb means the way of life practiced in Western-style liberal democracies – the way of the infidel, the Westerner, the non-Muslim. Similarly, "the lordship of one man over others" means the system of democracy – which is the political system of the infidel, the Westerner, the non-Muslim.

Among those who acted on Mawdudi and Qutb's injunctions with respect to jihad were the assassins of Egyptian president Anwar Sadat. The followers of Ayman al-Zawahiri and his group, Egyptian Islamic Jihad (EIJ), produced a pamphlet called *The Neglected Duty*, which exalted violent jihad to "enjoin the good and forbid evil"[110] as the heart and soul of Islam. *The Neglected Duty* exhorts Muslims to be aggressive and to "exert every conceivable effort" to establish truly Islamic government, a restoration of the caliphate, and the expansion of Dar al-Islam.[111]

Then, there is a volume whose title says it all: *The Quranic Concept of War*, written in 1979 by Brigadier General S. K. Malik when he was chief of staff of the Pakistani army.[112] Then-Pakistani Army Chief of Staff Zia ul Haq declared this book to be his country's doctrine.[113] The Advocate General in Pakistan said that it constitutes a "Restatement" of the law.[114]

OTHER SOURCES ON JIHAD

Modern means of communication allow for an even broader dissemination of Islamic thinking on the subject than ever before. For instance, the online Arabic language magazine *Moheet*, which has offices in Egypt and the United Arab Emirates, carried an article on March 13, 2010 by Islamic cleric Iman al-Khashab. The article extolled the virtues of jihad, provided doctrinal references for his position and described violent warfare against infidels as the "sixth pillar of Islam."[115] Al-Khashab wrote:

> Jihad in the path of Allah is a mainstay of the religion and a great religious duty, as the Prophet (PBUH) said: "The most important thing is Islam, and it is supported by prayer, and its

apex is jihad in the path of Allah." Allah has commanded us in many verses (of the Quran), and urged us, as has also our Prophet (PBUH), regarding the issue of jihad. The Prophet desired it himself, and urged (others) to it. He declared its virtues so often that some scholars consider it the sixth pillar of Islam, due to its importance, which is attested by how often it appears in the Quran and hadith.

THE SHIITE AND IRANIAN VIEWS OF JIHAD

The Sunni and Shiite schools of jurisprudence differ in a number of respects. One difference has been with respect to the doctrine under which "offensive" jihad could be conducted, with traditional Shiites holding that it may not be waged in the absence of an imam to lead it. According to Shia Islam, the 12th and final Shiite imam, directly descended from the Prophet, disappeared in the 10th century. For centuries afterward, Shiite scholars held that renewal of offensive jihad must await his reappearance as Shiism's messianic figure at the End of Times.

But in practice and in historical example, Shia and Sunni doctrines on jihad were fundamentally the same.116 Even the so-called "requirement" for the "hidden" Shia Imam's "consent" to wage jihad, was already argued away regarding "defensive jihad" by Abu Jaffar al-Tusi during the 11th century as the Shia of Iraq were beset by the Sunni Seljuk Turks.117 This position was reiterated in the 13th century by al-Hilli.118 These legists maintained—in a deliberately vague and elastic formulation—that Shia Muslims could be summoned to jihad by the Imam's so-called "designee(s)"—which came to mean the "fuqaha," or doctors of the (Shiite) Muslim Law. 119 With the advent at the outset of the 16th century of the very aggressive Shiite Safavid theocracy under Shah Ismail, who claimed direct descent from the Imams, we see "non-fuqaha" rulers declaring unabashed offensive, expansionist jihad throughout this dynasty. 120

Demonstrating how Safavid Shi'ite jurisprudence was in agreement with the Sunni consensus on the basic nature of jihad war, including offensive jihad, here is an excerpt from the Jami-i-Abbasi [the popular Persian manual of Shi'a Law] written by al-Amili (d.1622), a distinguished theologian under Shah Abbas I: [121]

> Islamic Holy war [jihad] against followers of other religions, such as Jews, is required unless they convert to Islam or pay the poll tax.

The 18th century Qajar Shiite theocratic dynasty saw the role of declaring jihad—again, including offensive, expansionist jihad—restored in theory to the Shiite fuqaha. [122] Finally re-emphasizing how such campaigns under the both Safavids and Qajars no longer required endorsement by the Imam, an early 18th century Qajar treatise on jihad states, "It is possible to say that jihad during the Imam's concealment is more praiseworthy than during his presence."[123]

The ascendancy of the Khomeini theocracy marked a revitalized militancy of Shiite jihadism unparalleled since the 16th to early 18th century Safavid dynasty. In 1970, the Iranian Ayatollah Ruhollah Musavi Khomeini outlined a personal ideology he called *Velayat-e Faqih* (Rule of the Jurisprudent). In it, he asserted – within this branch of Shia scholarly tradition – that Shiites should not have to wait interminably for the return to earth of their Mahdi to wage jihad.

Khomeini set himself up as a kind of stand-in for the 12th Imam as a grand ayatollah and arrogated to himself the title of "Imam." Following his revolution and rise to power in Tehran, the policy of his Iranian theocracy to bear in advancing the sort of offensive jihad shariah-adherent Sunnis had always espoused.

For example, Khomeini declared himself unequivocally committed to jihad:

Islam says: Whatever good there is exists thanks to the sword and in the shadow of the sword! People cannot be made obedient except with the sword! The sword is the key to Paradise, which can be opened only for Holy Warriors! There are hundreds of other [Koranic] psalms and *Hadiths* [sayings of the Prophet] urging Muslims to value war and to fight. Does all that mean that Islam is a religion that prevents men from waging war? I spit upon those foolish souls who make such a claim.[124]

Khomeini's ideology found its way into the 1989 Iranian constitution, as well. In the chapter dealing with the "Religious Army," better known as the Islamic Revolutionary Guard Corps (IRGC), the constitution pronounces: "The [IRGC has] the responsibility not only for the safeguarding of the frontiers, but also for a religious mission, which is Holy War (JIHAD) along the way of God, and the struggle to extend the supremacy of God's Law in the world."

Immediately following this chapter, the constitution quotes directly from Quranic verse 8:60: "Against them make ready your strength to the utmost of your power, including steeds of war, to strike terror into the hearts of the enemies of God and your enemies, and others besides." Interestingly, that is the same verse displayed on the Sunni Muslim Brotherhood's coat of arms.

It was this pan-Islamic perspective that brought the Iranian regime and its terror proxy Hezbollah to work with Osama bin-Laden, Ayman al-Zawahiri and an incipient al Qaeda in Sudan in the early 1990s in an operational alliance to conduct a unified jihad against the West. That Sunni-Shia alliance, formed under the aegis of the Sudanese Islamic figure, Hasan al-Turabi, solidified and intensified throughout the 1990s, with joint attacks against Khobar Towers (1996), two American embassies in East Africa (1998), the USS *Cole* (2000) and the attacks of September 11, 2001.

In short, each of these sources makes plain the supremacist character of shariah and the instrument for realizing its global dominance, jihad. The bottom line: There is no basis in doctrinal Islam for concluding that jihad means anything other than waging holy war for the implementation of shariah and the establishment of the caliphate throughout the world. Indeed, a scholarly consensus on the definition of jihad was achieved over a thousand years ago – because it was impossible *not* to have consensus on the question: Allah commanded it and Mohammed confirmed it. In both direct and indirect divine revelation, the meaning of jihad as holy war was made clear.

JIHAD IS OBLIGATORY[125]

With the correct meaning of jihad within shariah thus established, it is important next to note the compulsory nature of participating in jihad, which is founded in Quranic verse 2:216: "Prescribed for you is fighting, though it be hateful to you."

In his renowned *Muqaddimah*, the first work of Islamic historical theory, Ibn Khaldun, an acclaimed historian, jurist, philosopher, and early social scientist who lived from 1332-1406, picked up the theme of the Muslims' sacred duty to participate in jihad. He noted that, "In the Muslim community, the holy war is a religious duty, because of the universalism of the Muslim mission and [the obligation to] convert everybody to Islam either by persuasion or by force." Ibn Khaldun asserts that this is because Islam is "under obligation to gain power over other nations."[126]

In general, the obligation to jihad is a collective one (*fard kiffayah*) and only becomes a personal one (*fard 'ayn*) when Muslim lands are invaded or occupied by an infidel force that is uninvited. Ibn Rushd, writing in 12th Century Seville and Cordoba, Spain during the so-called "Golden Era" of Islam invoked the consensus of the scholars in his seminal *Bidayat al-Mujtahid wa-Nihayat al-Muqtasid*:

... This obligation [to jihad], when it can be properly carried out by a limited number of individuals, is cancelled for the remaining Muslims, is founded on [Q 9:122]: "It is not for the believers to go forth totally," "Yet to each Allah has promised the reward most fair" [Q 4:95] and, lastly, on the fact that the Prophet never went to battle without leaving some people behind. All this together implies that this activity is a collective obligation. ...

Scholars agree that all polytheists should be fought [According to some modern shariah authorities, this includes anyone who holds secular law as superior to Allah's shariah.] This is founded on: "Fight them until there is no persecution and the religion is Allah's entirely ...." [Q 8:39]

Damage inflicted upon the enemy may consist in damage to his property, injury to his person or violation of his personal liberty, i.e., that he is made a slave and is appropriated. This may be done, according to *ijma* [the consensus of the shariah authorities] to all polytheists: men, women, young and old, important and unimportant. ...

Most scholars are agreed that, in his dealings with captives, various policies are open to the Caliph or Imam [head of the Islamic State]. He may pardon them, enslave them, kill them, or release them either on ransom or as *dhimmi* [non-Muslim subjugated to the Muslim regime], in which latter case the released captive is obliged to pay poll-tax (*jizya*)."[127]

WAGING JIHAD

Muhammad ibn al-Hasan al-Shaybani, who lived in the 8th and 9th Centuries, was an important jurist of the Hanafi school of jurisprudence and the first to write extensively on the *Siyar* or Islamic Law of Nations. An important staple of Islamic jurisprudence, *Shaybani's Siyar* was translated and annotated by the respected contemporary scholar, Majid Khadduri, in 1966.

Shaybani wrote that a constant state of war must exist between the *Dar al-Islam* and the *Dar al-Harb* and explained the protocols to be followed in waging jihad.

> Fight in the name of Allah and in the "path of Allah." Combat those who disbelieve in Allah. Do not cheat or commit treachery, nor should you mutilate anyone or kill children. Whenever you meet your polytheist enemies, invite them [first] to adopt Islam. If they do so, accept it, and let them alone. . . .If they refuse, then call upon them to pay the *jizya* [poll tax imposed on dhimmis]; if they do, accept it and leave them alone. . . .If the army [of Islam] attacks *Dar al-Harb* and it is a territory that has received an invitation to accept Islam, it is commendable if the army renews the invitation, but if it fails to do so it is not wrong. The army may launch the attack by night or by day and it is permissible to burn [the enemy] fortifications with fire or to inundate them with water.[128]

Ibn Abi Zayd al-Qayrawani (10th century), a leading Maliki jurist, echoes al-Shaybani's injunction about the requirement to issue the call to Islam (*dawa*) before launching an attack (jihad) against the infidel. This legal requirement remains valid and relevant today. Al-Qayrawani also notes the choice given to People of the Book (Christians and Jews), who are not compelled to convert, but may submit to Islam, pay the jizya, and live under Muslim domination as *dhimmis*:

> Jihad is a precept of Divine institution. Its performance by certain individuals may dispense others from it. We Malikis maintain that it is preferable not to begin hostilities with the enemy before having invited the latter to embrace the religion of Allah except where the enemy attacks first. They have the alternative of either converting to Islam or paying the poll tax (*jizya*), short of which war will be declared against them.[129]

Finally, there is Ibn Taymiyya, a Hanbali jurist of the 14th century, and a favorite of contemporary jihadis, who, although primarily focused on defensive jihad, nevertheless wrote:

> Since lawful warfare is essentially jihad and since its aim is that the religion is Allah's entirely and Allah's word is uppermost, therefore according to all Muslims, those who stand in the way of this aim must be fought. As for those who cannot offer resistance or cannot fight, such as women, children, monks, old people, the blind, handicapped and their likes, they shall not be killed unless they actually fight with words (e.g., by propaganda) and acts (e.g., by spying or otherwise assisting in the warfare).[130]

Seething anger at the presence of hated non-Muslim influence anywhere in the "Muslim world" or in those parts of the world once under the dominion of Dar al-Islam infused Taymiyya's writings, including *Al-Ubudiyyah. Being a True Slave of Allah* and *Public and Private Law in Islam: Or Public Policy in Islamic Jurisprudence*.[131] It is in part Ibn Taymiyya's characterization of defensive jihad as a personal obligation (*fard 'ayn*) to fight "false" Muslim leaders (those who do not uphold strictly the obligations of shariah and allow Western/infidel troops on their soil) that has made him such a favorite source for contemporary jihadists.

CIVILIZATION JIHAD

Jihad in the form of violent acts, often referred to by some as "kinetic" jihad, dominates the attention of those responsible for national and homeland security. But the more dangerous threat, especially in the long run, is what the Muslim Brotherhood calls "civilization jihad" – a form of warfare that Robert Spencer has more popularly dubbed "stealth jihad."

According to shariah, this "pre-violent" form of jihad is considered an integral, even dominant element of jihad that is at least as obligatory for shariah's adherents as the violent kind. *Da-*

wa, the call to Islam that by Islamic law must precede jihad, is all-too-often dismissed – as are its manifestations under the rubric of non-violent jihad – simply because this kind of assault does not kill but intends "merely" to subjugate. Absent an appreciation of the threat posed by stealth jihad, the pre-violent jihadist is free to proceed unimpeded under the radar in Western societies, infiltrating and subverting along lines specifically tailored to today's liberal, multicultural-minded non-Muslim populations in ways that are genuinely difficult to recognize, oppose or counter. (See chapter seven.)

To be clear: The objective of the stealth jihad is the same as the violent: subjugation *of Dar al-Harb* to shariah, which would result in the non-Muslim world being subsumed under *Dar al-Islam*.

This subject will be dealt with at length in chapter five's discussion of the Muslim Brotherhood, because it is the Brotherhood that has the dominant role with respect to the prosecution of the pre-violent form of jihad in the United States, and the West more generally. The insinuation of shariah and its adherents into America's academic, banking and finance, government, intelligence, law enforcement and military institutions and society more generally is quite far advanced.

Official U.S. doctrine on threat development requires that threat assessment begin with an unconstrained analysis of the enemy's stated threat doctrine. The first two sections of this report make plain that it *is* possible to know the enemy and his intentions with certitude.

If adherents to shariah have sworn to destroy us, it is *their* doctrine we are required to know. Whether that doctrine is judged by us to be accurate, appropriate or even identifiable with "genuine" Islam is wholly irrelevant. If it can be demonstrated that the enemy that attacks and kills Americans and seeks to subvert our Constitution refers to and relies on this doctrine to guide and justify his actions, then that is all that matters in terms of the enemy threat doctrine U.S. civilian and military leaders must thoroughly understand and orient upon for the purpose of defeating such foes. (It is only in what the military calls the "course of action" development phase that issues concerning the actual validity of the threats adherence to Islamic law entails come into play.)

Failing to orient on an enemy's self-identified doctrines not only violates our own doctrine on threat analysis but renders us unable to defeat the enemy because we have failed properly to identify him. As noted at the beginning of this report, such failure defies the rules of warfare reaching back to Sun Tzu on the requirement to "know the enemy." It also completely defies common sense and the canons of professional conduct of our leadership.

SHARIAH'S SECURITY-RELEVANT ATTRIBUTES

Successfully assuring American security in the face of a determined jihadist effort to destroy this country will depend in part on an understanding of several attributes inherent in this seditious doctrine that have direct bearing on the character and insidiousness of the threat.

TREATIES AND TRUCES

Although the objective of the Muslim community, in the eyes of its jurists, is to spread submission to shariah through jihad, there are circumstances when the forces of Islam are not strong enough to prevail. Governed as they are by Islamic law in all they do, it is incumbent upon Muslims accurately to judge their capabilities at any point in time. When Muslims are powerful, they are commanded to mount offensive jihad without hesitation, relying on the Quranic verse 47:35 for authority: "So do not be faint-hearted and call for peace, when it is you who are the uppermost."

When infidel forces are too powerful to defeat, however, Muslims are obligated under the laws of war as defined in shariah to refrain from engaging in violence until such time as their forces once again are strong enough not just to take on the enemy, but to defeat him. This injunction against "transgressing the limits" also derives from the Quran: "Fight in the cause of Allah those who fight you, but do not transgress limits; for Allah loveth not transgressors." (Q 2:190)

Transgressing the limits of war in the context of shariah means launching jihad against superior enemy forces without ensuring adequate Muslim forces first. If the result of such rash action is that the enemy then retaliates by invading Muslim lands, with the result that (innocent) Muslims are killed, this becomes a "transgressing the limits" issue and may be consonant with what, according to the Quran, Allah viewed as the terrible crime of "spreading mischief in the land."

> On that account: We ordained for the Children of Israel that if any one slew a person - unless it be for murder or for spreading mischief in the land - it would be as if he slew the whole people: and if any one saved a life, it would be as if he saved the life of the whole people. Then although there came to them our messengers with clear signs, yet, even after that, many of them continued to commit excesses in the land. (Q 5:32)

The following verse, Quran 5:33, specifies the gruesome punishments that Allah ordains for those who violate this prohibition:

> The punishment of those who wage war against Allah and His Messenger, and strive with might and main for mischief through the land is: execution, or crucifixion, or the cutting off of hands and feet from opposite sides, or exile from the

land: that is their disgrace in this world, and a heavy punishment is theirs in the Hereafter." [132]

One of the reasons that Osama bin Laden and al Qaeda came in for criticism from shariah-oriented entities after the attacks of 9/11 was not because he launched terror attacks that killed thousands of innocent civilians, but because some Islamic authorities viewed the attacks as precipitous and premature. The fact that the U.S. was still powerful enough after 9/11 to invade Muslim lands with a large military force and exact massive retribution against Muslim populations may be considered evidence that bin Laden exceeded Muslim abilities, that is, "transgressed the limits."

It is important for national security leadership to pay attention when prominent Islamic entities or individuals, especially Salafis, appear to condemn the killing of non-Muslims in non-Muslim lands to determine whether the condemnation was made in an unqualified and outright manner or whether it was in some way associated with downstream acts that merely caused "mischief" to be brought down upon Muslim lands. This becomes especially relevant when jihadi forces come to be perceived as violating Islamic law themselves, especially actions that cause such downstream "killing without right" – meaning the unjust killing, not of non-Muslim innocents, but of *Muslims.*

This discussion about causing "mischief in the land" and the shariah prohibitions against launching jihad without the ability to carry through and prevail leads to situations in which Muslim forces might lawfully enter into a treaty or truce with the enemy. The classic example of such circumstances occurred in the year 628 when Mohammed, then in control of Medina, agreed to a 10-year truce with the pagan Qurashi tribe of Mecca.

Although he had set out to attack Mecca, Mohammed realized en route that his forces were not yet strong enough to prevail; so, he agreed to the Treaty of Hudaybiyyah. Two years later, with 10,000 men now under his command, Mohammed broke the treaty and marched into Mecca. Sahih hadith from Bukhari attributed to Mohammed, "War is deceit"[133] and "By Allah, and Allah willing, if I take an oath and later find something else better than that, then I do what is better and expiate my oath"[134] clearly demonstrate this doctrinal or moral justification of deception and truces.

Yasser Arafat's repeated references to the Treaty of Hudaybiyyah following his signature of the Oslo Accords in 1993 on behalf of the Palestinian Liberation Organization (PLO) is a good example in modern times of Muslim awareness of the Quranic position on entering into truces with the enemy. Arafat was careful to reassure his followers (in Arabic) that his commitment at Camp David was nothing more than a temporary hiatus in jihad (a *hudna*) at a time of PLO weakness vis-à-vis the Israelis – and entirely in keeping with shariah. Similarly, in 2006, the leadership of Hamas offered Israel a ten-year truce to break the deadlock over its refusal to recognize the Jewish State. At the time, few in the West seemed to realize that Palestinian Prime Minister Ismail Haniyeh was in perfect accord with the example of Mohammed and would predictably break any such hudna the moment it proved advantageous for the Muslim side to do so.

In practice, though, truces are generally disfavored under shariah "because it entails the nonperformance of jihad."[135] As noted above, the Quran enjoins its followers "So do not be faint-hearted and call for peace, when it is you who are the uppermost." (Q 47:35). Consequently, under Islamic law, the maintenance of a peaceful status quo cannot serve as the basis for a truce when the milestones favor Islamic success in Jihad.

As Majid Khadduri, the translator of Mohammed ibn al-Hasan al-Shaybani's highly revered *Siyar*[136] puts it: "Muslim authorities concluded peace treaties with the enemy only when it was to the advantage of Islam, whether because it found itself in a state of temporary weakness following a military defeat or because of engagement in war in another area."[137]

SACRED SPACE

The concept of "sacred space" is well-developed in shariah, which centuries of commentary have established as authoritative. Indeed, shariah is an aggressively territorial system that holds all land on earth has been given by Allah to Muslims in perpetuity: Since the world already belongs in its entirety to Muslims – whether currently in reality or prospectively – they are both destined and obligated to dominate it.[138]

Land already conquered and occupied by Muslims as well as any space ever gained in the past for the forces of the faith are *waqf* and considered sacred ground, endowed by Allah to the *ummah* or Muslim people forever. If ever such space has been lost, it is the duty of all Muslims to regain it, by jihad, if necessary. Chechnya, the State of Israel, Iberian Peninsula (or al-Andalus), and Indian subcontinent (Hind) are all examples of such territory, once conquered by the armies of Islam but now under the control of non-Muslims (infidels, or *kuffar*). In keeping with the shariah principle of sacred space, each of these places is to remain the target of declarations of ownership by the forces of jihad and repeated terrorist attacks and plots by Muslim jihadis intent upon returning them to the *Dar al-Islam*.

Sacralizing new or reclaimed territory for Islam is an ongoing venture in which migrant and converted Muslim communities in the West are constantly engaged, according to Patrick Sookhdeo, who has written extensively about the concept of Sacred Space in Islam.[139] Such Muslims may first sacralize the spaces within their own homes and mosques while later generations typically move outward to claim an ever-expanding share of the public space.

This Muslim mission to sacralize new physical ground for Islam has been especially obvious in Europe. There gigantic mosques (some have been dubbed "mega-mosques") have been going up across the continent since the mid-20th century, when infusions of Saudi oil money began to make such massive buildings possible. The mosques, with their towering minarets, attest in a deliberately physical way to the presence and dominance of Islam. As Turkish Prime Minister Erdogan stated in 1998, "The mosques are our barracks, the domes our helmets, the minarets our bayonets, and the faithful our soldiers."[140]

The neighborhoods around such mosques often are purchased in an incremental way, too, gradually expanding to encompass apartment buildings and even entire city blocks occupied exclusively by Muslims. This tactic (in the U.S.) often involves Muslim real estate agents who ensure that homes occupied by Muslims will always be occupied by Muslim families. By establishing such a network of Muslim-controlled space, in which adherence to shariah is enforced and from which non-Muslims are excluded, Islamic communities seek the ability to live in imitation of Mohammed and the earliest Muslims after the *hijra* (the move from Mecca to Medina). Muslims also demonstrate their dominance by requiring non-Muslims who may be permitted access to such areas to comply with shariah while in Muslim space.[141]

In many cases, as these segregated areas expand, they become not only ghettos where crime flourishes among an immigrant population that refuses to assimilate, but actual sacred space where shariah is practiced in contravention and supersession of local law. All too often, as is the case in France and elsewhere, such enclaves are avoided by the security forces, which literally cede sovereignty by abrogating their duty to enforce local law in such areas.[142]

The concept of sacred space also explains why Muslims who conquer enemy territory traditionally erect mosques and Islamic centers literally on top of the destroyed sacred places of other faiths. Examples of this practice include: the great Hagia Sophia mosque in Istanbul (formerly the Cathedral of St. Sophia in Constantinople); the al-Aqsa Mosque and Dome of the Rock Mosque, both built on Jerusalem's Temple Mount, directly above the remnants of the Jewish Second Temple; and the Cordoba mosque complex – the third largest in the world – which transformed a Christian cathedral in the capital city of the Moorish kingdom. The city was conquered in the 8th Century and was the headquarters of what came to be known as the "Cordoba Caliphate" for the next 500 years.

Most recently, plans were announced to construct a $100 million, 13-story Islamic center and mega-mosque complex two blocks from Ground Zero in New York City, the site of the World Trade Center, which was destroyed in jihadi attacks on September 11, 2001. The name of the organization leading the Ground Zero mosque project is likewise revealing of Islamic traditions: it is called the "Cordoba Initiative."

Sometimes, mere proximity to Muslims' sacred space, where displays of Islamic supremacy are expected, is sufficient to compel Westerners to censor their speech or alter their behavior or dress. Examples include female journalists who don a headscarf for an interview with a Muslim personage and Western political figures who do the same thing, even when they are visiting Muslim heads of state whose own wives do not wear the hijab. This sort of behavior demonstrates a kind of pre-emptive submission on the part of non-Muslim Westerners who adopt a subservient mentality of *dhimmitude*, erroneously believing their diplomacy, interview or outreach will go the better for it.

APOSTASY

To understand what is meant by *kufr*, or unbelief, it is instructive to move on to Book O, "Justice" in the *Reliance of the Traveller*. In the chapter on "Apostasy from Islam," [143] it states:

- "Leaving Islam is the ugliest form of unbelief and the worst."

- "Whoever voluntarily leaves Islam is killed."

- "When a person who has reached puberty and is sane voluntarily apostatizes from Islam, he deserves to be killed."

This is an absolute rule in shariah that does not admit of an alternate interpretation. A modern case in point is Abdul Rahman, the Afghan national who, in 2006, converted to Christianity. When the Islamic authorities found out about his conversion, Rahman was sentenced to death for apostasy. The European Union determined this was a human rights violation and they reacted by threatening to withhold five hundred million euros in economic aid from Afghanistan.

This created a significant political and legal issue for Afghan President Hamid Karzai. If he failed to put Rahman to death for apostasy, he would be violating Islamic law (and the Afghan Constitution in which shariah is the law of the land) and failing in his duty as a Muslim leader. If Karzai allowed the sentence to be carried out, he would lose the European economic aid.

The solution: Rahman was declared insane.[144] Under Islamic law, declaring a person insane is one of the only ways a Muslim leader (who is required to follow shariah) can avoid putting the apostate to death.

In the Western world, declaring a sane man to be insane would be an abominable human rights violation, but under shariah, it can be the only thing that allows the authorities to avoid imposing the death sentence that is prescribed by Islamic law for apostasy.

The enumerated reasons in shariah for declaring a Muslim an "apostate" include: "to deny any verse of the Koran or anything which by scholarly consensus…belongs to it" and "to deny the obligatory character of something which by the consensus of Muslim…is a part of Islam."[145] This means that Islamic law makes violation of scholarly consensus an unambiguous act of apostasy.

So, if one were to disagree with something where there is consensus among the scholars, one could be charged with apostasy and put to death. *This shariah concept of "scholarly consensus" effectively precludes any effort to moderate or reform any element of shariah sustained by such consensus.*

Reliance underscores the magnitude of the crime of apostasy in Book C, "The Nature of Legal Rulings"[146]: Here, the author notes, "Scholars distinguish between three levels of the unlawful: (1) minor sins…; (2) enormities…; and (3) *unbelief (kufr)*, sins which put one beyond the pale of Islam… and necessitate stating a Testification of Faith…."

The only way a Muslim who is declared a *kufr* can escape this is to recant and recite the *Shahada* (the declaration of Islamic faith in Allah and the Prophet), thus declaring a new testimony of faith. He has to re-enter the Islamic faith, as it were.

As Louay Safi, a top Muslim Brotherhood member operating in the United States who is nonetheless considered by many officials to be a respected "moderate," wrote in his 2001 book *Peace and the Limits of War — Transcending Classical Conception of Jihad*: "The war against the apostates is carried out not to force them to accept Islam, but to enforce the Islamic law and maintain order."[147]

Safi then adds:

Therefore, the individual apostasy which takes place quietly, and without causing any public disorder, should not be of concern to Islamic authority…. Only when the individual openly renounces Islam and violates Islamic law should he be punished for breaking the law.

In other words, Safi is saying, in effect: We do not put people to death for becoming apostates. We put people to death when we find out that they have become apostates.

In the final analysis, defining elements of shariah are intolerant of any deviation. There is freedom of belief in Islam only to the extent that matters of individual conscience do not threaten the *ummah,* whose cohesion and public appearance of rigid compliance with shariah is paramount and takes precedence over any individual's personal preferences.

PERMISSIBLE LYING

It is imperative that national security professionals with responsibility for defending the U.S. Constitution from encroachment by shariah understand that, under Islamic law, lying is not only permissible, but *obligatory* for Muslims in some situations. This complicates efforts to understand the true nature of the threat – and to have confidence in those Muslims at home and abroad with whom the government hopes to make common cause in countering that threat.

What is particularly confusing is the fact that shariah has two standards of truth and falsehood: In general, the Quran disapproves of Muslims deceiving other Muslims. It declares, "Surely God guides not him who is prodigal and a liar."[148] Yet, Quranic passages and statements attributed to Mohammed in reliable *hadiths* provide exceptions even to the usual prohibitions on lying to fellow Muslims.

For example, *Reliance of the Traveler* provides practical examples of where lying even to Muslims can be appropriate: "Giving directions to someone who wants to do wrong" is one such example, explaining that "It is not permissible to give directions

96

and the like to someone intending to perpetrate a sin, because it is helping another to commit disobedience."[149] Such disobedience, as understood under Islamic law, is defined as: "Giving directions to wrongdoers includes: (1) showing the way to policemen and tyrants when they are going to commit injustice and corruption."[150]

Reliance also shows in quotes from Mohammed that there are other grounds for lying even to Muslims: "He who settles disagreements between people to bring about good or says something commendable is not a liar."[151] And "I did not hear him permit untruth in anything people say, except for three things: war, settling disagreements, and a man talking with his wife or she with him (in smoothing over differences.)"[152] These exceptions are sufficiently broad to cover most instances in which lying would be expedient.

Shariah demands, moreover, that its adherents lie where it will be advantageous in dealings with infidels whose submission is an obligation. Consider the legal guidance provided in the authoritative *Reliance of the Traveler*. In Book R, "Holding One's Tongue," one finds sections on "Lying" (r8.0) and "Permissible Lying," (r8.2). These cite the iconic Islamic legal jurist Imam Abu Hamid Ghazali:

> This is an explicit statement that lying is sometimes permissible for a given interest...When it is possible to achieve such an aim by lying but not by telling the truth, it is permissible to lie if attaining the goal is permissible (N: i.e., when the purpose of lying is to circumvent someone who is preventing one from doing something permissible) and obligatory to lie if the goal is obligatory.[153]

An example of the Quranic basis for the shariah standard on lying is: "Allah has already sanctioned for you the dissolution of your vows."[154] Indeed, in some places, it is Allah himself who is described approvingly as a capricious deceiver: "Say, 'God leads whosoever He wills astray."[155]

As noted above, Sahih Bukhari writes that Mohammed, too, authorized a permissive attitude toward telling the truth: "The Prophet said, 'If I take an oath and later find something else better than that, then I do what is better and expiate my oath.'"[156]

Besides lying, there is also guidance in *Reliance* about giving a misleading impression: "Scholars say that there is no harm in giving a misleading impression if required by an interest countenanced by Sacred Law."[157]

TAQIYYA

Closely associated with shariah doctrine on lying is the concept of *taqiyya*, which is generally described as lying for the sake of Islam. *Taqiyya* is a concept in Islamic law that translates as "deceit or dissimulation," particularly towards infidels. It is based on Quran 3:28 and 16:106 as well as *hadiths*, *tafsir* literature, and judicial commentaries that permit and encourage precautionary dissimulation as a means for hiding true faith in times of persecution or deception when penetrating the enemy camp.

Take, for example, Quran 3:28: "Let not the believers take the disbelievers as friends instead of the believers, and whoever does that, will never be helped by Allah in any way, *unless you indeed fear a danger from them.* And Allah warns you against Himself, and to Allah is the final return." (Emphasis added.)

The authoritative commentary on the Quran, *Tafsir Ibn Kathir* [158] notes the prohibition on "taking disbelievers as friends" then explains the Quranic phrase "unless you indeed fear a danger from them":

> The Prohibition of Supporting the Disbelievers. Allah prohibited His servants from becoming supporters of the disbelievers, or to take them as comrades with whom they develop friendships, rather than believers. Allah warned against such

behavior when He stated ... *"unless you indeed fear a danger from them"* meaning, except those believers who in some areas or times fear for their safety from the disbelievers. In this case, such believers are allowed to show friendship to the disbelievers outwardly, but never inwardly.... "We smile in the face of some people although our hearts curse them."

Another authoritative Arabic text, *Al-Taqiyya fi Al-Islam*, states definitively the standing *taqiyya* enjoys in shariah:

Taqiyya [deception] is of fundamental importance in Islam. Practically every Islamic sect agrees to it and practices it. We can go so far as to say that the practice of *taqiyya* is mainstream in Islam, and that those few sects not practicing it diverge from the mainstream. ... *Taqiyya* is very prevalent in Islamic politics, especially in the modern era.[159]

A respected modern-day authority on Islam, William Gawthrop, has observed in connection with the practice of *taqiyya*:

Concealing or disguising one's beliefs, convictions, ideas, feelings, opinions, and/or strategies at a time of eminent danger, whether now or later in time, [is permissible] to save oneself from physical and/or mental injury. *Taqiyya* has been used by Muslims since the 7th century to confuse and split 'the enemy.' One result is the ability to maintain two messages, one to the faithful while obfuscation and denial is sent – and accepted – to the non-Muslim audience.[160]

It is worth noting how closely this language from Gawthrop's "Islam's Tools of Penetration" maps to the language used by Omar Ahmad, an unindicted co-conspirator[161] in the 2008 Holy Land Foundation terrorism financing trial, when discussing separating the information role of CAIR from the operations role of the HLF. From the transcript of a secretly recorded meeting in Philadelphia which was identified as "Philly Meeting – 15," and entered into evidence in the *U.S. v. HLF* trial,[162] Ahmad had this to say regarding an dual-message information campaign against the United States:

> Omar Ahmad: I believe that our problem is that we stopped working underground. We will recognize the source of any message which comes out of us. I mean, if a message is publicized, we will know…, the media person among us will recognize that you send two messages; *one to the Americans and one to the Muslims.* If they found out who said that – even four years later – it will cause a discredit to the Foundation as far as the Muslims are concerned as they say "Look, he used to tell us about Islam and that is a cause and stuff while he, at the same time, is shooting elsewhere."

Raymond Ibrahim, another contemporary scholar on Islam, quoted one of the principal Quranic authorities to address this circumstance:

> Al-Tabari's (d. 923) famous tafsir (exegesis of the Koran) is a standard and authoritative reference work in the entire Muslim world. Regarding [the Quranic Sura] 3:28, he writes: "If you [Muslims] are under their [infidels'] authority, fearing for yourselves, behave loyally to them, *with your tongue,* while harboring inner animosity for them.…Allah has forbidden believers from being friendly or on intimate terms with the infidels in place of believers – except when infidels are above them [in authority]. In such a scenario, let them *act* friendly towards them."[163]

* * *

> Regarding 3:28, Ibn Kathir (d. 1373, second in authority only to Tabari) writes, "Whoever at any time or place fears their [infidels'] evil may protect himself through outward show." As proof of this, he quotes Mohammed's close companion, Abu Darda, who said, "Let us smile to the face of some people [non-Muslims] while our hearts curse them"; another companion, al-Hassan, said, "Doing *taqiyya* is acceptable till the Day of Judgment [i.e., in perpetuity]."[164]

A classic example of the shariah practice of *taqiyya* can be found in the dual messaging of Yousuf al-Qaradawi, best known as the spiritual leader of the Muslim Brotherhood. For an intended Muslim audience, he wrote in the *Saudi Gazette* on June 11, 2010:

> ... The acceptance of secularism means abandonment of sha-riah, a denial of the divine guidance and a rejection of Allah's injunctions....For this reason, the call for secularism among Muslims is atheism and a rejection of Islam. Its acceptance as a basis for rule in place of shariah is downright apostasy....[165]

At an earlier "Democracy and Political Reform" conference held in Qatar in June 2004, al-Qaradawi also declared: "There are those who maintain that democracy is the rule of the people, but we want the rule of Allah."[166]

In these two instances, al-Qaradawi's rejection of Western-style liberal democracy could not have been more clearly stated. He was making these statements in his role as an Islamic jurist, providing legal opinions specifically sourced back to the Quran and shariah. This is not the message he gives to other audiences, however.

For instance, during a January 2010 interview in the Egyptian newspaper, *Al-Shorouk*, he saw advantage for the Muslim Brotherhood and shariah in extolling the virtues of democracy – as a means of ending the rule of President Hosni Mubarak (who mostly suppresses the Muslim Brotherhood) and bringing the Ikhwan to power: "Egypt will not regain its status, its wellbeing and its role unless it opens the windows of freedom. It must open the doors completely and make way for [new] figures and competition as real democracy is the solution, not fake [democracy]."[167]

Similarly, in the Brotherhood's online forum, IslamOnline.net, which is published in English and aimed at a Western audience, al-Qaradawi went so far as to suggest that shariah actually *embraces* democracy: "Islam calls for democracy and grants people the right to choose their governor."[168]

In short, what Muslim audiences are required to know about Islam is not the same thing as what non-Muslim Western audiences are allowed to know – or encouraged to think – by Islamic authorities. *Taqiyya* provides the legal basis under shariah for this sort of deceptive dual messaging.

The practice of *taqiyya* is sometimes erroneously described as one in which only Shiites engage. While it is true that the Shiites, being the minority sect in Islam, have historically had reason to engage in deception (i.e., to conceal their religious identity from the majority Sunni population who would otherwise persecute them), Sunni Muslims living in the West are themselves in the minority among societies full of non-Muslims. Shariah is permissive of their lying in such conditions.

Such examples from shariah sources should suffice to alert national security professionals to the mainstream position of Islamic doctrine on the subject of lying. In view of the Prophet Mohammed's statement that "War is deceit," and cognizant of the requirement under shariah for Dar al-Islam to be in a constant state of animosity, hatred, and jihad with *Dar al-Harb* until "all religion belongs to Allah," it is imperative that those whose duty it is to protect the United States. from shariah grasp the centrality of *taqiyya* in the arsenal of its adherents. This is critical because the consequences of *taqiyya* extend to real world issues related, for example, to Muslim overtures for interfaith dialogue, peace and mutual tolerance – all of which must be viewed in the light of Islamic doctrine on lying.

This is not an argument for trusting or mistrusting someone in any particular instance. It is, though, an argument for professionals to be aware of these facts, to realize that they are dealing with an enemy whose doctrine allows – and at times even *requires*

– them not to disclose fully all that they know and deliberately to misstate that which they know to be the truth.

As is discussed at greater length below, American officials charged with national and homeland security have a duty to understand that which is within the sphere of their professional competence. For anyone with such responsibilities, knowledge of these attributes of Shariah is a requirement.

SLANDER

Given the importance the enemy's doctrine attaches to information dominance evident in the legitimacy shariah assigns to lying and *taqiyya*, it is hardly surprising that this threat doctrine also seeks through other means to keep the *harbi* (residents of *Dar al-Harb*) unaware of the true character and intentions of shariah's adherents. In fact, Islamic law provides, in tandem with the right (described above) to deceive *harbi*, an enforceable requirement to make disclosure of those rules of Islam a punishable offense. This is among the purposes of the shariah concept of slander, which differs significantly from its Western counterpart.

Reliance of the Traveler has the following relevant passages (emphasis added throughout):

- "Slander (*ghiba*) means to mention anything concerning a person that he would dislike."[169]

- "As for talebearing (*namima*), it consists of quoting someone's words to another in a way that worsens relations between them."[170]

- "The Prophet (Allah bless him and give him peace) said:

- (1) "The talebearer will not enter paradise."

- (2) "Do you know what slander is?" They answered, "Allah and His Messenger know best." He said, "It is to mention of your brother that which he would dislike." Someone asked, "What if he is as I say?" And he replied,

"If he is as you say, you have slandered him, and if not, you have calumniated him."

- (3) "The Muslim is the brother of the Muslim. He does not betray him, lie to him, or hang back from coming to his aid." [171]

- "...In fact, talebearing is not limited to that, but rather consists of revealing anything whose disclosure is resented, whether presented by the person who originally said it, the person to whom it is disclosed, or by a third person. ... The reality of talebearing lies in divulging a secret, in revealing something confidential whose disclosure is resented. A person should not speak of anything he notices about people besides that which benefits a Muslim to relate or prevents disobedience." [172]

From such definitions, it is easy to see how a legally sanctioned code of silence could be imposed and enforced. Taken together with the rules on lying and *taqiyya*, it is easy to understand how self-identified "moderate" Muslims can insist that acts of terrorism undertaken by "extremists" had nothing to do with Islam – even in cases where the perpetrators and their supporters explicitly claim Islam as the motivation, often on television broadcasts receiving rapturous applause from other Muslims.

These attributes of shariah have two significant implications for U.S. security policymakers. In accordance with the definition of "talebearing" in *Reliance's* chapter r2.6, the disclosure of any sensitive information to non-Muslims is forbidden, where sensitive means any information that puts Islam or a Muslim at a disadvantage. Hence, a shariah-adherent Muslim risks eternal damnation if he discloses to a non-believer information that would cause the non-believer to question either Islam or a Muslim.

In other words, law enforcement, military and intelligence services may be relying on individuals whose behavior is governed by shariah must subordinate national security collection requirements and practices to potentially restrictive and manipulative disclosure rules dictated by Islamic law. This is submission. It also turns all professional notions of competent analysis and information security on their heads.[173]

BLASPHEMY

For non-believers, the corollary to the Islamic rule against disclosing anything disadvantageous to Islam is shariah's prohibition against blasphemy. This requires that infidels refrain from engaging in discussions about Islam that extend beyond what is permitted of them or would give offense to Muslims.

Such suppression of information is invaluable to the shariah enterprise because a straightforward reading of Islamic doctrine lends credence to claims by its adherents to be in the mainstream and orthodox. The current approach enshrined in U.S. national intelligence and security policy, which conforms to shariah blasphemy dictates, has the effect of removing these facts from discovery.

This submission to shariah is evident in the failure of U.S. government agencies accurately to describe the enemy and his threat doctrine described elsewhere in this report. It also is reflected in other, less obvious but highly insidious ways. These include gaps in the professional education of senior civilian and military personnel and in possible biases based on such failures inherent in the promotion process for federal employees across the governmental bureaucracy.

Such policies are systematically corroding the U.S. government's situational awareness by effectively imposing, via explicit or implicit gag orders, a system of self-censorship. The practical effect is that the truth about shariah and its adherents is suppressed, as is informed deliberation about appropriate responses to the threats it poses. This amounts to a collective act of submission to shariah by the national leadership of the U.S. that emboldens our enemies even as it disables our defenses against them.

By contrast to current U.S. government policy about the shariah threat that avoids facts as unwanted disclosures, an effective analytic process could be tailored *specifically* to answer questions concerning the enemy's doctrine by direct reference to those same facts. There can be no successful intelligence analysis – or appropriate national security strategy – where the underlying facts are barred.

Arguably, not since the days of the first Team B report – when unwelcome information about Soviet communism's agenda, doctrine and capabilities was discounted or suppressed – has there been a greater need for unconstrained analysis using all relevant facts to contribute to the development of an awareness of the self-identified enemy's stated doctrine. The "second opinion" on shariah offered by this Team B II analysis is intended to be a catalyst for such an all-source analysis, and for a national debate about the inadequacies of the present, official ("Team A") assessment of the threat.

THE MUSLIM BROTHERHOOD: THE THREAT DOCTRINE OPERATIONALIZED

As was shown in chapter three, shariah places great importance on its adherents' exercise of information dominance. Accordingly, the shariah campaign of civilization jihad against the United States prominently features propaganda, political and psychological warfare, influence operations and other techniques for neutralizing and, ultimately, subverting our American foundational institutions – political, military, law enforcement, educational, religious, financial and media – as integral parts of the campaign to secure this country's destruction and the triumph of shariah.

The information war in the West and the civilization jihad of which it is a central element is driven by an organization called the International Muslim Brotherhood (IMB), also known by its Arabic title "Ikhwan."[174] The Muslim Brotherhood (MB) is the "vanguard"[175] or tip-of-the-spear of the current Islamic Movement in the world. While there are other transnational organizations that share the MB's goals (if not its tactics) – including al Qaeda, which was born out of the Brotherhood – the Ikhwan is by far the strongest and most organized.

The Muslim Brotherhood is now active in over 80 countries around the world.[176] Each nation in which the Brotherhood has a presence is structured with an Organizational Conference (planning group), a Shura Council (legal body), and a General Masul (Leader) or "General Guide." The "Supreme Guide" is the individual leader of the International Muslim Brotherhood (IMB) and is based in Cairo, Egypt.[177]

The MB's "civilization-jihadist process" (the Ikhwan's term which will be described in depth below) is primarily conducted by groups posing as peaceable, "moderate" and law-abiding Muslim community organizations. Yet, the Muslim Brotherhood's bylaws (viewable in English on the Ikhwan's website[178]), MB doctrinal books published in English, and a series of Muslim Brotherhood strategic documents found in an FBI raid in Virginia in 2004 and entered uncontested into evidence in the largest terrorism-financing trial in American history, the 2008 Holy Land Foundation (HLF) trial in Dallas, Texas, make one thing plain: The Ikhwan's mission in the West is sedition in the furtherance of shariah's supremacist agenda, not peaceful assimilation and co-existence with non-Muslim populations.[179]

Thanks to the HLF trial, it is now public knowledge that nearly every major Muslim organization in the United States is actually controlled by the MB or a derivative organization. Consequently, most of the Muslim-American groups of any prominence in America are now known to be, as a matter of fact, hostile to the United States and its Constitution.

This chapter will detail the history of the Muslim Brotherhood and its arrival in America, its key objectives and supporting doctrine, the individuals and organizations working to achieve its objectives, and some examples of how they are achieving them.

WHAT IS THE MUSLIM BROTHERHOOD?

The Muslim Brotherhood was founded in Egypt in 1928. Its express purpose was two-fold: (1) to implement shariah worldwide, and (2) to re-establish the imperial Islamic state (caliphate).[180] Therefore, Al Qaeda and the MB have the same objectives. They differ only in the timing and tactics involved in realizing them.

The Brotherhood's creed is: "God is our objective; the Koran is our law; the Prophet is our leader; jihad is our way; and death for the sake of Allah is the highest of our aspirations."[181] It is evident from the creed, and from the Brotherhood's history (and current activities) detailed below, that violence is an inherent part of the MB's tactics. The MB is the root of the majority of Islamic terrorist groups in the world today.[182]

The Ikhwan believes that its purposes in the West are, for the moment, better advanced by the use of non-violent, stealthy techniques. In that connection, the Muslim Brotherhood seeks to establish relations with, influence and, wherever possible, penetrate government circles in executive and legislative branches at the federal, state and local levels; the law enforcement community; intelligence agencies; the military; penal institutions; the media; think tanks and policy groups; academic institutions; non-Muslim religious communities; and other elites. The Brothers engage in all of these activities and more for one reason: to *subvert* the targeted communities in furtherance of the MB's primary objective – the triumph of shariah.[183]

THE GENESIS OF THE MUSLIM BROTHERHOOD

The defeat of the Ottoman Empire and its allies in World War I led to the Empire's dissolution as a unified entity in July

1923, and the establishment of the modern state of Turkey by Mustapha Kemal, who was given the title "Ataturk" or "Father of the Turks."[184] Determined to tie his country firmly to the West, Ataturk sought to diminish its Islamic character, notably by abolishing the caliphate in favor of secular rule. Ataturk also banned the growing of beards by men and wearing of headscarves by women; banned the call to prayer by muezzins; abolished the Turkish language's script and replaced it with the Latin alphabet; and made the Turkish military the custodian of secular tradition.

The dissolution of the caliphate and the transformation of Turkey from the center of the Islamic world to a secular nation did not sit well with some in the global Islamic community (*ummah*). One of those determined to restore the caliphate was Hassan al Banna, the son of a Muslim imam who lived outside of Cairo, Egypt. In 1928, he founded an organization known as the *al-Ikhwan al-Muslimin*, the Society of Muslim Brothers or the Muslim Brotherhood (MB), for the purpose of unifying the Islamic States under a new caliphate and subordinating all lands to the Caliph's rule pursuant to shariah.[185]

The Muslim Brotherhood's bylaws make clear the Ikhwan's objectives and means to achieve them:[186]

> "The Muslim Brotherhood is an International Muslim body which seeks to establish Allah's law in the land by achieving the spiritual goals of Islam and the true religion which are namely the following:
>
> ... F) The need to work on establishing the Islamic State;
>
> G) The sincere support for a global cooperation in accordance with the provisions of the Islamic Sharia.
>
> Chapter II, Article 3:
>
> The Muslim Brotherhood in achieving these objectives depends on the following means:

...D) Make every effort for the establishment of educational, social, economic, and scientific institutions and the establishment of mosques, schools, clinics, shelters, clubs, as well as the formation of committees to regulate *zakat* affairs and alms;

E) The Islamic nation must be fully prepared to *fight* the tyrants and the enemies of Allah as a prelude to establishing the Islamic State."   (Emphasis added.)

By the early 1930's, the Brotherhood had developed a formal organizational structure around groups of men with special spiritual and physical training called "Battalions." By 1940, the Brotherhood created the "secret apparatus" which was the military wing of the Society of Muslim Brothers, and in 1943 abandoned the Battalions. The MB's military wing continues to operate today, and is referred to as the "Special Section." Its operations are known as "special work," meaning military fighting or armed actions.[187]

During World War II and the years that followed, the Brotherhood became increasingly aggressive and violent, and called for the removal of all British forces ("non-Muslim Forces") from Egypt ("Muslim Lands"), as required by Islamic Law (shariah). During the late 1940's, the Brotherhood targeted Egyptian officials, British soldiers, and their families, and in December of 1948, a Muslim Brother assassinated Egyptian Prime Minister Mahmud Fahmi al-Nuqrashi.[188] In February 1949, the Egyptian security services killed Muslim Brotherhood founder Hassan al Banna in Cairo.

The period following the assassination of al Banna was marked with significant MB violence against the Egyptian monarchy and the British. After a ban on Brotherhood activities was lifted in 1951, the MB coordinated actively with Gamal Abdel Nasser and the young officers who overthrew King Farouk in 1952. As soon as the Ikhwan felt powerful enough to confront the

111

government on their own, however, it turned against the new president Nasser. Nasser launched a crackdown against the Brotherhood in 1954 that accelerated an exodus of many top Brothers and the expansion of the organization around the world, including into the West.

MOVEMENT OF THE MUSLIM BROTHERHOOD INTO THE WEST

Among the most prominent members of the Ikhwan during this transitional period were: Youssef Nada, Said Ramadan, Ghaleb Himmat, Mohamed Akef, and Yousef Qaradawi, who is today known as the International Muslim Brotherhood's "spiritual guide" and is a leading Islamic legal scholar. Each of these men played an important role in transforming the Ikhwan into the international Muslim mafia it is today. The history of their penetration of Western societies in Europe is instructive for those seeking to understand how and the extent to which similar influence operations are being run against the United States.

Of these men, Said Ramadan is particularly noteworthy as he was al Banna's assistant for years, married his daughter and became a driving force in the Brotherhood leadership after al Banna was killed by the Egyptian security services. His son, Tariq Ramadan, is a member of Brotherhood elite and one of today's most assiduous practitioners of the stealth jihad. In January 2010, Secretary of State Hillary Clinton reversed a six-year ban on the younger Ramadan's entry into the United States. He has used his renewed access to American audiences to advance the Brotherhood's civilization jihad.[189]

Post-war Germany offered the Brotherhood a valuable safe haven in the heart of Europe, primarily because the Brothers had established a relationship with the Nazis during World War II and maintained ties to powerful Germans after the war. Additionally, the West Germans were especially welcoming of Syrians and

Egyptians because of a state policy that offered assistance to any "refugees" from nations that formally recognized Bonn's rival, East Germany – something both Egypt and Syria did.

The Brotherhood leadership, which insinuated itself into the societies of Germany, Austria, Switzerland, and other European countries, established numerous front organizations for the Ikhwan – a pattern the organization follows aggressively around the world and especially in the West to this day. For example, Said Ramadan moved to Cologne, where he received a law degree, and founded the Islamic Society of Germany. He presided over it from 1958-1968. In 1962, Ramadan founded the Muslim World League in Saudi Arabia.

Ghaleb Himmat was a Syrian who was a citizen of Italy, who directed the Islamic Society of Germany from 1973-2002.[190] He established the Al-Taqwa Bank, which Italian intelligence dubbed "the bank of the Muslim Brotherhood." Himmat ran Al-Taqwa and a group of front companies in Switzerland, Liechtenstein, and the Bahamas with Youssef Nada. Before it was shut down in 2002, Al-Taqwa became known for its funding of: al Qaeda; the Brotherhood's Palestinian arm, known as Hamas; Iran's Ayatollah Khomeini and his supporters; and other terrorist movements and organizations.

In the 1960's, these senior Muslim Brotherhood leaders planned and built a huge complex known as the Islamic Center of Munich which became an important staging point for the Muslim Brotherhood in Europe. A new book by Ian Johnson entitled *A Mosque in Munich* describes the powerful force-multiplier this facility became for Ikhwan operations in Europe and beyond. The book also reveals longstanding U.S. government ties to the Brothers, including Said Ramadan who contributed to the construction of this mosque.[191]

In 1973, several dozen Muslim Brothers attended a meeting of the Islamic Cultural Centres and Bodies in Europe in London, England in order to organize the Muslim Brotherhood Movement in Europe. Ghaleb Himmat was present as the head of the Islamic Community of Southern Germany. While no agreement on strategy to develop a European Islamic network was reached, this meeting laid the foundation for such a plan.[192]

Four years later, the senior Muslim Brotherhood leaders met in Lugano, Switzerland, near the homes of Ghaleb Himmat and Youssef Nada to discuss the strategy for moving the Brotherhood forward.[193] Yousef al-Qaradawi was among those present at this meeting. One of the first actions taken afterwards was the establishment of the MB front known as the International Institute for Islamic Thought (IIIT). IIIT's role was to maintain the ideological purity and consistency of the Brotherhood's expanding operations. During a subsequent meeting in Saudi Arabia in 1978, the Ikhwan decided to set up IIIT near Temple University in Philadelphia, an institution where leading Islamic thinker and Muslim Brother Ismail Faruqi was teaching at the time.[194] Later, the IIIT moved its headquarters to Herndon, Virginia.

In the 1980s, Mohammed Akef (the MB's Supreme Guide for several years until early 2010), who was then serving as the imam at the Munich mosque, moved the MB's European headquarters into the Markfield Conference Centre, a small community near Leicester in the United Kingdom.[195] The Federation of Islamic Organizations in Europe (FIOE) is housed there and led by an Iraqi named Ahmed al-Rawi. FIOE has become one of Europe's largest MB organizations.[196] The Markfield Conference Centre is owned by the Islamic Foundation which is an affiliate of the Muslim Council of Britain – both Muslim Brotherhood front groups. Yousef al-Qaradawi is heavily involved with this network.

The Federation has become the starting point for a number of other Muslim Brotherhood entities, including the Institute for the Study of Human Sciences and the European Council for Fatwa and Research. The latter is headed by al-Qaradawi.[197]

In France, the Brotherhood has the Union of Islamic Organizations in France,[198] and its partner organization in Italy is the Union of the Islamic Communities and Organizations in Italy.[199] Those groups work, respectively, with the French and Italian governments in order to advance the Muslim Brotherhood agenda and subvert their respective nations, while using claims of victimhood and demands for equality and tolerance to mask their true intentions and marginalize or silence critics.

In the United Kingdom, the Muslim Council of Britain and Muslim Association of Britain are two of the most prominent MB organizations.[200] Like their counterparts on the continent, the MCB and MAB work with the British government at the highest levels toward the same end: subverting Her Majesty's Government and nation from within.

The late 1990s saw the MB launching the Forum for European Muslim Youth and Student Organizations (FEMYSO), which is headquartered in Brussels. FEMYSO describes itself in its own literature as "a network of 42 national and international organizations bringing together youth from over 26 different countries,"[201] and credibly claims to be the primary organization in Europe for Muslim youth. This Muslim Brotherhood organization – like most of the Ikhwan's other fronts – has significant influence and appears to have encountered little resistance from European security services.

In short, Muslim Brotherhood organizations exist across Europe today. As we shall see with respect to the MB footprint in the United States, virtually without exception, the leading Muslim organizations across the continent are fronts for the Muslim Brotherhood. Even though the affiliation with the Brotherhood for most of these organizations is easily established, and the true, seditious objectives of these organizations are readily discernable, most European governments are unwilling to face reality – let alone deal effectively with the threats posed by MB penetration of the highest levels of their societies.

As illustrations of the problem, two of the most prominent Muslim Brothers in Europe, Ghaleb Himmat and Yousef Nada, were designated as terrorism financiers by the U.S. Treasury Department in the wake of the 9/11 attacks. Treasury also deemed their bank, Al-Taqwa, as an entity that funds terrorism.[202] For his part, the Muslim Brotherhood's spiritual leader, Yousef al-Qaradawi, was named in the HLF trial as an unindicted co-conspirator for his involvement with that Hamas front.

All three of these individuals have, nonetheless, been allowed to continue doing business with and, in some cases, actually *in* Europe.[203]

One reason for Europe's unwillingness to confront and counter the danger posed by the Muslim Brotherhood and its operatives is that in parliamentary politics of some nations, Muslim communities are increasingly seen as critical voting blocs.[204] To the extent that the Ikhwan is able to capitalize on such perceptions long before Muslims achieve majority status in the demographics of a number of European nations, it has greatly facilitated the MB's efforts to insinuate shariah into and otherwise exercise influence over these states.

Growing unease about the success of the Islamization of Europe has begun translating into push-back, however – most notably in the Netherlands, where Geert Wilders' party rooted in opposition to shariah has garnered unprecedented support. The question is: Will it amount to much and, if so, will it happen in time?

THE MUSLIM BROTHERHOOD IN AMERICA

In 1953, Princeton University hosted a group of "prominent Muslims" for an "Islamic Colloquium." Ikhwan delegates asked for and were granted a meeting with President Dwight D.

Eisenhower, who agreed to the meeting on advice from his defense and intelligence advisors, who saw it as an opportunity for the U.S. to influence the Muslim world and use them against the communists.

One of the delegates at the meeting was the "Honorable Saeed Ramahdan, Delegate of the Muslim Brothers," as described in the official White House documents. A now-declassified CIA documents recording the events of this meeting described Ramadan as follows: "Ramadan seems to be a Fascist, interested in the grouping of individuals for power. He did not display many ideas except for those of the Brotherhood."[205]

It is critical to recall the MB's aforementioned bylaws, and specifically that the approved "means" to achieve the Ikhwan's objectives in America includes this mandate: *"Make every effort for the establishment of educational, social, economic, and scientific institutions and the establishment of mosques, schools, clinics, shelters, clubs."* (Emphasis added.)

As the Muslim Brothers "settled" in North America, they did so according to their stated bylaws. At the University of Illinois in Urbana, the Ikhwan created its first front organization in North America, the Muslim Students Association (MSA) in 1963. Today, MSA chapters are present on many college campuses across the country, serving as recruiting nodes for the MB and, in some cases for violent jihadist organizations (some of which are described in chapter five). As will be explained, out of the MSA came nearly every Muslim organization in America today. Initially, as MSA chapters sprang up on American campuses, they presented Islam in public as an acceptable alternative to other religions, never mentioning its revolutionary aspects. In recent years, MSA members have become ever more aggressive in their demands for accommodations and silencing those who oppose them.[206]

In the 1970s, the Brotherhood formed a number of trade organizations for the purpose of insinuating its members more deeply into American society. These included the Association of Muslim Social Scientists (AMSS), the Association of Muslim Scientists and Engineers (AMSE), the Islamic Medical Association (IMA), the Muslim Communities Association (MCA), and others. The Brothers also formed other student groups in the 1970s, including the Muslim Arab Youth Assembly (MAYA) and Muslim Youth of North America (MYNA).[207]

In 1973, the Saudis created an important new enabler of Brotherhood operations in the United States and domination of American Muslim communities: the North American Islamic Trust (NAIT). NAIT "controls" approximately 80 percent of the titles/deeds to the mosques, Islamic organizations and Islamic schools in this country.[208] Typically, along with such ownership comes Saudi-trained and appointed imams, textbooks for the madrassas, jihadist literature and videos for the bookstore, paid hajj pilgrimages (the obligatory trip to Mecca) and, in some cases, training for jihad.

In 1980, the Brotherhood created a new organization to extend the footprint made possible by the swelling ranks of Muslim Students Association alumni. It brought together most of its groups under the authority of the Islamic Society of North America (ISNA), which is today the largest Muslim Brotherhood front in North America.

The creation of ISNA ushered in an era of massive growth of the movement in North America. Through the 1980s and 1990s, the Brotherhood created hundreds of new organizations and built hundreds of mosques and Islamic schools across the U.S. and Canada. It did so primarily with funding from Saudi Arabia.[209]

BREAKING THE CODE

In August of 2004, an alert Maryland Transportation Authority Police officer observed a woman wearing traditional Islamic garb videotaping the support structures of the Chesapeake Bay Bridge, and conducted a traffic stop. The driver of the vehicle was identified as Ismail Elbarasse and detained on an outstanding material witness warrant issued in Chicago, Illinois, in a Hamas case.

The FBI's Washington Field Office raided Elbarasse's residence in Annandale, Virginia, and in the basement of his home, a hidden sub-basement was found. In the sub-basement, the FBI discovered the archives of the Muslim Brotherhood in North America. The documents *confirmed* what investigators and counterterrorism experts had previously suspected and contended about the myriad Muslim-American groups in the United States – namely, that nearly all of them are controlled by the MB and, therefore, as shariah dictates, are hostile to this country, its Constitution and freedoms. The documents make clear the groups' sole objectives are to implement Islamic law in America in furtherance of re-establishing the global caliphate.[210]

THE HOLY LAND FOUNDATION TRIAL[211]

Between July and September 2007, prosecutors from the U.S. Attorney's Office in Dallas, Texas, along with attorneys from the main Department of Justice (DOJ) in Washington, working with FBI case agents and analysts from the FBI Dallas Field Office, tried the Holy Land Foundation for Relief and Development (HLFRD or simply HLF) and its senior leadership in U.S. Federal Court, Northern District of Texas. At the time, HLF was the largest Muslim charity in North America, and funneled money and assistance to Hamas overseas in support of its terrorist operations. Hamas had been designated a Foreign Terrorist Organization

119

(FTO) by the U.S. government in 1995, and is a Palestinian wing of the Muslim Brotherhood.

In the course of the HLF trial, scores of exhibits and testimony were introduced into evidence uncontested by the defense. Taken together, the evidence provided unprecedented insights into the web of connections among a handful of alleged Hamas front groups that have operated on American soil throughout the 1990s to this day. This network serves as a central node in the Muslim Brotherhood's wider U.S. organizational infrastructure. HLF was the largest Hamas front organization ever prosecuted by the U.S. government; its trial was the largest in the history of official efforts to counter terrorism financing in America.

On October 22, 2007, after 19 days of deliberation, a jury was unable to reach a unanimous verdict on any of the charges against the defendants. U.S. District Judge Joe A. Fish declared a mistrial after a decision could not be reached.

In September 2008, the second Holy Land Foundation trial began. On November 24, 2008, after six weeks of testimony and seven days of deliberation, the jury convicted HLF and five of its leaders on charges of providing material support to Hamas. As the Department of Justice stated at the time:

> The government presented evidence at trial that, as the U.S. began to scrutinize individuals and entities in the United States who were raising funds for terrorist groups in the mid-1990s, the HLF intentionally hid its financial support for Hamas behind the guise of charitable donations. HLF and these five defendants provided approximately $12.4 million in support to Hamas and its goal of creating an Islamic Palestinian state by eliminating the State of Israel through violent jihad.

Commenting on the verdicts, Patrick Rowan, Assistant Attorney General for National Security, observed:

> Today's verdicts are important milestones in America's efforts against financiers of terrorism. For many years, the Holy Land Foundation used the guise of charity to raise and funnel millions of dollars to the infrastructure of the Hamas terror organization. This prosecution demonstrates our resolve to ensure that humanitarian relief efforts are not used as a mechanism to disguise and enable support for terrorist groups."
> 212

The following sentences were handed down for the defendants:

- Shukri Abu Baker, 50, of Garland, Texas, was sentenced to a total of 65 years in prison. He was convicted of 10 counts of conspiracy to provide, and the provision of, material support to a designated foreign terrorist organization; 11 counts of conspiracy to provide, and the provision of, funds, goods and services to a Specially Designated Terrorist; 10 counts of conspiracy to commit, and the commission of, money laundering; one count of conspiracy to impede and impair the Internal Revenue Service (IRS); and one count of filing a false tax return.

- Mohammad El-Mezain, 55, of San Diego, California, was sentenced to the statutory maximum of 15 years in prison. He was convicted on one count of conspiracy to provide material support to a designated foreign terrorist organization.

- Ghassan Elashi, 55, of Richardson, Texas, was sentenced to a total of 65 years in prison. He was convicted on the same counts as Abu Baker, and one additional count of filing a false tax return.

- Mufid Abdulqader, 49, of Richardson, Texas, was sentenced to a total of 20 years in prison. He was convicted on one count of conspiracy to provide material support to a designated foreign terrorist organization, one count of conspiracy to provide goods, funds, and services to a specially designated terrorist, and one count of conspiracy to commit money laundering.

- Abdulrahman Odeh, 49, of Patterson, New Jersey, was sentenced to 15 years in prison. He was convicted on the same counts as Abdulqader.

- HLF, now defunct, was convicted on 10 counts of conspiracy to provide, and the provision of, material support to a designated foreign terrorist organization; 11 counts of conspiracy to provide, and the provision of, funds, goods and services to a Specially Designated Terrorist; and 10 counts of conspiracy to commit, and the commission of, money laundering.

It should be emphasized that all these defendants were proven to be leaders of Hamas in the United States and, therefore, Muslim Brothers.

The North American Islamic Trust (and perhaps other unindicted co-conspirators) has appealed the court's ruling on their listing.[213] According to press reports, a panel of the 5th Circuit held a closed-door hearing on the matter in 2010. As of this writing, neither the government's position nor the judgment of the court of appeals is known.

'AN EXPLANATORY MEMORANDUM'

One of the most critical documents found at the FBI raid in Annandale, Virginia, in 2004 entered into evidence during the HLF trial was the Muslim Brotherhood's Strategic Plan for North America entitled, *An Explanatory Memorandum: On the General Strategic Goal for the Group.*" It was written by a member of the Board of Directors for the Muslim Brother in North America and senior Hamas leader named Mohammed Akram. This document was approved by the Brotherhood's Shura Council and Organizational Conference in 1987, and it establishes the mission of the Muslim Brother in North America in this following passage:

The process of settlement is a "Civilization-Jihadist Process" with all the word means. The Ikhwan must understand that their work in America is a kind of grand jihad in eliminating and destroying the Western civilization from within and "sabotaging" its miserable house by their hands and the hands of the believers so that it is eliminated and God's religion is made victorious over all other religions.[214]

In other words, the Ikhwan's strategy for destroying the United States is to get us, specifically our leadership, to do the MB's bidding. The Ikhwan intends to conduct civilization jihad by co-opting our leadership into believing a counterfactual understanding of Islam and the nature of the Muslim Brotherhood, thereby manipulating or coercing these leaders to enforce the MB narrative on their subordinates.

At the ground level, this means that when police officers, federal agents, military personnel, or any another Americans who have sworn an oath to protect and defend the Constitution challenge their leadership with facts, the latter is faced with a hard choice: admit a lack of understanding of the threat and that he or she has been duped, or the leader must suppress the facts and his subordinates in the interest of protecting his or her professional reputation.

Copious anecdotal evidence obtained from law enforcement professionals, federal agents, and military service members suggests that there is considerable suppression of the facts about shariah and efforts by the Muslim Brotherhood and its allies to bring it to America. This behavior frequently impedes ongoing investigations and countervailing efforts.

For instance, police officers in a number of communities around the country have been pushed out of their Joint Terrorism Task Force (JTTF) or counterterrorism positions by their chiefs or deputy chiefs for factually articulating that certain MB operatives working with their police leadership are, in fact, hostile to the

United States and the police department in question.[215] A similar phenomenon has also been evidenced within the FBI, the Department of Homeland Security and other federal, as well as state and local, entities. [216] That is what is meant by "'sabotaging' Western civilization by 'their hands.'"

THE MUSLIM BROTHERHOOD'S 'PHASED PLAN'

We know from, among other things, the Elbarasse trove of MB documents, that the goal of destroying Western civilization from within is to be achieved by the Brotherhood in accordance with a "phased plan." The plan is a stepped process modeled directly after Sayyid Qutb's *Milestones* and the shariah doctrine of progressive revelation.

One such document is an undated paper entitled, "Phases of the World Underground Movement Plan."[217] It specifies the five phases of the Muslim Brotherhood Movement in North America. They are described, together with comments about the Ikhwan's progress in realizing each goal as follows:

> *Phase One:* Phase of discreet and secret establishment of leadership.
>
> *Phase Two:* Phase of gradual appearance on the public scene and exercising and utilizing various public activities (It greatly succeeded in implementing this stage). It also succeeded in achieving a great deal of its important goals, such as infiltrating various sectors of the Government. Gaining religious institutions and embracing senior scholars. Gaining public support and sympathy. Establishing a shadow government (secret) within the Government.
>
> *Phase Three:* Escalation phase, prior to conflict and confrontation with the rulers, through utilizing mass media. Currently in progress.

Phase Four: Open public confrontation with the Government through exercising the political pressure approach. It is aggressively implementing the above-mentioned approach. Training on the use of weapons domestically and overseas in anticipation of zero-hour. It has noticeable activities in this regard.

Phase Five: Seizing power to establish their Islamic Nation under which all parties and Islamic groups are united.[218]

This document offers a chilling operational insight into the mindset, planning, and vision of the Islamic Movement in North America.

THE IMPLEMENTATION OF SHARIAH BY THE MUSLIM BROTHERHOOD

The Elbarasse archives and close observation of the Brotherhood's operations reveal the following as the most important of the techniques employed by the Ikhwan in America to achieve the seditious goals of its civilization jihad:

- Expanding the Muslim presence by birth rate, immigration, and refusal to assimilate;
- Occupying and expanding domination of physical spaces;
- Ensuring the "Muslim community" knows and follows MB doctrine;
- Controlling the language we use in describing the enemy;
- Ensuring we do not study their doctrine (shariah);
- Co-opting key leadership;
- Forcing compliance with shariah at local levels;
- Fighting all counterterrorism efforts;
- Subverting religious organizations;

- Employing lawfare - the offensive use of lawsuits and threats of lawsuits;

- Claiming victimization/demanding accommodations;

- Condemning "slander" against Islam;

- Subverting the U.S. education system, in particular, infiltrating and dominating U.S. Middle East and religious studies programs;

- Demanding the right to practice shariah in segregated Muslim enclaves;

- Demanding recognition of shariah in non-Muslim spheres;

- Confronting and denouncing Western society, laws, and traditions; and

- Demanding that shariah replace Western law.

Note that many of the foregoing techniques entail, in one way or another, influencing and neutralizing the American government at all levels.

MUSLIM BROTHERHOOD PENETRATION OF THE U.S. GOVERNMENT: A CASE STUDY

In that connection, one of the most successful Brotherhood influence operations in support of this phased plan that has been uncovered to date involved arguably the Ikhwan's preeminent figure in America during the 1990s: Abdurahman Alamoudi. His is a tale of a sustained effort to penetrate and compromise both Democratic and Republican administrations and their partisan organizations.

Alamoudi immigrated from Eritrea in 1979 and became a naturalized U.S. citizen in 1996.[219] During the 1990s, he parlayed his role as founder and executive director of the American Muslim

Council and his involvement with nearly two-dozen other Muslim organizations in this country into entrée to the White House itself.

This access afforded Alamoudi various opportunities for mounting influence operations against the Clinton administration. According to multiple sources:

> In 1995, Alamoudi helped President Clinton and the ACLU develop a presidential guideline entitled "Religious Expression in Public School."[220] In November of that year, Alamoudi and 23 other Muslim leaders met with President Clinton and Vice President Al Gore. On December 8, Clinton's National Security Adviser, Anthony Lake, met with Alamoudi and several other AMC Board members. On February 8, 1996, Hillary Clinton penned a newspaper column based on talking points provided by Alamoudi. Later that month, Mrs. Clinton asked AMC to draw up a guest list for a reception marking the end of Ramadan that was to be held at the White House.[221]

Alamoudi also parlayed his access at the highest levels of the U.S. government into the lead role in establishing the Muslim Chaplain Program for the Department of Defense, and then serving as the certifying authority for Muslim chaplains serving U.S. servicemen and women. He was also the founder and leader of the American Muslim Armed Forces and Veterans Affairs Council (AMAFVAC).[222]

In 1993, the Defense Department certified AMAFVAC as one of two organizations (the other was the Graduate School of Islamic and Social Sciences) authorized to approve and endorse Muslim chaplains. From about 1993 to 1998, the Pentagon would retain Alamoudi on an unpaid basis to nominate and approve Muslim chaplain candidates for the U.S. military. Among the chaplains Alamoudi hired was James Yee, who was arrested in 2003 by the U.S. government on charges he was supporting the jihadis detained at Guantanamo Bay, Cuba.[223]

The Muslim men working with Yee at Guantanamo, uniformed and contract employees (linguists), were all convicted on charges including mishandling classified information and espionage.

In 1998, Alamoudi provided at least $20,000 in checks enabling Republican activist Grover Norquist to establish what would become a Muslim Brotherhood front organization targeted at penetrating GOP circles and the presidential campaign of then-Governor George W. Bush.[224] The new entity was called the Islamic Free Market Institute (better known as the Islamic Institute, or II). Alamoudi also detailed his long-time deputy, Khaled Saffuri, to serve as II's first executive director, with Norquist as the Chairman of the Board.[225]

As a result of these connections, Alamoudi was among a group of Muslim Brotherhood operatives who were invited on May 1, 2000, to meet with Bush in the Texas governor's mansion. Saffuri was designated the Bush campaign's Muslim outreach coordinator and Norquist assisted another prominent Ikhwan operative, Sami al-Arian, to obtain a commitment from candidate Bush that, if elected, he would prohibit the use of classified intelligence evidence in deportation proceedings against foreigners suspected of terrorist ties. This was a priority for al-Arian since his brother-in-law was being held at the time by federal immigration authorities on the basis of such evidence.[226]

After the election, a member of the Islamic Institute's board of directors with myriad and longstanding connections to other Muslim Brotherhood organizations, Suhail Khan, was appointed to be the gatekeeper for the Muslim community in the White House Office of Public Liaison. Such relationships and placements afforded the Ikhwan unprecedented opportunities for influence operations against the U.S. government, especially after 9/11.[227]

Unfortunately for Alamoudi, his own ability directly to exploit such opportunities had by that time been irreparably damaged by his appearance at an anti-Israel rally outside the White House in October 2000. On that occasion, he carelessly gave the game away, when he declared on video: "I have been labeled…as being a supporter of Hamas. Anybody supporters of Hamas here? [Roars of approval from the crowd.] We are all supporters of Hamas. [More roars.] I wish they added that I am also a supporter of Hezbollah. [More roars.]"[228]

Then, in 2003, Alamoudi was arrested at Heathrow Airport (UK) on his way back from Libya with $340,000 in cash given to him by Libyan President Muammar Qaddafi for jihad. The money was to be used to underwrite a plot involving two U.K.-based al Qaeda operatives intending to kill Crown Prince (now King) Abdullah of Saudi Arabia.[229]

Alamoudi was extradited to the United States where, in the Eastern District of Virginia, he pled guilty to and was convicted of terrorism-related charges. He was proven to be a senior al Qaeda financier, who moved at least $1 million dollars to the terrorist organization. Alamoudi had also been caught on recorded conversations supporting acts of terrorism, terrorist organizations like Hamas and Hezbollah, and clearly stated his objective of making America a Muslim nation. Alamoudi is now serving a 23-year sentence in federal prison.[230]

Before his fall, Abdurrahman Alamoudi was one of the leaders of the global Islamic Movement and one of its most successful influence operatives. His arrest and conviction should have sent shock waves through the U.S. intelligence community, particularly its counterintelligence units, since Alamoudi's blown cover provided a reality check on the extent of shariah's stealth jihad in this country, and how badly we have been penetrated.

Here was, after all, proof that an al Qaeda financier, Hamas operative and Muslim Brotherhood agent had enjoyed access to the most senior levels of the American government. Thanks to that access, he was allowed – among other things – to create and run the program for selecting and placing members of his team to proselytize as Muslim chaplains in what can be the two most lucrative target populations for jihadist recruiters: the U.S. military and imprisoned felons.

Far from regarding the Alamoudi revelations as a wake-up call, however, administrations of both parties transferred his responsibilities for the chaplains to the Islamic Society of North America (ISNA), the largest Muslim Brotherhood front in this country.

In the absence of a serious effort to understand the true nature of shariah and the determined campaign being mounted to insinuate it into this country, together with an aggressive counter-intelligence operation aimed at defeating such influence and penetration operations, it is predictable that the next Alamoudi will be able to do vastly more damage than did the original.

MAPPING THE BROTHERHOOD

The "process of settlement" outlined in the *Explanatory Memorandum* and in published Muslim Brotherhood doctrine, such as *Toward a Worldwide Strategy for Islamic Policy*[231] and *Methodology of Dawah Ilallah in American Perspective*,[232] has been operationalized in the United States by one MB-related front group after another, starting with the very first, the Muslim Student Association (MSA), and continuing to the present day. As noted above, through this process, the Muslim Brotherhood has, as a matter of historical fact, established, built and maintained control over most of the prominent Muslim organizations in America. [For the complete text of the Memorandum, see Appendix II.]

The identified MB fronts and the other, as-yet-unknown groups share an inherent enmity for the United States and the West. It follows that when any friendly entity – to include federal, state and local law enforcement or intelligence units in the United States, other public officials, media organizations and religious institutions – works with individuals representing a self-described "Muslim" group, there is the probability that those with whom such outreach is being conducted and the group with whom it is being undertaken, are actually *hostile* to the United States.

The Muslim Brotherhood's own *Explanatory Memorandum* (reprinted in full as Appendix II of this book) identifies the following groups under the heading "a list of our organizations and the organizations of our friends"[233] :

- Islamic Society of North America (ISNA)
- Muslim Student Association (MSA)
- Muslim Communities Association (MCA)
- Association of Muslim Social Scientists (AMSS)
- Association of Muslim Scientists and Engineers (AMSE)
- Islamic Medical Association (IMA)
- Islamic Teaching Center (ITC)
- North American Islamic Trust (NAIT)
- Foundation for International Development (FID)
- Islamic Housing Cooperative (IHC)
- Islamic Centers Division (ICD)
- American Trust Publications (ATP)
- Audio-Visual Center (AVC)
- Islamic Book Service (IBS)
- Muslim Businessmen Association (MBA)
- Muslim Youth of North America (MYNA)
- ISNA Fiqh Committee (IFC)
- ISNA Political Awareness Committee (IPAC)
- Islamic Education Department (IED)

- Muslim Arab Youth Association (MAYA)
- Malasian [sic] Islamic Study Group (MISG)
- Islamic Association for Palestine (IAP)
- United Association for Studies and Research (UASR)
- Occupied Land Fund (OLF)
- Mercy International Association (MIA)
- Islamic Circle of North America (ICNA)
- Baitul Mal Inc (BMI)
- International Institute for Islamic Thought (IIIT)
- Islamic Information Center (IIC)

Several of the preeminent Muslim-American organizations in the United States today (notably, the Council on American Islamic Relations, the Muslim Public Affairs Council and the Islamic Free Market Institute) had not been established at the time in 1991 when this document was adopted by the Muslim Brotherhood. As will be discussed below, the ties of such groups to the Muslim Brotherhood can nonetheless be readily established by the involvement in their founding and/or operations of individuals associated with other Ikhwan fronts.

In order to be considered by the Muslim Brotherhood to be one of "our organizations" or an "organization of our friends," *all* of these entities had to have embraced the aforementioned Ikhwan creed: "Allah is our goal; the Messenger is our guide: the Koran is our law; Jihad is our means; and martyrdom in the way of Allah is our inspiration."

As we have seen, the actualization of the Muslim Brotherhood creed demands the triumph of shariah globally and the re-establishing the caliphate on a global basis. This end-state will entail subordinating to shariah the governing system of non-Islamic nations like ours (and Muslim nations not currently adhering to Islamic law) and, in due course, the destruction of such alternatives.

The inherently seditious nature of the Muslim Brotherhood's agenda and its incompatibility with Western civilization and governments is typically obscured in the free world by the assertion that the Ikhwan only seeks to achieve its objectives through non-violent means. As a result, the Brothers, their allies and proxies are all-too-often considered to be acceptable and reliable "moderate" partners for governments seeking to counter violent jihad.

Such openness to the Ikhwan is astounding not only because of the toxic nature of the MB's ambitions. The act of openness also ignores the fact that *Brotherhood doctrine recognizes that violence must be used when needed to achieve shariah's supremacist objectives.* For example, the Brotherhood bylaws call for Muslims to "fight the tyrants" when necessary to establish the Islamic state, indicating violence is approved when the time is appropriate.

Even more dispositive is the fact that the U.S. State Department-designated Foreign Terrorist Organization, Hamas, was formed out of the Palestinian Muslim Brotherhood. In addition, jihadi organizations such as al Qaeda sprang out of the Muslim Brotherhood and have among their leaders senior Muslim Brothers.

These realities underscore the inadvisability of any "outreach" to American Muslim organizations that espouse shariah, whether or not they acknowledge a tie to the Muslim Brotherhood.

UNDERSTANDING THE DEPTH OF MUSLIM BROTHERHOOD CONTROL

To reiterate, most Muslim organizations in North America are controlled by the Muslim Brotherhood or a derivative group (Hizb ut-Tahrir, Tablighi Jamaat, Jamaat-e-Islami, etc.). If an individual is the president, vice president, executive director, general secretary, board member or otherwise carries a significant leadership title within a Muslim organization controlled by the Muslim Brotherhood in America – particularly if he is responsible for the group's financial affairs, or sits on the Fiqh Council of North America – he is a Muslim Brother. The Ikhwan simply will not entrust such stature and responsibility to anyone unless he enjoys the trust that derives from being a member in good standing of the Muslim Brotherhood.

There are seemingly a few exceptions to this rule. Females have been utilized more often of late as "leaders" in several of these organizations (notably, the Muslim Students Association and the Islamic Society of North America) in order to project a softer image for these hostile organizations. This is particularly useful in confusing non-Muslims insofar as it would appear that such groups could not adhere to shariah's misogynistic practices and yet confer upon women positions of true responsibility.

Even a cursory examination, however, of the views of the current ISNA president, Ingrid Mattson, and former MSA President Hadia Mubarak reveals their philosophies are right in line with Muslim Brotherhood doctrine. And, in both organizations, the male leadership within the Brotherhood continues to make operational decisions, despite the title conferred upon such women.

A second exception to this rule involves some of the more recently established Muslim American organizations, especially where younger men and women are at the helm.

While they are not technically Brotherhood fronts, the message is nonetheless communicated in fairly explicit terms to these newer groups at major MB conferences (such as the annual ISNA conclaves): So long as these organizations observe the policy and doctrinal parameters set by the Brotherhood, they will be afforded access to the Brotherhood's infrastructure and financial support.[234]

On the other hand, historically any Muslim individual or organization that does *not* embrace shariah and the MB line has not been able to gain broad recognition as a Muslim-American force in America. Instead, they are systematically ostracized, delegitimized and, in some cases, directly threatened. We saw this in the Alamoudi network's bid to marginalize the Islamic Supreme Council of America, a Sufi organization led by Sheikh Muhammad Hisham Kabbani who warned early and often about Muslim Brotherhood operations against the United States as they were being put into place. The Brotherhood's strong-arm tactics are made all the more effective by the Ikhwan's ability to demonstrate that its doctrine is in line with Islamic law and backed by the threat of declaring the deviating Muslim an "apostate" (or, to non-Muslim audiences, simply dismissing the deviator as unrepresentative or irrelevant, with no real following), undercutting the authority and any opportunities for leadership among Muslims of those working against the MB.[235]

As a result of this modus operandi, the Muslim Brotherhood is not only able to prevent any appreciable challenge to its efforts to dominate the Muslim-American community. It is also able to exercise effective control over nearly all the Muslim organizational infrastructure in the United States, including most of those Muslim-American groups that are nominally outside its network. In any event, the latter pale by comparison in terms of their influence to those U.S.-based Islamic groups that are Ikhwan operations.

WHO'S WHO IN THE AMERICAN IKHWAN

The following are among the most worrisome of the Muslim Brotherhood front groups operating in the United States:

As we have seen, the Muslim Student Association was the first Muslim Brotherhood entity formed in the United States at the University of Illinois, Urbana campus in 1962-63. The MSA has chapters at nearly every major college and university campus in the United States, making it the most visible and influential of all Islamic student organizations in North America. The MSA is a point of recruitment for the Muslim Brotherhood and for jihadis.

The MSA's own website previously noted that all major Muslim organizations in America grew out of the MSA.[236] These references have been removed from the MSA website, however. It is nonetheless indisputable that among the MSA's offshoots are: the Islamic Medical Association (IMA), the Muslim Arab Youth Association (MAYA), the Association of Muslim Social Scientists, the Islamic Circle of North America (ICNA), and the Islamic Society of North America (ISNA).[237]

While presenting itself as just another moderate Muslim group working on college campuses, MSA in fact promotes a shariah-based Islamic agenda dedicated to spreading Islam among North American youth by way of an aggressive *dawa* program. The ideology that underpins the MSA mission is the same ideology as defines the Muslim Brotherhood and al Qaeda. The MSA perspective is global and its aspirations are closely linked to those of the "global Islamic Movement."[238]

MSA leaders have made statements condemning the United States and calling for the killing of all Jews.[239] Several MSA presidents have publicly supported jihad, and in the case of at least one, Omar Hammami from Alabama, have actually participated in violent jihad overseas.[240] MSA members routinely express admiration and support for terror organizations such as Hamas and Hezbollah and for the foundational leaders of the Muslim Brotherhood such as Hasan al-Banna and Sayyid Qutb.[241]

In addition to promoting aggressive political influence and intimidation operations like "Israel Apartheid Week" on many campuses, MSA chapters are also focal points for efforts to impose shariah blasphemy rules or otherwise control speech. To this end, members frequently engage in disruptive actions aimed at preventing speakers from exposing students to information about shariah Islam, jihad and their targets – notably, the United States and Israel – that would be deemed "offensive" or otherwise contrary to the ambitions of the Ikhwan.

THE ISLAMIC SOCIETY OF NORTH AMERICA

In 1980, the Muslim Brotherhood created the Islamic Society of North America (ISNA) "to be a nucleus for the Islamic Movement in North America."[242] From the time of its founding in Plainfield, Indiana, ISNA has been run by the senior leaders of the Muslim Brotherhood's Movement in the United States and Canada, and has emerged as the largest of the MB fronts in North America.

ISNA's prominent role in the Ikhwan operations in America is suggested by its listing at the top of the Explanatory Memorandum's roster of its front groups. The subheading on that list is: "Imagine if they all march according to one plan." ISNA was established as an umbrella organization to help foster such a plan, and ensure that all MB organizations "march" according to it.

Over the past three decades, thanks largely to its numerous chapters, its "over 300 community and professional organizations in North America,"[243] its substantial resources and aggressive influence operations, the U.S. government has accorded ISNA considerable stature as its leading "educational" and "outreach" partner in the Muslim-American community. For agencies with national and homeland security responsibilities like the White House, the FBI, the Departments of State, Defense and Homeland Security, and the intelligence community to confer such legitimacy on ISNA is all the more astounding given the results of the successful prosecution of the Holy Land Foundation in 2008.

ISNA and the HLF Trial: As this report discusses elsewhere, this trial was the largest involving Hamas and terrorism financing in U.S. history. In the course of its proceedings, the Justice Department established ISNA's role as a leading Muslim Brotherhood organization and its hostility to U.S. interests. In particular, thanks to evidence of financial transactions between ISNA and Hamas that the government introduced, along with scores of MB documents, it became clear that the Islamic Society of North America directly supports Hamas and its operations.

On the basis of such evidence, ISNA was named an unindicted co-conspirator in the HLF trial. ISNA, along with the North American Islamic Trust (NAIT), filed a motion with the court to be removed from the unindicted co-conspirator list. On July 10, 2008, the government filed a response to ISNA/NAIT's request. It is worth citing relevant parts of that response at some length:

> Although the indictment in this case charges the seven named individual defendants and the Holy Land Foundation for Relief and Development, it will be obvious that the defendants were not acting alone....The defendants were operating in concert with a host of individuals and organizations dedicated to sustaining and furthering the Hamas movement. Several of the individuals who hold leading roles in the operation of Hamas are referenced by name in the indictment. A list of unindicted coconspirators is attached to this trial brief. (Attachment A).

> The object of the conspiracy was to support Hamas. The support will be shown to have taken several forms, including raising money, propaganda, proselytizing, recruiting, as well as many other types of actions intended to continue to promote and move forward Hamas's agenda of the destruction

of the State of Israel and establishment of an Islamic State in its place." (p. 5)

Attachment A to the Trial Brief listed 246 different individuals and organizations as either unindicted co-conspirators and/or joint venture partners under one or more headings:

(1) individuals/entities who are and/or were part of the Hamas social infrastructure in Israel and the Palestinian territories;

(2) individuals who participated in fundraising activities on behalf of HLF;

(3) individuals/entities who are and/or were members of the U.S. Muslim Brotherhood's Palestine Committee and/or its organizations;

(4) individuals/entities who are and/or were members of the Palestine Chapter of the International Muslim Brotherhood;

(5) individuals who are and/or were leaders of Hamas inside the Palestinian territories;

(6) individuals who are and/or were leaders of the Hamas Political Bureau and/or Hamas leaders and/or representatives in various Middle Eastern/African countries;

(7) individuals/entities who are and/or were members of the U.S. Muslim Brotherhood;

(8) individuals/entities that are and/or were part of the Global Hamas financing mechanism;

(9) individuals/entities that [Hamas official Musa Abu] Marzook utilized as a financial conduit on behalf and/or for the benefit of Hamas;

(10) individuals who were HLF employees, directors, officers and/or representatives; and

(11) Hamas members whose families received support from the HLF through the Hamas social infrastructure." (p. 5)

ISNA and NAIT are listed in the attachment under the seventh heading, individuals/entities who are and/or were members of the U.S. Muslim Brotherhood." (p. 6)

During the trial, the Court entered into evidence a wide array of testimonial and documentary evidence expressly linking ISNA and NAIT to the HLF and its principals; the Islamic Association for Palestine and its principals; the Muslim Brotherhood in the United States and its Palestine Committee, headed by Hamas official Musa Abu Marzook; and the greater Hamas-affiliated conspiracy described in the Government's case-in-chief." (p. 7)

The evidence introduced at trial, for example, established that ISNA and NAIT were among those organizations created by the U.S.-Muslim Brotherhood." (p. 12)

ISNA and NAIT, in fact, shared more with HLF than just a parent organization. They were intimately connected with the HLF and its assigned task of providing financial support to Hamas." (p 13) [244]

The judge ruled against ISNA and NAIT, left them on the list of Unindicted Co-conspirators in the HLF trial and permitted the public release of the list.

Based on the facts presented herein, several questions demand answers: Why are ISNA and its leadership still given access to the U.S. government at the highest levels, to include the White House, the intelligence community, the military, and other obvious targets for Muslim Brotherhood influence operations? For example, ISNA President Ingrid Mattson was invited to attend President Obama's 2010 Iftar dinner where he announced his support for the Ground Zero mega-mosque.

Why are ISNA subsidiaries still the certifying authority for all Muslim Chaplains at the Department of Defense and within the U.S. Bureau of Prisons? Why was ISNA selected to provide training for U.S. Army senior enlisted men and officers to orient them about Islam prior to their deployments to Iraq and Afghanistan? Why has ISNA become the U.S. government's leading partner for "outreach" to the Muslims of America – including for the FBI and DHS, the very organizations mandated by law to protect and defend us from domestic enemies?

NORTH AMERICAN ISLAMIC TRUST

The North American Islamic Trust was created by the Saudis in 1973 and is often called "the bank" for the Muslim Brotherhood in North America. The following description of NAIT and its function was found on the website of its parent organization, ISNA:

> The North American Islamic Trust (NAIT) is a *waqf*, the historical Islamic equivalent of an American trust or endowment, serving Muslims in the United States and their institutions since 1973. NAIT is a not-for-profit entity, a tax-exempt organization under Section 501(c) (3) of the Internal Revenue Code. NAIT supports and provides services to ISNA, MSA, their affiliates, and other Islamic centers and institutions.
>
> NAIT holds titles to mosques, Islamic centers, schools and other real estate to safeguard and pool the assets of the American Muslim community, develops financial vehicles and products that are compatible with both the shariah and the American law, publishes and distributes credible Islamic literature, and facilitates and coordinates community projects.
>
> **Islamic Centers Division:** Islamic Centers Division (ICD) manages Waqf program services of NAIT to Islamic centers, mosques and schools. NAIT's Waqf program for the properties of Islamic centers, mosques and schools is based on

NAIT holding titles to these assets. *NAIT holds titles of approximately 300 properties. NAIT safeguards these community assets, and ensures conformity to the Islamic purpose(s) for which their founders established them.* NAIT does not administer these institutions or interfere in their daily management, but is available to support and advise them regarding their operation in conformity with the shariah." (Emphasis added.)[245]

As the foregoing makes plain, given the ties the Islamic Society of North America and the Muslim Students Association have to the Muslim Brotherhood, NAIT serves as the bank for the Ikhwan in the United States and Canada. The ISNA website goes on to say that NAIT "ensures conformity to the Islamic purpose(s) for which their founders established them." Since the MB exists to further the Islamic Movement, in pursuit of bringing the world under shariah and with the end goal of re-establishing the global Islamic State (i.e., the caliphate), NAIT serves, as a practical matter, as both an enabler and, through its financial leverage, an *enforcer* of the collective pursuit of those objectives.

As noted in connection with the foregoing discussion of ISNA, NAIT was also an unindicted co-conspirator in the HLF trial. In the course of those proceedings, numerous checks and other documents were made a part of the public record detailing financial transactions between NAIT and known Hamas entities. NAIT joined ISNA in requesting its name be removed from the unindicted co-conspirator list in the HLF trial. The judge denied the motion due to the overwhelming evidence that NAIT, in fact, serves as a support structure for the terrorist group Hamas.

COUNCIL ON AMERICAN ISLAMIC RELATIONS

The Council on American Islamic Relations (CAIR) was created in 1994 by the leadership of Hamas following a meeting of its senior U.S. operatives in 1993 in Philadelphia. According to FBI Assistant Director for Counterterrorism Dale Watson, the

Bureau wiretapped the Pennsylvania conclave meeting because it was "a meeting...among senior leaders of Hamas, the Holy Land Foundation for Relief and Development and the Islamic Association for Palestine." [246]

The CAIR Leadership: In an analysis of the meeting entered into evidence at the HLF trial, the FBI stated that "all attendees of this meeting are Hamas members."[247] Among those present were Omar Ahmad and Nihad Awad – the two founders of CAIR. Ahmad and Awad were both recorded in numerous intercepted conversations discussing Hamas' plans for America. On the tapes, Omar Ahmad was described as a leader of the Islamic Movement in the United States and a proposal was made to create a new public relations arm for the organization not connected with the Brotherhood's other entities, to include the HLF. Less than a year after this meeting, CAIR was formed with Omar Ahmad and Nihad Awad at the helm.

Ahmad and Awad were both senior leaders of the Islamic Association of Palestine (IAP), of which Ahmad was the President. The IAP's chairman was designated terrorist and Hamas leader Musa Mohammed Abu Marzook, who was also the chairman of the United Association for Studies and Research (UASR) and the Occupied Land Fund (OLF). The latter subsequently became the Holy Land Foundation (HLF), not to be confused with a Christian charity with a similar name.

Marzook was at the time the leader of Hamas in the United States and one of the top three Hamas leaders in the world. The U.S. Treasury Department designated him as a terrorist (SDT-145769). IAP, UASR, and OLF are all listed in the *Explanatory Memorandum* as Muslim Brotherhood affiliated organizations, and all are Hamas entities.

The Action Plan for Palestine: Another MB document entered into evidence at the HLF trial entitled "Islamic Action for Palestine" was dated October 1992.[248] It details the International

Muslim Brotherhood's creation of "Palestine Committees" to serve as leading Hamas elements in countries around the world for the purpose of raising money, recruiting jihadis and their supporters, and using propaganda to support the Palestinian cause:

> With the growth of the blessed Intifada and the spread of the spirit of Jihad amidst the children of Palestine and the nation, it became incumbent upon the remainder of the Ikhwan to play a role in attributing this Intifada and this Islamic action to Palestine. Therefore, a resolution was issued by the Guidance Office and the Shura Council of the International Movement to form "Palestine Committees" in all the Arab, the Islamic and the Western nations whose job it is to make the Palestinian cause victorious and to support it with what it needs of media, money, men and all that."[249]

This "resolution" was issued by the senior ranks of the leadership of the International Muslim Brotherhood as part of a global strategic move to draw support to the Palestinian cause and the leadership of that cause, Hamas, officially known as the Islamic Resistance Movement:

> The Islamic Resistance Movement: With the increase of the Intifada and the advance of the Islamic action inside and outside Palestine, the Islamic Resistance Movement (Hamas), provided through its activities in resisting the Zionist occupation a lot of sacrifices from martyrs, detainees, wounded, injured, fugitives, and deportees and it was able to prove that it is an original and effective movement in leading the Palestinian people. This movement – which was bred in the bosom of the mother movement, "The Muslim Brotherhood" – restored hope and life to the Muslim nation and the notion that the flare of jihad has not died out and that the banner of Islamic Jihad is still raised."[250]

Under chapter five of the "Islamic Action for Palestine" document is the title "Islamic Action for Palestine Cause for North America." This chapter then details the creation of three entities: IAP, UASR, and OLF to be the front organizations for Hamas in North America.

> When work developed, the Intifada started and the Islamic Resistance Movement (Hamas) was formed and the general apparatus for Palestine developed, and in light of the resolutions of the Guidance Office and the Shura Council of the International Movement to form Palestine committees in all the countries, the General Director of the apparatus came and met with the leadership of the Movement in America in 1988. After discussions and agreement, a "Palestine Committee" was formed under the supervision of the executive office. The Committee was then tasked with supervising all the organizations which serve the plan of the Movement domestically and internationally in addition to the Palestinian cause. Among these organizations were "The Islamic Association," "The Occupied Land Fund" and "The United Association."[251]

During the HLF trial, the prosecutors made it clear that the International Muslim Brotherhood created the Palestine Committee to oversee the work of the Palestine Sections in each country. These were the operational arms of Hamas, serving Hamas and its efforts. One key document entered into evidence is the list of the members of the Palestine Section in America.

Of the 35 names on the list of Hamas operatives in the United States, the first two names on the list are Musa Abu Marzook and Mohammed Akram, respectively. Name number 25 is "Omar Yeheya", an alias for Omar Ahmad, and name number 32 is "Nihad Awad".

CAIR *is* Hamas: In other words, according to a Muslim Brotherhood document entered into evidence by the prosecution – *and stipulated to by the defense attorneys as being true or at least what it purports to be* – the founders of CAIR have been officially identified as members of the Ikhwan's Palestinian franchise, the jihadist terror organization known as Hamas. In addition, another piece of Holy Land Foundation trial evidence, the organizational charts for the Central (Palestine) Committee's Executive staff, includes Omar Ahmad as the President of the IAP.

In light of the massive amount of evidence that CAIR is a Hamas entity operating in the United States on behalf of Hamas, CAIR and its president, Omar Ahmad, were both named as unindicted co-conspirators in the HLF trial. Like ISNA and NAIT, CAIR petitioned the court to have its name removed from the Unindicted Co-conspirator List. In the government's Memorandum in Opposition to CAIR's Request dated September 4, 2007, prosecutors stated:

> As of the date of this response, the Court has entered into evidence a wide array of testimonial and documentary evidence expressly linking CAIR and its founders to the HLF and its principals; the Islamic Association of Palestine and its principals; the Palestine Committee in the United States, headed by Hamas official Musa Abu Marzook; and the greater Hamas-affiliated conspiracy described in the Government's case-in-chief." [252]

The aforementioned Prosecutorial response to the ISNA/NAIT petition for removal of their names from the Unindicted Co-conspirator List also noted:

> Shortly after Hamas was founded in 1987, as an outgrowth of the Muslim Brotherhood, Govt. Exhibit 21-61, the International Muslim Brotherhood ordered the Muslim Brotherhood chapters throughout the world to create Palestine Committees, whose job it was to support Hamas with "media, money, and men." Govt. Exhibit 3-15. The U.S. Muslim Brotherhood created the U.S. Palestine Committee, which documents reflect was initially comprised of three organizations: the OLF (HLF), the IAP, and the UASR. *CAIR was later added to these organizations."*[253] (Emphasis added.)

As with ISNA and NAIT, the presiding judge ruled against CAIR and left it on the list of Unindicted Co-conspirators in the HLF trial and permitted the list's publication.

It was not until June 2008 that the FBI formally cut off all official relations with CAIR, ending, at last, its bizarre practice of having Hamas and the Muslim Brotherhood conducting "sensitivity training" for Bureau personnel. Unfortunately, the FBI's leadership at the Bureau's headquarters and some Special Agents in Charge at field offices around the nation continue to work with CAIR and other hostile entities over the objections of subordinates and evidence demonstrating why these entities are hostile.

The putative benefits of official outreach to Muslim Brotherhood fronts remain to be officially documented. Details are lacking, at least in the open source world, about tangible leads provided by any of the prominent Muslim organizations mentioned in this report that have resulted in the arrest of a terrorist or prevented a significant terrorist-related event. To the contrary, CAIR, for instance, issued a notice to its members as recently in May 2010 that advised them against cooperating with the FBI.[254]

CAIR and *The Muslim Mafia*: In October 2009, a book titled *Muslim Mafia: Inside the Secret Underworld That's Conspiring to Islamize America*[255] was published. It was authored by Paul Sperry, a best-selling author and investigative reporter, and David Gaubatz, a former Air Force investigator.

As it happens, the latter's son, Chris Gaubatz, had assumed the guise of a newly-converted Muslim and volunteered as an intern for CAIR. He was initially assigned to the organization's branch office in Herndon, Virginia. Herndon has long been known as a center of what Sperry has dubbed "the Wahhabi Corridor" – a concentration of shariah-adherent mosques (notably, the terrorist-tied Dar al Hijra mosque in Falls Church, Virginia) and Ikhwan fronts stretching from Washington's bedroom communities all the way to Richmond. When the Herndon office was closed, the younger Gaubatz was asked to work at CAIR's headquarters in Washington, D.C.

At the latter location, Chris Gaubatz was tasked with shredding large quantities of CAIR documents. Concerned that among these materials might be evidence of criminal activity, he removed over what was reported to be over 12,000 documents for more careful review. Drawing upon this data, along with the evidence from the Holy Land Foundation trial and considerable research previously done by Sperry on the Muslim Brotherhood in the United States (some of it detailed in an earlier book entitled *Infiltration: How Muslim Spies and Subversives Have Penetrated Washington*[256]), the authors produced *Muslim Mafia*.

Muslim Mafia explores the relationships between CAIR, Hamas, al Qaeda, and other entities. It documents how CAIR goes about manipulating information and conducting political influence operations, intelligence collection and counterintelligence activities. The book provided a call for action against not just "terrorism," but the sort of civilization jihad that CAIR and other MB fronts mount to insinuate shariah into the United States.

Some Members of Congress have begun to express concern about the efforts of the Muslim Brotherhood to penetrate our government and destroy us from within. On October 15, 2009, four Representatives, led by U.S. Congresswoman Sue Myrick of North Carolina, held a press conference on Capitol Hill asking, based on the primary source evidence presented in *Muslim Mafia*, that the Department of Justice investigate revelations in the book that CAIR/Hamas had, among other things, systematically tried to place interns on key national security committees in Congress. The targeted panels include the Armed Services, Homeland Security, and Intelligence Committees. Rep. Myrick also called on the Justice Department to brief all members of the U.S.

Congress on the evidence provided through the Holy Land Foundation trial and its implications.

In a written response dated February 12, 2010, Assistant Attorney General Ronald Weich stated:

> Enclosed are four copies of the trial transcripts on CD-ROM that contain testimony and other evidence that was introduced in that trial which demonstrated a relationship between CAIR, individual CAIR founders, and the Palestine Committee. Evidence was also introduced that demonstrated a relationship between the Palestine Committee and Hamas, which was designated as a terrorist organization in 1995."[257]

In short, an official communication between a senior Justice Department official and a sitting Member of Congress confirms what has been documented in this report: The Council on American Islamic Relations is a Hamas front. CAIR *is* Hamas.

CAIR Observatory: In addition, materials available at CAIRObservatory.org, a website sponsored by the Center for Security Policy,[258] suggest that the Council on American Islamic Relations is functioning as *an unregistered foreign agent* – an apparent violation of the Foreign Agent Registration Act (FARA). Enforcement of the act gained considerable publicity in 2010 when prosecutors used it to compel the forced deportation from the United States of ten Russian agents. The CAIR Observatory documents how the organization has received millions in contributions and financial pledges from abroad, including from foreign governments, organizations and individuals to conduct influence operations on their behalf.

The Center has conveyed information about CAIR's violation of federal law to targets of the latter's influence operations and to the relevant division in the Department of Justice, which is also responsible for counterintelligence. A federal grand jury reportedly was asked to review evidence of CAIR's apparent criminal wrongdoing.[259]

The Muslim American Society's articles of incorporation are dated June 11, 1993, and provide as its address 77 West Washington Street in Chicago, Illinois.[260] The founding directors, Omar Soubani, Jamal Badawi, and Ahmad Elkadi, are three of the most prominent Muslim Brothers in the world.

- Omar Soubani was listed as a "Member of the Board of Directors" of the Muslim Brotherhood in North America in evidence entered at the HLF trial.[261] His name appears as well on the list of members of the Palestine Section in America, making him a member of the Designated Terrorist Organization, Hamas.

- Jamal Badawi is today one of the world's senior Muslim Brothers. He is a member of the Fiqh Council of North America, one of the most influential and prominent Muslim Brotherhood organizations in the country. He was also a named unindicted co-conspirator in the HLF trial.

- Ahmad Elkadi was the General Masul, or General Guide, of the Muslim Brotherhood in America from the mid-1980s to the mid-1990s. In that capacity, he was the leader of the Ikhwan in America for nearly 10 years.

The fact that these three men founded the Muslim American Society makes MAS a significant Muslim Brotherhood operation. The MAS merged with the Islamic Circle of North America (ICNA), in 2000. ICNA is listed in the Ikhwan's *Explanatory Memorandum* as an MB-affiliated organization.

A further indication of the MAS' real role was provided in the course of a terrorism trial against a jihadist named Sabri Benkahla. When the case was heard before the Fourth Circuit Court of Appeals, the prosecution noted: "MAS was founded as the *overt* arm of the Muslim Brotherhood in America." (Emphasis added.)

As such, the Muslim American Society has been more directly politically active than ISNA. Today, MAS is a national organization with nearly 50 chapters and is known for its alliances with such far-left groups as the North Korea-affiliated organization called International ANSWER. Through its 501(c)(4), the MAS Freedom Foundation, the Muslim Brotherhood has a vehicle for engaging directly in lobbying activities and trying to influence elections.

A prominent fixture in Brotherhood influence operations is Mahdi Bray, the executive director of the Muslim American Society Freedom Foundation. Bray is a Muslim convert who has been exposed[262] as a convicted felon on myriad counts, ranging from drug use to grand larceny. He has been a vocal exponent of such other Muslim criminals as Abdurrahman Alamoudi, the MB operative now serving 23 years on terrorist-related convictions; Sami al-Arian, the senior Palestinian Islamic Jihad official who served federal prison time; and Jamil Abdullah Al-Amin (better known as H. Rap Brown), in prison for the murder of a law enforcement officer.[263] Bray has also been a visible critic of U.S.-led wars against the Taliban and al Qaeda, and a proponent of the Ground Zero mega-mosque.[264] (On the basis of serious concerns about the Muslim American Society, MAS was rebuffed despite a concerted charm offensive[265] when the Catholic church that owned a former convent in Staten Island and the community opposed an MAS bid to turn the property into its own mosque and Islamic center complex.[266])

Bray has been associated with a number of other Ikhwan front groups, serving on the advisory boards of Alamoudi's American Muslim Council and the Muslim Public Affairs Council.[267] He also served as president of the Coordinating Council of Muslim Organizations, a Brotherhood-dominated operation with which the Obama administration has been meeting for the purpose of providing government grants to its members and their projects.[268]

FIQH COUNCIL OF NORTH AMERICA

The Fiqh Council of North America, previously called the ISNA Fiqh Committee, is a known member of the Muslim Brotherhood movement and is listed in the *Explanatory Memorandum*'s roster as such.[269] The purpose of the Fiqh Council is to ensure the activities of the Muslim Brotherhood in North America are in compliance with shariah.

The Arabic term "fiqh" means "comprehension" or "understanding" and is related to Islamic legal scholars' comprehension of Islamic jurisprudence. Ensuring their activities are compliant with shariah is of the utmost importance to the Brotherhood, hence the North American Council.

The founding trustees of the Fiqh Council were Jamal Barzinji, Taha al-Awani, and Abdurahman Alamoudi.

Jamal Barzinji was one of the first Muslim Brothers to come to the United States in the late 1950's. Of Iraqi origin, Barzinji helped establish the entire first generation of Muslim organizations in America. He was present at significant international Muslim Brotherhood meetings and his home and offices were raided by the U.S. government after the attack on September 11, 2001.

Taha al-Awani has been the leader of several significant Muslim Brotherhood entities, to include the International Institute of Islamic Thought (IIIT). He is also a significant leader in the international MB Movement.

Abdurrahman Alamoudi is the Muslim Brother whose exploits as an al Qaeda financier and Hamas operative have been previously detailed. Alamoudi admitted to his role in a plot with two UK-based al Qaeda operatives to kill then-Saudi Crown

Prince, now King, Abdullah. He is currently serving a 23-year sentence on terrorism-related charges at Colorado's Supermax prison.

The Fiqh Council works closely with ISNA whose charter includes requirements for shariah adherence and for arbitration panels for the community. *These represent a ready-made infrastructure for insinuating shariah into America as a parallel legal code,* notwithstanding the U.S. Constitution's Article VI, which establishes it as "the supreme law of the land."

MUSLIM PUBLIC AFFAIRS COUNCIL

The Muslim Public Affairs Council (MPAC) was formed in 1986 as the Political Action Committee for the Islamic Center for Southern California, one of the largest Wahhabi mosques in America.[270] In 1988, the Political Action Committee separated from the Islamic Center of Southern California and became the Muslim Public Affairs Council. The founders of the Islamic Center for Southern California are Hassan Hathout and his brother Maher Hathout. The late Hassan Hathout was a senior member of the Muslim Brotherhood movement. The two brothers spent time in an Egyptian prison during the early days of the Muslim Brotherhood's activities there, led by the Brotherhood's founder Hassan Al Banna. MPAC's own publication, *The Minaret*, has proudly called Hassan a "companion of" and Maher "a close disciple of" the Brotherhood founder.

Maher Hathout was also one of the founders of MPAC. He currently serves as a senior advisor for MPAC and, along with other members of the organization, works for and maintains a close relationship with the Islamic Center of Southern California. Hathout was on the board of directors and a member of the American Muslim Council (AMC) from 1993 to 1997. As previously discussed, the AMC was founded by al Qaeda financier and Hamas operative Abdurrahman Alamoudi, who served as its executive director during the period Maher Hathout served on the AMC board of directors.

Maher Hathout has publicly voiced his approval of Designated Terrorist Organizations such as Hezbollah; decried many U.S. counterterrorism efforts; called for the destruction of Israel; and, openly supported known terrorists such as Hasan al Turabi, the leader of the National Islamic Front of Sudan. Yet, the organization he founded, MPAC, enjoys a reputation in official U.S. circles as a "moderate" Muslim organization. Salam al-Marayati is the current president of MPAC. Al-Marayati was denied a leadership position on the National Commission on Terrorism by then-House Democratic Leader Richard Gephardt when it came to light that Al-Marayati claimed that Hezbollah was a legitimate organization and had the right to attack the Israeli Army. Marayati's wife, Dr. Laila al-Marayati, was the White House appointee to the U.S. Commission on International Religious Freedom.

Edina Lekovic is MPAC's communications director. Previously, Lekovic was editor of the magazine *Al-Talib* when it editorialized that Osama bin Laden was a freedom fighter and warrior for Allah, who should be defended by Muslims. *Al-Talib* is the magazine published by the UCLA chapter of the Muslim Students Association. As discussed above, the MSA was the first Muslim Brotherhood organization established in the United States.

MPAC's role in the Muslim Brotherhood movement is significant. MPAC is an aggressive propaganda arm for the Ikhwan, contributing through taqiyya and disinformation to the MB's efforts at information dominance in the United States. For example, MPAC attacked the language used to describe the events of September 11, 2001 detailed in the 9/11 Commission Report. MPAC demanded an end to the use of words such as jihad, *ummah*, caliphate, shariah and others in relation to terrorist doctrine.

In subsequent years, the National Counterterrorism Center, the Department of Homeland Security and the Federal Bureau of Investigation have all issued strategic counterterrorism documents devoid of these terms. As described in chapter seven, such conformity to shariah by U.S. government entities such as the FBI and DHS is an extraordinary strategic victory for the enemy in the information and psychological battlespace.

THE DISAPPEARING LANGUAGE OF TERROR

	9/11 Commission Report[1] (2004)	FBI Counter-terrorism Analytical Lexicon[2] (2008)	National Intelligence Strategy[3] (2009)
Violent Extremism	3	29	9
Enemy	39	0	0
Jihad	126	0	0
Muslim	145	0	0
Islam	322	0	0
Muslim Brotherhood	5	0	0
Religious	65	3	1
Hamas	4	0	0
Hezbollah	2	0	0
al Qaeda	36	0	1
Caliph/Kalif	7	0	0
Shariah	2	0	0

SOURCES:

1 9/11 Commission Report, 2004, http://www.9-11commission.gov/
2 FBI Counter-Terrorism Lexicon, 2008, http://cryptome.org/fbi-ct-lexicon.pdf
3 National Intelligence Strategy , 2009, http://www.dni.gov/reports/2009_NIS.pdf

Most recently, Salam al-Marayati has been a prominent champion of the Ground Zero mosque, using the occasion of his advocacy to mislead American audiences about the nature of shariah and its compatibility with the U.S. Constitution. For example, in an interview published by the *Huffington Post* on August 22, 2010, the MPAC president engaged in world-class *taqiyya* when he made this declaration in response to the question "What about shariah (Islamic law) in the U.S.?":

> If what you mean by shariah is what is practiced in the Muslim world – No! Many Muslims fled the Muslim world because of corrupt regimes, injustice, misogyny, and downright discourtesy. I love the Muslim peoples throughout the world, and to borrow from Thomas Jefferson, my heart trembles for the Muslim world when I reflect that God is just. Shariah, to me, means living up to God's will of establishing justice. It is driven by five noble goals (as agreed upon uniformly by Muslim scholars throughout the ages), namely to secure and promote individuals' rights to life, expression, faith, property and family. When we see stoning of women in Afghanistan or Nigeria, or child marriages in the Arabian Peninsula, *that is not shariah*. It is an exploitation of Islam to oppress people, especially women.
>
> In reality, *the U.S. Constitution fulfills my obligation as a Muslim to achieve the five principles of shariah*. When I pledge allegiance to the flag of the United States of America, I make a pledge with God to uphold liberty and justice for all. Among our vast challenges today as Muslim Americans is the urgent need to develop a corpus of thinking and action that promotes a progressive approach to applying Islam in the modern era. We must find a way to keep the principles but do away with customs, cultural biases, and archaic traditions.[271] (Emphasis added throughout.)

Chapter six addresses in detail the untenability of claims like al-Marayati's about the compatibility of shariah with the U.S. Constitution.

The American Muslim Task Force (AMTF) used to have an enormously revealing description of itself on its website:

> The American Muslim Task Force on Civil Rights and Elections (AMT), an umbrella organization representing American Muslim Alliance (AMA), American Muslims for Palestine (AMP), Council on American Islamic Relations (CAIR), Islamic Circle of North America (ICNA), Islamic Society of North America (ISNA), Muslim Alliance in North America (MANA), Muslim American Society (MAS), Muslim Public Affairs Council (MPAC), Muslim Students Association – National (MSA), Project Islamic Hope (PIH), and United Muslims of America (UMA).[272]

At this writing, the "About Us" tab on the AMTF website is not functioning; likewise, its "Search" capability is "broken." The "Links" tab, however, takes the visitor to a page full of the names of the most prominent Muslim Brotherhood organizations and affiliates in the U.S., including: the AMA, CAIR, ICNA, ISNA, MAS, MPAC and MSA. Plentiful advice elsewhere on the website provides tips to motivate this group's membership to activism in the political arena. These kinds of efforts by a major Islamic organization with openly-advertised affiliations to Muslim Brotherhood-linked organizations and to focus on lawmakers and election campaigns at national and state levels must be cause for concern, and are key parts of the enemy's civilization jihad, being conducted pursuant to its "phased plan."

THE ORGANIZATION OF THE ISLAMIC CONFERENCE

The Muslim Brotherhood's goal of promoting civilizational jihad is strongly supported by the activities of the Organization of the Islamic Conference (OIC). The OIC is the second-largest supranational body in the world. It is an umbrella organization of fifty-six Muslim countries plus "Palestine"; only the United

Nations includes more member states[273]. Its members are represented annually at the heads of state level.

The OIC purports to represent the entire Islamic world, and styles itself as the Ummah – the collective of all those who worship Allah, follow Mohammed, and revere the Quran. Like the Ikhwan, the OIC has laid out explicitly how it intends to subjugate the *Dar al-Harb* to Islam.

So what is the OIC? Here is an excerpt from a speech give by the Conference's Secretary General, Professor Ekmeleddin Ihsanoglu, at the 35th session of the Council of Foreign Ministers of the OIC in June, 2008. Notice in particular how the Secretary General's words bear on freedom of speech issues[274]:

> In confronting the Danish cartoons and the Dutch film "Fitna," we sent a clear message to the West regarding the red lines that should not be crossed. As we speak, the official West and its public opinion are all now well-aware of the sensitivities of these issues. They have also started to look seriously into the question of freedom of expression from the perspective of its inherent responsibility, which should not be overlooked.

To whom precisely does that "we" refer in the context of the OIC? A visit to the OIC homepage is very informative, where a little drop-down lists its charter, its rules of procedure, and its organizational structure[275].

> The Organization of the Islamic Conference (OIC) is the second largest inter-governmental organization after the United Nations which has membership of 57 states [*sic.*] spread over four continents. *The Organization is the collective voice of the Muslim world* and ensuring to safeguard and protect the interests of the Muslim world in the spirit of promoting international peace and harmony among various people of the world. [Emphasis added.]

Given the many rivalries and divisions between the OIC's member states, such assertions of a monolithic position on anything – let alone claims to be an institutionalized "collective voice" – sounds presumptuous, if not utterly fatuous. Yet, when it comes to promoting Shariah via *dawa* backed by the threat of violence, it would be a grave mistake to discount the increasing potential for malevolence of an organization made of up of many of the richest and certainly some of the most dangerous countries in the world (notably, Iran, Libya, Sudan, Somalia, Saudi Arabia and Persian Gulf emirates).

A case in point is the present OIC Charter adopted by the Eleventh Islamic Summit held in Dakar on 13-14 March 2008. It lays down the objectives and principles of the organization and fundamental purposes to strengthen the solidarity and cooperation among the member states and describes the mandate of its main bodies. Several are noteworthy.

> **The Islamic Summit**, composed of Kings and Heads of State and Government of Member States, is the supreme authority of the Organization. It convenes once every three years to deliberate, take policy decisions and provide guidance on all issues pertaining to the realization of the objectives and consider other issues of concern to the Member States and the Ummah.

This statement underscores the fact that, when the OIC holds summits, the participants are *heads of state*, conferring on the organization a prominence it might not otherwise enjoy. It also suggests that, at the summits at least, participants are able to exercise considerable governmental authority, not merely represent their respective states.

> The **Council of Foreign Ministers**, which meets once a year, considers the means for the implementation of the general policy of the Organization by, *inter alia*:

(a) Adopting decisions and resolutions on matters of common interest in the implementation of the objectives and the general policy of the Organization;

(b) Reviewing progress of the implementation of the decisions and resolutions adopted at the previous Summits and Councils of Foreign Ministers;

In short, the OIC is comprised of real state actors using real state power to undertake collective actions in furtherance of transnational objectives. As many of its members' treasuries have been infused with vast oil export-driven revenues, this Muslim "bloc" has taken on greater influence internationally, particularly within the United Nations.

The question occurs: Whom does the Organization of the Islamic Conference actually represent? The OIC asserts that the answer is all Muslims – the *Ummah*. Consider the following examples of such claims:

From the Charter of the Organization of the Islamic Conference:

Chapter IV "Islamic Summit," Article 7: The Islamic Summit shall deliberate, take policy decisions and provide guidance on all issues pertaining to the realization of the objectives as provided for in the Charter and consider other *issues of concern to the Member States and the Ummah*[276]. (Emphasis added.)

Article 9: Extraordinary Sessions will be held, whenever the interests of the Ummah warrant it, to consider *matters of vital importance to the Ummah* and coordinate the policy of the Organization accordingly[277]. (Emphasis added.)

Chapter V, "Council of Foreign Ministers," Article 10, Section 3: "The Council of Foreign Ministers may recommend convening other sectorial Ministerial meetings to deal with the *specific issues of concern to the Ummah*."[278] (Emphasis added.)

The Secretary General of the OIC also routinely asserts that the OIC represents the Ummah. For example, in his speech in June, 2008 at the 35th session of the Council of Foreign Ministers, Prof. Ihsanoglu said[279]:

> In one word, we have managed to affirm our presence and draw attention to the fact that the OIC is considered an international organisation worthy of representing the *collective will and concerns of the Ummah* on the global level. (Emphasis added.)

The most recent OIC Summit (conducted at the heads of state level) goes so far as to identify the session as being convocation of the "Muslim Ummah." Here is the final communiqué of the meeting held in March, 2008 in Senegal[280]:

> In response to the kind invitation of H.E. Maitre Abdoulaye WADE, President of the Republic of Senegal, the Eleventh Session of the Islamic Summit Conference, **Session of the Muslim Ummah** in the 21st Century, was convened in Dakar, capital of the Republic of Senegal, on 6-7 Rabiul Awwal 1429 H.(13-14 March 2008). (Emphasis added.)

What seems indisputable is that the OIC is trying to forge a political force that is not merely the unachievable utopian ideal of a monolithic Ummah, as many Westerners assume. At the very least, for the participating heads of state and their foreign ministers, the OIC's claim to speak for the Muslim world is absolutely real, absolutely present in everyday life and a force behind their policy-making. To deny this is to ignore an obvious reality. Indeed, if the Caliphate is ever reestablished, it seems likely that it will grow directly out of the Organization of the Islamic Conference.

This prospect takes on additional moment against in light of the *Ummah's* goals as professed by the OIC. Particularly noteworthy is the arrogation to the OIC of a supranational, interventionist role "to defend," "to support," and "to assist" Muslims achieve the stated objectives, even on behalf of those Muslims who live as citizens of discrete sovereign non-member states:

- To defend the universality of Islamic religion;
- To support the struggle of the Palestinian people, who are presently under foreign occupation, and to empower them to attain their inalienable rights;
- To assist Muslim minorities and communities outside the Member States to preserve their dignity, cultural and religious identity;
- To support the restoration of complete sovereignty and territorial integrity of any Member State under occupation, as a result of aggression, on the basis of international law and cooperation with the relevant international and regional organizations;
- To promote and defend unified position on issues of common interest in the international fora.

OIC ACTIONS TO ENFORCE SHARIAH

The OIC is a primary international institution designed systematically to enforce shariah in Muslim and most importantly, non-Muslim countries. The obligation to enforce shariah doctrine globally is central to the OIC mission, and to its concept of unifying the *ummah*. In the OIC's "Ten-Year Programme of Action To Meet the Challenges Facing the Muslim Ummah in the 21st Century" of the 3rd Extraordinary Session of the Islamic Summit Conference[281], December 2005, Article VII calls for "deterrent punishments" to be imposed by all states – not just Muslim states – against critics of Islam:

VII. Combating Islamophobia

1. Emphasize the responsibility of the international community, including all governments, to ensure respect for all religions and combat their defamation.

2. Affirm the need to counter Islamophobia, through the establishment of an observatory at the OIC General Secretariat to monitor all forms of Islamophobia, issue an annual report thereon, and ensure cooperation with the relevant Governmental and Non-Governmental Organizations (NGOs) in order to counter Islamophobia.

3 Endeavor to have the United Nations adopt an international resolution to counter Islamophobia, and call upon all States to enact laws to counter it, including deterrent punishments.

4. Initiate a structured and sustained dialogue in order to project the true values of Islam and empower Muslim countries to help in the war against extremism and terrorism.

The OIC is also dedicated to opposing western traditions of liberty, freedom and human rights, since those traditions assert the rights of the individual rather than the submission of the individual to shariah. In 1990, the OIC member states adopted The Cairo Declaration of Human Rights in Islam[282] (CDHRI), a declaration which provides an overview on the Islamic perspective on human rights, and affirms Islamic shariah as its sole source. This declaration is usually seen as a shariah-adherent counter to the post-World War II United Nations' Universal Declaration of Human Rights (UDHR) of 1948, as well as the U.S. Constitution and Bill of Rights. Among its many declarations in direct opposition to definitions either of civil liberties or human rights are the following:

The Islamic Sharia is the only source of reference for the explanation or clarification to any of the articles of this Declaration (Article 25)

All the rights and freedoms stipulated in this Declaration are subject to the Islamic Shari'ah. (Article 24)

Everyone shall have the right to express his opinion freely in such manner as would not be contrary to the principles of the Shari'ah (Article 22)

> 1. Everyone shall have the right to advocate what is right, and propagate what is good, and warn against what is wrong and evil according to the norms of Islamic Shari'ah.

> 2. Information is a vital necessity to society. It may not be exploited or misused in such a way as may violate sanctities and the dignity of Prophets, undermine moral and ethical Values or disintegrate, corrupt or harm society or weaken its faith.

> 3. It is not permitted to excite nationalistic or doctrinal hatred or to do anything that may be an incitement to any form or racial discrimination.

Since its inception, the OIC has attempted to enforce – in all countries, not just Muslim-majority ones -- the shariah doctrine that any speech or expression offensive to shariah authorities is criminally-sanctioned blasphemy or slander. Since 1998, the OIC has substituted the term "Islamophobia" for blasphemy to make the charge more acceptable to Western governments. Where a charge of "racism" can be criminally prosecuted, as in Europe, the OIC has also tried to assert "Islamophobia" as legally equivalent to "racism" and therefore subject to government legislation and prosecution. Since 1999, the OIC has submitted numerous resolutions to the UN to censor free speech as "defamation against religion," with special emphasis on "Islamophobia."[283]

The OIC and its affiliated institutions provide an intellectual justification for terrorism that exempts jihad outright, and a comprehensive list of endorsed acts of violence against anyone they decide is an enemy. In the publication *Journal Islam Today* published by the OIC-established "specialized institution": "Islamic Educational, Scientific and Cultural Organization," in the article "Terrorism: Factors and Countermeasures," the author defines terrorism with these terms[284]:

> "The violent nature of an act is no longer a criterion in labeling it as a terrorist act...In light of this definition, we can identify the paradigms used to describe an act as terrorist. We can affirm that these attributes do not apply to:
>
> A. National resistance operations conducted exclusively against occupiers and colonialists.
>
> B. The resistance of peoples against forces imposed on them by force.
>
> C.The rejection of dictatorship and any form of tyrannical rule.
>
> D. Struggle against inhumane movements such as Nazism and racism.
>
> E. Retaliation in the same fashion to aggression when no other options exist.
>
> F. **Legitimate jihad with its moral conditions and human objectives as defined and clarified by our scholars.** (Emphasis added.)
>
> These attributes do not apply either to any peaceful action (involving no terrorist act), even if the underlying purpose is not a humanitarian one, **nor do they cover individual destructive acts** with no effect on society. Such acts and similar ones, even if they are condemned on another level, cannot be considered as terrorist acts.

The OIC's refusal to define" individual destructive acts" as terrorism (and indeed, endorsement of such acts as jihad) provided the policy framework for the U.S. Department of Defense's refusal to define the murder of thirteen people by Major Nidal

Hasan as an act of either jihad or terrorism in the August 18, 2010, "Department of Defense Implementation of Recommendations from the Independent Review Related to Fort Hood."[285] Hasan's act was instead treated as an individual destructive act – in compliance with OIC publications on terrorism.

THE MUSLIM BROTHERHOOD'S U.S. OPERATIONS: EXEMPLARS

By the mid-1990s, thanks to the successful application of the techniques employed pursuant to the phased plan by the Muslim Brotherhood's organizational footprint in the United States, the Ikhwan was in a position to target American society at all levels. With growing aggressiveness in recent years, its operatives have been mounting influence operations against this country's government, educational institutions, media, churches and synagogues, and local communities from coast to coast.

Here are a few illustrative examples of the MB's progress:

- Federal, state, and local law enforcement agencies and the intelligence community have been targeted in order to: blunt investigative efforts that might interfere with the Ikhwan's activities; keep homeland defenders and military personnel from being educated on the true nature of shariah, jihad and the Muslim Brotherhood; and ensure the MB is the only Muslim entity from which the U.S. government seeks advice on Islamic matters.

- The Department of Education and school boards across America have been penetrated for the purpose of encouraging, subliminally at first, submission to shariah in textbooks and pedagogy. The object is to control and soften the history of Islam and how it is taught to American students. Middle East Studies and "interfaith" programs at several leading U.S. universities have received $20 million apiece from a prominent Saudi prince and enabler of the Brotherhood, Prince Alwaleed bin Talal, with predictable results regarding their curriculum.

- Many well-meaning leaders of other faiths and their churches and synagogues have been penetrated and compromised through MB influence operations under the guise of "interfaith dialogue." Some have provided invaluable political cover for the Ikhwan by decrying objections to the establishment of mosques associated with it – for example, at Ground Zero in Lower Manhattan, in Roxbury, Massachusetts, in Murfreesboro, Tennessee and elsewhere – in the name of safeguarding religious tolerance.

- Prominent secular leadership figures in communities across the country have also been induced to provide what amounts to political cover for the Brotherhood. This is done when they lend their prestige and authority to MB *taqiyya* and publicly consort with Ikhwan operatives. Perhaps the most egregious example has been New York City Mayor Michael Bloomberg's repeated insistence that the Ground Zero mega-mosque must be built. Those who oppose the construction of the mosque near Ground Zero, or even seek to establish whether the $100 million to construct it are coming from problematic sources (perhaps including Iran), according to Bloomberg, are "un-American."[286]

- The financial community has been deeply penetrated via the promotion of shariah-compliant finance into Wall Street, with encouragement from the U.S. government. In fact, the American taxpayer now owns the largest purveyor of shariah-compliant insurance products in the world: AIG. (For more on this subject and a federal lawsuit challenging its constitutionality, see Appendix I.)

In short, the enemy among us – organized and guided by the Muslim Brotherhood and disguised by deceit – poses a grave long-term threat to our Constitution, government, freedoms and way of life. When the Brotherhood's stealth jihad operates in conjunction with overtly or covertly violent jihadist organizations like those described in the following chapter, joining forces to operate as a sort of strategic pincer-movement, they become toxic to freedom-loving and open Western societies like ours.

OTHER SHARIAH-ADHERENT ORGANIZATIONS

The division of labor within the community of adherents to shariah that has the Muslim Brotherhood promoting their agenda, for the moment, mostly through non-violent means has counterpart efforts being made by other groups that seek the same goals – the triumph of Islam worldwide and the restoration of the caliphate – *through violence.* Since September 11, 2001, the best known of these is the perpetrator of the murderous attacks launched that day: al Qaeda. Its prominence has only grown with repeated declarations by U.S. government officials to the effect that Osama bin Laden's group is *the* enemy we confront.

In fact, as the foregoing sections have demonstrated, al Qaeda is but *one* of the threats we confront, and not necessarily the most dangerous. The following pages discuss al Qaeda and a representative sample of other organizations in the world of adherents to shariah that are actively seeking to compel our submission and, ultimately, our destruction, through force and terror.

AL QAEDA

Contrary to popular opinion and stated U.S. national security policy, the real threat from al Qaeda is not its international network of jihadist training camps and cells, or even its trademark multiple, simultaneous suicide explosion attacks. Rather, the greatest danger arises from this group's singular ability to distract our leadership away from the stealth jihad aimed at insinuating shariah into our society and legal system.

Since the horrific 9/11 attacks, we have allowed ourselves to be sapped of blood and treasure, lured into faraway battlefields in Muslim lands, where the best and bravest American patriots have been asked to fight and die, too often with no clear strategy for victory and bereft of any understanding of shariah – even as they defend U.S. interests in shariah-dominated lands..

Such confusion at the top of U.S. national security ranks is inexcusable so many years after 9/11. That is especially so given that the enemy has explained his strategy clearly and repeatedly. Jihadist online postings from 2002 described in forthright terms the al Qaeda strategy to draw the American military machine into the Afghan maw to be bloodied and drained:

> And it is known and transmitted amongst the pioneers in the fields of sacrifice that al Qaeda Organization adopted a new plan to lure [enemies] into Afghanistan; that is, attacking the Americans directly and in three different pillars of governance – politics, economy, and military power – in order to achieve a number of very important goals...[among which were]:
>
> 9 - To lure the American Forces into an Asymmetric battle, to liquidate the power of the enemy and have him bankrupt [himself], just like their Russian counterpart.
>
> 10 - To start a struggle between the American forces and the [Islamic] nation's men (not the armies of the rulers) in a long and unlimited battle that starts in America and expands from

Afghanistan to Mauritania, and with it the spirit of the Islamic resistance comes back and in it the Muslims youth will carry the weapons.[287]

As envisioned by al Qaeda strategists, years of grinding warfare in Afghanistan with no clear victory for Western forces not only have taken their toll on budgets and troops, but most importantly of all, have sowed doubts about America's military and political leadership in the hearts and minds of the American people.

Brigadier S.K. Malik wrote the Pakistani military doctrine in 1979 in a slim volume called *The Quranic Concept of War*. In it, he describes jihad as "a continuous and never-ending struggle, waged on all fronts including political, economic, social, psychological, domestic, moral and spiritual...."[288] and says that "The whole philosophy [of the Quranic military strategy] revolves around the human heart, his soul, spirit and Faith." He went on to add, "In war, our main objective is the opponent's heart or soul..."[289]

Then, in July 2010, the *Washington Times* highlighted significant differences between the war-fighting doctrine of General David Petraeus, the new Afghan theater commander, and the Obama administration about the very nature of the jihadist enemy. Whereas the 2006 Petraeus counterinsurgency field manual refers explicitly to "Islamic insurgents," "Islamic extremists," and "Islamic subversives," current national leadership literally has banned the use of such terminology. The story only deepened the perception of an American leadership crisis in the jihad wars.[290]

From the perspective of the jihadist enemy, such developments contribute to the aforementioned pincer-movement against the West – in which violent terror demoralizes and intimidates even as it simultaneously distracts attention from and reinforces the Muslim Brotherhood's mission of "eliminating and destroying the Western civilization from within and 'sabotaging' its miserable house by their hands."[291]

As U.S. civilian, intelligence and military leadership attention is consistently diverted to conflicts abroad, and new plots for terrorist attacks at home are uncovered at an alarming rate, the mantra of U.S. leadership remains narrowly focused on the threat of "violent extremism" – a euphemism often substituted for al Qaeda. At best, American attention, rhetoric and resources are as a result addressed to stopping al Qaeda, even though it is *just one of the many jihadist groups* (several of the most prominent of which are described below) that are using kinetic means to advance shariah – or preparing to do so.

Such a myopic characterization of the terror threat as the full extent of the jihadist enemy's strategy to destroy our society and impose shariah has no basis in reality. It can only be considered a product of the enemy's successful psychological offensive and information dominance. (For more on this strategy and its success, see chapter seven.)

If, in fact, the real threat is only *partly* about jihadist violence, then Western civilization must face up to the genuinely terrifying reality that the enemy we face is not al Qaeda per se or alone. We must instead come to grips with the jihadist imperative that derives from shariah doctrine itself – and the reality that all who know and actively follow that doctrine are dedicated to jihad for the purpose of imposing Islamic law on this country and all non-Islamic societies worldwide.

As will be discussed at greater length below, if the enemy at war with the United States is not just al Qaeda, but also a significant percentage of the hundreds of millions of Muslims who are dedicated to the imposition of shariah on us by violence or by stealth, and the U.S. leadership willfully is misconstruing the threat, then that leadership is failing in its constitutional responsibility to "support and defend the Constitution against all enemies foreign and domestic." This is the actual meaning of the Muslim Brotherhood Memorandum and mission in America: its stated purpose is to so blind U.S. strategic thinkers to the existence of doctrinal justification for Islamic terror that they themselves, "by their own hand," will cripple America's ability to respond effectively.

For all the horrific destruction of human life and endeavor thus far perpetrated by al Qaeda and its allies, both national (Iran) and sub-national (e.g., Hezbollah, Hamas and the Taliban), those atrocities have no power to threaten our way of life – unless we allow them to undermine our morale and erode our faith in ourselves, our abilities and our leadership. If America permits al Qaeda to instill the terror about which S.K. Malik (among many other shariah-adherents) have spoken, then we will have granted al Qaeda and its ilk the power to set the conditions for our acquiescence, appeasement and surrender.

Refusal to name the enemy or describe his ideology accurately is but the first step in the enemy's program to divorce U.S. strategic thinking from confronting the real threat or having any hope of developing an effective strategy to defeat it. *It is imperative that we as Americans recognize and openly identify shariah as the font of Islamic terror.* The ultimate objective of al Qaeda and other perpetrators of that terror is not merely to inflict death and mayhem on infidels like us, but to advance our subjugation to shariah.

FORCES OF THE ISLAMIC REPUBLIC OF IRAN

The Islamic Republic of Iran is, according to its own constitution, dedicated to revolution and "the religious fight of Islam…inside and outside the country." The duties of the vanguard in that fight, the Islamic Revolutionary Guard Corps (IRGC), are likewise set out in Iran's 1989 constitution:

> "…The corps of Revolutionary Guards…have responsibility not only for the safeguarding of the frontiers, but also for a re-

ligious mission, which is jihad along the way of Allah, and the struggle to extend the supremacy of Allah's law in the world."[292]

In 1979, Iran's Ayatollah Ruhollah Khomeini and his followers were the second group of jihadists, after the House of Saud earlier in the 20th Century, to seize control of a nation state with vast natural resources. While the Saudi population is predominantly Sunni and that of Iran predominantly Shiite, both regimes are completely committed to the supremacy of shariah and its realization across the globe via jihad – whether by the pen, the purse or the sword.

As noted in chapter two, Khomeini's ideology of *Velayat-e Faqih* (or Rule of the Jurisprudent) calls for theocratic governance under a senior Shiite cleric. It derives from Khomeini's own deeply hostile attitude towards modernization and secularization in an increasingly Western-dominated world.

Velayat-e Faqih mandates strict implementation of shariah along 7th Century lines. Even though a 1989 referendum by the Iranian people suggested popular support for this official ideology, it imposes draconian *hudud* punishments, the death penalty for homosexuals and an institutionalized misogyny that are deeply resented and increasingly opposed by Iran's youthful population. Especially in the wake of the massive nationwide popular protests following the fraudulent June 2009 presidential elections, demonstrators in the street and senior members of the Iranian Shiite clergy alike have demanded an end to the institution of the Supreme Leader and *Velayat-e Faqih* itself, correctly declaring both to be perversions of traditional Shia Islam.[293]

In the face of such opposition, the clerical clique in Tehran maintains power today by means of draconian repression domestically and the projection of its ideology and power abroad. The latter is accomplished through proxy and allied terrorist organizations – which include Sunni organizations like al Qaeda and

Hamas, as well as Shiite ones like Hezbollah and a variety of Iraqi militias.

The mullahs' drive for a deliverable nuclear weapons capability is the *sine qua non* of this regime and will not be denied it, absent a credible threat to regime survival – or, perhaps, by its destruction alone. Their implacable antisemitism and declarations of genocidal intent toward the State of Israel provide inspiration, guidance and material support to entities bent on preventing an Arab-Israeli peace process.

At the same time, Tehran's aggressive drive for expanded geo-strategic influence in the Persian Gulf and the broader Middle East, in conjunction with its bid to seize leadership of the international jihad, alarms neighboring Sunni regimes, compounded by fear of an imminent withdrawal of traditional American power projection in the region by the Obama administration.

The Iranian Revolutionary Guards Corps, its Qods Force division, and the Ministry of Intelligence and Security (MOIS) are the lead Iranian organizations for jihadist terror projection. Each of these organizations requires urgent attention by U.S. security policymakers.

THE IRGC

The Iranian Revolutionary Guards Corps (IRGC), also known as the *Pasdaran* – derived from the more formal title *Sepah-e Pasdaran-e Inqilab-e Islami*, which literally translates from Farsi as "Army of the Guardians of the Islamic Revolution") was established by the Ayatollah Khomeini in March 1979 to augment the regular army in defense of the physical borders of the state. Its primary function, however, is maintaining the clerical regime in power. In the wake of the chaotic civil disturbances that followed the June 2009 presidential elections, widely seen as fraudulent, regime resources increasingly have flowed to the IRGC to augment its ability to suppress regime opposition. The growing power and influence of the *Pasdaran* is so notable that its evolution of late has been termed a "military coup."[294]

Today, the IRGC numbers some 125,000 and includes the Qods Force, the regime's international terror arm.[295] The Commander of the Guard directs and organizes the arming, equipping, and training of the Iraqi Shiite "Special Groups," and al Qaeda and other Sunni forces.[296]

As the direct commander of Hezbollah cells in Iran and Iraq, the IRGC oversees the training camps where Hezbollah explosives experts pass on the deadly skills that kill American and Coalition troops and Iraqi civilians alike.[297] Increasingly, the IRGC-Qods Force is also providing funding, training, and weapons to Taliban forces in Afghanistan, activity that had diminished for a time after 9/11.[298] Reporting out of West Africa, Europe, and North and Latin America suggests an expanding presence of IRGC-Qods Force, MOIS and Hezbollah elements in these regions, as well.[299]

The IRGC controls Iran's biological and chemical weapons programs, as well as its nuclear weapons program since being assigned the duty of acquiring the bomb by the Ayatollah Khomeini in the 1980s. It is also responsible for Iran's ballistic missile development program, which it manages in a kind of joint venture arrangement with North Korea.

The IRGC has been amassing control over a significant segment of the Iranian economy. It is estimated that the IRGC, its top commanders and affiliates now own outright 30 percent or more of the entire Iranian economy.[300] This situation contributed directly to the decision by the wealthy Rafsanjani clan to launch its election challenge in a bid to defend against further IRGC encroachment on its financial empire.

The Qods Force is specifically charged with extraterrito-
rial liaison with terrorist organizations and is Iran's tip of the spear
for arming, funding, training, and other support to groups such as
al Qaeda, Hamas, Hezbollah, the Iraqi Jaish al-Mahdi, Palestinian
Jihad and the Taliban.[301] The Qods Force also handles Iranian
relations with organized crime and narco-trafficking organizations, such as the Afghan opium drug lords.[302]

Numbering around 21,000 members, the Qods Force
members deploy to the field and also operate undercover out of
Iranian embassies worldwide. The organization has trained
members of dozens of international terrorist groups in guerrilla,
paramilitary and terror tactics. In the wake of the U.S. invasion of
Afghanistan in 2001, Qods Force commanders negotiated Iranian
safe haven for hundreds of al Qaeda fighters, including at least two
of bin Laden's sons, Saad and Hamza, and other bin Laden family
members, plus al Qaeda's military operations chief, Saif al-Adl.[303]
It was Qods Force that maintained Iran's operational relationship
with al Qaeda in Iraq's leader, Abu Musab al-Zarqawi, until his
elimination at the hands of U.S. forces in 2006.[304]

THE MINISTRY OF INTELLIGENCE AND SECURITY

The Iranian intelligence service is a "ministry" in name only, as its chain of command actually bypasses the cabinet and reports directly to the Supreme Leader. With up to some 30,000
officers and support staff, MOIS is one of the largest intelligence
services in the Middle East and has been termed by Magnus Ran-
storp, the renowned Scottish defense and security expert, "a su-
perpower in intelligence terms in the region," because of its global
reach and sophistication.[305]

MOIS performs all the usual functions of a national intelligence agency, such as collection, analysis, and dissemination of
reporting. It is also tasked with keeping the regime in power by

any and all means, including but not limited to: infiltrating and disclosing conspiracies that threaten the regime; suppressing internal dissent; arresting, assassinating, jailing, intimidating, kidnapping, torturing and forcibly repatriating regime opponents; and maintaining liaison relationships not only with foreign intelligence services, but with terror organizations worldwide with whom the MOIS actively collaborates.[306]

The Iranian intelligence service has been faulted for failing to keep control of the situation following the 2009 elections and reportedly has lost status, particularly vis-à-vis the IRGC, as a result. The MOIS director was replaced and resources are flowing to augment the Intelligence Unit of the IRGC, a small but increasingly favored rival to the MOIS.

THE 'IRAN LOBBY'

In addition to the formidable capabilities the IRGC, Qods Force, MOIS and their proxies represent for influencing and, where desirable, violently attacking the Tehran regime's enemies, the Islamic Republic of Iran also can rely upon a well-organized network of influential individuals and groups in this country that its own government-controlled media have dubbed "the Iran lobby in America."

That network generally operates from a common script to urge a U.S. foreign policy towards the Tehran regime that features accommodation, concessions and unconditional dialogue, while arguing strenuously against coercive measures – notably, the imposition of political and economic sanctions and most especially military action against Iran's nuclear weapons facilities.[307]

The preeminent figure in the "Iran lobby" is an Iranian-born agent of influence named Trita Parsi. Emulating the Sunni Muslim Brotherhood model of spawning front organizations, Parsi founded the National Iranian-American Council (NIAC) in 2002. Under his leadership, NIAC has, in turn, helped to found and/or established relationships with a variety of sympathetic organizations, including: some MB fronts like the Council on American Islamic Relations (CAIR, founded as noted above by Hamas in 1994); the Campaign Against Sanctions and Military Intervention in Iran (CASMII, founded in December 2005); the Center for a New American Security (CNAS, founded in February 2007), the Campaign for a New American Policy on Iran (CNAPI, founded in June 2008), and the American Foreign Policy Project (AFPP, founded in December 2008).[308]

It is of considerable concern that individuals associated with the Iran Lobby network, often through one or more of these organizations, have found their way into influential posts in the Obama administration. Even as events in the Middle East move inexorably toward renewed conflict and Iran defiantly accelerates its nuclear weapons program, such "friends of Iran" as Dr. Vali Nasr (now the senior advisor to Ambassador Richard Holbrooke for Afghanistan/Pakistan issues), Dr. Susan Rice (U.S. Ambassador to the United Nations) and John Limbert (until July 2010 a top official at the State Department's Iran desk) – have helped ensure that U.S. policy towards Iran remains incoherent and contrary to long-term U.S. national security interests.[309]

The magnitude of damage Iranian elements are capable of perpetrating in America in furtherance of their shariah agenda is greater if, as seems to be the case, senior U.S. national security policymaking circles have been penetrated by agents of influence and those influenced by them whose actions, intentional or otherwise, serve to support the objectives of a hostile foreign power. To date, there is no evidence that such a possibility has been seriously considered, let alone thwarted by American counterintelligence.

HEZBOLLAH

Hezbollah (literally, the Party of God) is a Shiite Lebanese terrorist organization founded in the early 1980s by the Iranian government's Islamic Revolutionary Guard Corps. Former Deputy Secretary of State Richard Armitage once said that Hezbollah may well be the "A team" and al Qaeda the "B team" of global terrorism. As such, the organization, its role and capabilities warrant close study.

Hezbollah's purpose is to advance Tehran's agenda of: promoting shariah; destroying Israel; dominating Lebanon; and the readying of a global strike force. Although the immediate justification for Hezbollah's emergence was in response to Israel's invasion of southern Lebanon in 1982, an influx of Shia scholars from Najaf fleeing the 1968 Baathist coup in Iraq had laid the groundwork for the Islamicization of Lebanon more than a decade earlier.[310]

Iranian sponsorship of Hezbollah enabled it to become not only a regional organization fighting against the Israelis, but also a global terrorist network. Hezbollah today is a tightly disciplined, superbly trained, and fanatically dedicated cadre of shariah-adherent jihadis that effectively controls Lebanon on behalf of Iran. The Party of God's expansion into politics, with representatives in the Lebanese cabinet and parliament, demonstrates the totality of the stranglehold Iran and Hezbollah jointly exercise over Lebanon.

CURRENT MILITARY CAPABILITIES

Hezbollah fields up to 20,000 fighters, of whom perhaps one-third have undergone advanced combat training in Iran. Such training involves a rigorous three-year basic course, which emphasizes: advanced individual commando skills; small unit tactics; terror training (such as assassination, bomb-making, explosives, kidnapping and suicide-bombing); and weapons expertise across a broad range of light infantry arms.

Hezbollah's vaunted rocket and missile arsenal and other armaments were massively resupplied by Iran and Syria after the 2006 Lebanese war with Israel. Its current inventory includes Fajr-3 and Fajr-5 surface-to-surface missiles, Zelzal-2 ballistic missiles, tens of thousands of Katyusha rockets, and Chinese-model cruise missiles. In April 2010, Defense Secretary Robert Gates said Hezbollah had "far more rockets and missiles than most governments in the world." [311]

In addition, Hezbollah has an array of unmanned aerial vehicles, Russian-made anti-tank guided missiles and anti-aircraft missiles, tanks, and armored personnel carriers. It also operates a state-of-the art military-grade fiber optic communications network that is directly integrated with the Iranian IRGC network.[312]

ROOTED IN SHARIAH

Hezbollah literally burst onto the world scene in 1983 when it killed 241 U.S. Marines in a suicide attack on their barracks in Lebanon. Operating in coordination with senior levels of Ayatollah Khomeini's revolutionary regime – which armed, funded, inspired and trained it, Hezbollah subsequently launched a campaign of global terror marked by bombings, hijackings, kidnappings, and incessant attacks against Israel.

These attacks included ones Hezbollah carried out (under Iranian direction), notably the 1992 and 1994 bombings in Buenos Aires against the Israeli Embassy and AMIA Jewish Cultural Center, respectively. As noted elsewhere in this report, at about the same time, Hezbollah joined its Shiite Iranian sponsors in an operational relationship with al Qaeda, under the aegis of the Sudanese government and the pan-Islamic Sunni cleric, Hassan al-Turabi. That partnership made possible the Khobar Towers suicide attack of 1996, the East Africa Embassy bombings in 1998, the USS *Cole* attack in 2000 and, ultimately, 9/11 itself.

Hezbollah styles itself a violent movement in the service of shariah. Its official symbol is a globe and an upraised arm brandishing an AK-47 rifle. There is real meaning to the imagery of that symbol: It starkly shows that Hezbollah is an Islamic jihadist organization dedicated to the imposition of shariah across the world. Hezbollah's official name in Arabic, *Hizb Allah-Al-thawra Al-Islamiya fi Lubnan,* appears below the globe and means "The Islamic Revolution in Lebanon."

Visually, the positioning of the character "A" of "Allah" is linked above to the upraised arm with the AK-47, to signify divine sanction for the group. A Quran rests atop the letter "b" of the word "Hizb" (party), which is fashioned in the shape of a traditional lectern for the Muslim scriptures, conveying the message that Hezbollah is legitimate and based upon the Quran. Finally, emblazoned above the Hezbollah symbol is the Quranic verse, *"Fa-inna Hizb Allah hum alghalibun,"* which means "Lo, the Party of God, they are the victorious ones."[313]

Hezbollah was founded on and continues to follow the principles of not only traditional Shia Islam, but also the untraditional ideology of Iran's Ayatollah Khomeini. As discussed below, Khomeini's concept of *Velayat-e Faqih* puts a Shiite cleric in control of both political and theological power and claims supreme rule over all Shiites everywhere.

The Iranian constitution dedicates the regime to jihad to achieve the global spread of shariah. Hassan Nasrallah, the fourth and current Secretary General of Hezbollah, has publicly pledged fealty to the Iranian Supreme Leader, Ayatollah Ali Khamenei, as his *Marja* or spiritual leader. Like Iran, Hezbollah and Nasrallah proclaim their dedication to the destruction of Israel and "death to America."

Nasrallah is an iconic figure to millions of Lebanese Shia. His fiery speeches evoking shariah and jihad contribute to the cult of personality that surrounds him. He was born in southern Lebanon and wears the black turban that signifies bloodline descent from the Prophet Mohammed. Nasrallah was educated in the Iraqi holy city of Najaf.

The Hezbollah leader is viewed as a tough, charismatic leader whose own son, Hadi, was killed in action against the Israelis in 1997. He lives under multiple layers of security in the Hezbollah stronghold of southern Beirut and is seldom seen in public for fear of Israeli assassination operations and rose to Hezbollah leadership in 1992 after Israeli forces killed his predecessor, Sheikh Abbas Musawi. He earned the sobriquet of "the man who never lies," because of his record of turning military success against the Israeli Defense Forces into political gains for Lebanese Shiites.

Hezbollah is run by the Executive Shura headed by Secretary General Nasrallah, who manages the group's day-to-day activities and makes all decisions related to financial, judicial, military, political, and social issues. The Consultative Council is comprised of 12 key figures among the Hezbollah leadership and meets on a weekly basis to discuss current matters. There is also a Supervisory Committee, or Politburo, comprised of 15 select Shiite clergy members, that conveys Consultative Council dictates to Lebanon's regional areas and coordinates propaganda and support services at the local level.

Thanks to an annual infusion of funding from Iran that amounts to hundreds of millions of dollars, Hezbollah operates civil defense centers, clinics, hospitals, and schools across Shiite areas of Lebanon otherwise underserved by the central government. Hezbollah has been exceptionally adept at developing a grassroots network and insinuating itself into Lebanese society.

Hezbollah runs youth groups, scout troops, and summer camps that inculcate hatred of Jews, infidels and Americans from the earliest ages. In addition, it also provides physical and weapons training to children in preparation for later military service. The legendary loyalty of Hezbollah's fighters is inspired in part through absolute guarantees to care for its injured members and the families of the fallen, to educate their children, and to provide lifelong pensions to their widows.

Hezbollah's "social" and "charitable" activities do nothing to diminish its jihadist agenda and terrorist operations. They not only serve to promote *dawa* and recruit new adherents to shariah; they serve as a visible form of taqiyya as well. Specifically, these activities are calculated – and shrewdly used – to blur the hard edges of its identity in the eyes of a poorly informed and credulous international community.

One indication of the success of such deflections is, as noted below,[314] that even the U.S. Central Command (CENTCOM) issued – albeit under the guise of a *plausibly deniable* "Red Team" study – a paean to Hezbollah in May 2010. The paper suggested that because, among other considerations, Hezbollah has been so successful in translating its social services into a popular following, a change in U.S. government policy towards the organization is now warranted, with a view to expressing American-support for the Party of God's integration into the Lebanese political mainstream.

HEZBOLLAH'S INTELLIGENCE OPERATION

The organization has developed and fielded an intelligence apparatus that is highly capable, tightly organized and exceedingly difficult to penetrate. In part, its effectiveness derives from the fact that it functions along the lines of, and benefits from, Lebanese Shia clan loyalties. That reality is also a function of the organization's professional training under the formidable Iranian services. Indeed, the Iranian IRGC and MOIS provide Hezbollah with secure training facilities on Iranian territory where Hezbollah cadres develop advanced intelligence and counterintelligence capabilities.

Hezbollah brings to bear double-agents, information and psychological operations and intelligence-gathering and penetration operations against both the Israelis and the United States. Busted cigarette-smuggling operations from North Carolina to Michigan suggest the presence of active Hezbollah cells in the United States.[315] The 2007 case of Hezbollah agent Nada N. Prouty, who obtained U.S. citizenship through a sham marriage, and then succeeded in infiltrating both the FBI and the CIA, provides an indication of the sophistication of Hezbollah's operations.[316]

HEZBOLLAH'S INFORMATION OPERATIONS

Al-Manar (The Beacon) is the Hezbollah official television station that reaches across the Middle East and, via satellite, around the world. Al-Manar amounts to a powerful propaganda, indoctrination and recruitment vehicle, although it masquerades as a full schedule of news, commentary and educational programming.

In addition, Al-Manar pumps out a steady stream of dramatic music videos about Hezbollah suicide bombers and military operations. The cumulative effect of this diet of violent content in shaping public understanding of and support for shariah and jihad – including by inciting hatred against Israel and the West – among millions of Arabs and Muslims cannot be overstated.

HEZBOLLAH'S TERROR OPERATIONS

Hezbollah's worldwide terrorist operations are directed by the Special Security Apparatus (SSA), which is also responsible for intelligence and security matters. Long led by Imad Mughniyah, the man Israeli intelligence called "a triple Hezbollah-Iran-al Qaeda agent and terrorist executive,"[317] the SSA is charged with carrying out Hezbollah terror operations on orders of the Iranian Supreme Leader.

Mughniyah was killed in 2008, reportedly by the Israelis with inside support from Syrian intelligence. He remains, however, an iconic figure for jihadis the world over, remembered for masterminding a long list of high-profile terrorist attacks that culminated in the attacks of September 11, 2001, carried out in coordination with Iran and al Qaeda. In an emotional eulogy, delivered at Mughniyah's funeral, Nasrallah promised Hezbollah revenge for Mughniyah's killing.

STATE SUPPORT FOR HEZBOLLAH

Hezbollah activities are enabled by the support of two state sponsors of terrorism: Iran and Syria. Both find utility in using Hezbollah to conduct proxy warfare against Israel. As noted above, Iran provides the financial underpinning, without which Hezbollah would be incapable of operations on its current scale. Additionally, Iran supplies Hezbollah with its massive modern arsenal of missiles and rockets, whose expanding ranges increasingly are capable of reaching Israel's major cities.

As noted above, Iran's IRGC Qods Force, whose ultimate commander is the Iranian Supreme Leader, the Ayatollah Ali Khamenei, serves in coordination with the Iranian MOIS as the Iranian regime's liaison in this exceptionally close relationship with Hezbollah.

For its part, Syria, under the Baath dictatorship of Bashar al-Assad, also uses Hezbollah as a strategic force-multiplier to give the Alawite regime a front-line capability against Israel. Analyst Rachel Ehrenfeld cites intelligence sources as finding that, "The Bashar Assad regime not only allows Hezbollah to carry out terror attacks from Lebanese territory, as one of the expressions of support for the [Palestinian] Intifada, but also provides direct aid to Hezbollah, a step from which [Hafez] Assad Senior refrained."[318] Syria views its ability to maintain military pressure against Israel as critical to its longstanding goal of forcing Israel to withdraw from the Golan Heights and, thereafter, resuming the effort to destroy the Jewish State outright.

Syria plays a key role in Iranian efforts to supply arms to Hezbollah. Typically, shipments of such arms arrive at Damascus airport and are then trucked to the Beka'a Valley and other Hezbollah strongholds. The importance of this overland route is evident in the successful interception by Israel or the United States of ships carrying arms from Iran on no fewer than six different occasions between 2001 and 2010. As a result, Hezbollah was denied tons of sophisticated Iranian weaponry, underscoring the premium it must place on logistical arrangements with Syria that are less susceptible to such setbacks and humiliations for both the terror group and its sponsors.[319]

HEZBOLLAH'S GLOBAL REACH

At Tehran's direction, and in support of the Iranian regime's global terror mission, Hezbollah has established cells throughout the world, including as noted above, in the United States. These cells are dedicated to fundraising, logistical support and terror operations and typically work in close liaison with Iranian IRGC/Qods Force and MOIS undercover operatives attached to Iranian diplomatic facilities. This arrangement gives Iran an expanded capability to attack American, Israeli and other Western interests while maintaining a measure of plausible deniability.

Two areas of Hezbollah activities outside of Lebanon warrant special mention:

Africa: Iran and Hezbollah have been expanding activities in West Africa since the 1990s, piggybacking off of large Shia Lebanese populations who pursue business interests there. Iran's African outreach serves two overt purposes: (1) to court diplomatic support, especially for its nuclear program, in international organizations such as the United Nations (UN) and International Atomic Energy Agency (IAEA), and (2) to extend Shia proselytizing to areas either traditionally Sunni or non-Muslim.

In addition, the Shia diaspora in West Africa, numbering hundreds of thousands, provides Hezbollah with millions of dollars in revenue each year. Besides voluntary contributions (*zakat*), Hezbollah levies an annual tax assessment on Shia businesses which is collected either in cash (by Hezbollah couriers) or remitted by electronic funds transfers directly to Lebanon.[320] The lenient security environment in much of Africa provides Hezbollah a benign area in which to find safe-haven and conduct recruitment, fundraising and racketeering operations.

Hezbollah also derives illicit income from criminal enterprises in West Africa: The organization has long been involved in the "conflict" or "blood" diamonds trade. Hezbollah operatives introduced al Qaeda representatives to that business in the months before 9/11. Hezbollah is also involved in the precious mineral trade in Sierra Leone, Liberia, the Democratic Republic of Congo and possibly Angola.[321] The money Hezbollah raises from its African gold and diamond business is used to buy weapons and fund jihadist operations, both in Lebanon and elsewhere around the world.[322]

Latin America: Hezbollah criminal and terrorist activity in the Tri-Border area of South America dates at least to the early 1990s. This region, where the borders of Paraguay, Argentina and Brazil come together, is notorious as a lawless safe-haven for arms-trafficking, contraband of all kinds, counterfeiting, drugs and terrorists. The Tri-Border area is a perfect breeding ground and recruiting venue for adherents to shariah, especially since a large percentage of the population in the region is Muslim Arab, with Lebanese Shiites being the most numerous.

The Tri-Border area served as the Hezbollah planning and recruitment nexus for the Iranian plots in Argentina to bomb the Israeli Embassy in 1992 and AMIA Jewish Cultural Center in 1994. Declassified National Security Agency reporting traced the initiative and direction of the Israeli Embassy attack to the Supreme National Security Council of Iran.[323] As Iran expands its diplomatic presence and influence throughout Latin America, Hezbollah, too, increasingly is active in Bolivia, Ecuador, Nicaragua, Panama, Mexico and elsewhere.

HEZBOLLAH AND THE DRUG TRADE

Hezbollah generates millions of dollars annually from the drug trade in the Balkans, Latin America and Lebanon. A benefit of Iran's expanding presence in South America is the opportunity it increasingly affords Hezbollah to derive significant income from the Andean cocaine trade, especially since Iran intensified its relationship with the Hugo Chavez regime in Venezuela.[324]

The Lebanese Beka'a Valley poppy and cannabis crop is another source of illicit narcotics income for Hezbollah. The Balkans serve as a major gateway to Europe for Hezbollah heroin which traverses the Balkan Road running through Albania, Kosovo and Macedonia.[325] The fact that European "infidels" are the primary end-user of these drugs adds motivation and a source of satisfaction for Hezbollah jihadis.[326]

HEZBOLLAH AND THE UNITED STATES

The narcotics trade is not Hezbollah's only criminal enterprise, including some involving America and its vital interests. For example, the group was the manufacturer and distributor of high-quality counterfeit U.S. $100 bills in the early 1990s, which were produced in the Beka'a Valley.[327] Hezbollah also has been involved with a laundry list of criminal scams, including the aforementioned cigarette smuggling operations, inside the United States that all contribute to the group's ability to conduct jihad in the service of Iran and their shared, worldwide mission of imposing shariah. They constitute a direct and material threat to this country and its people – one that is, to some extent, already present within the gates.

Still more Hezbollah operatives may be here soon, thanks to the organization's expanding presence just south of our border. The arrest in Mexico of one of the group's top terrorist commanders, Jameel Nasr, on charges of organizing and recruiting cadre there is deeply worrying.

Reports that such activities also involve converting Hispanics to Islam and the embrace of shariah greatly compounds a problem that has been evident for some time: A March 2009 report in the *Washington Times* described Hezbollah's use of Mexican drug cartel channels to run narcotics and illegals into the United States. According to Michael Braun, former assistant administrator and chief of operations at the U.S. Drug Enforcement Administration (DEA), Hezbollah relies on "the same criminal weapons smugglers, document traffickers and transportation experts as the drug cartels."[328] To the extent that Hezbollah terrorists not only can pass for but actually *are* illegal aliens from Mexico (rather than Lebanon or elsewhere in the Middle East), the already complicated job of shutting down its smuggling operations will be made more difficult.

In sum, the Hezbollah track record gives Western security officials good reason to consider it even more dangerous than al Qaeda. Hezbollah's sponsors in the Iranian, Syrian and Lebanese governments provide: secure geographic bases of operations; access to increasingly modern and lethal weapons; and nation-state financial, intelligence, logistical and training resources.

Hezbollah remains fanatically dedicated to shariah and jihad, sophisticated and tenacious. Its mastery of explosives makes it the indispensible trainer of choice for Islamic terrorists, including al Qaeda, Iraqi Shiite and Sunni militias, and the Taliban. Hezbollah's close links to al Qaeda, Hamas and Palestinian Islamic Jihad, coupled with bragging rights for having pressured Israel to withdraw from Lebanon and then fighting the Israeli Defense Forces (IDF) to a standstill in the Lebanese war during the summer of 2006, make it a force that commands and enjoys respect in all the wrong places.

Rising tensions across the Middle East fueled by Iran's aggressive ascendancy and its drive for a nuclear weapon, taken together with Hezbollah's unswerving allegiance to Tehran's mullahs[329] and the group's alliance with al Qaeda, justify serious concern about the circumstances under which Hezbollah operatives around the world – and especially those in the United States – might be ordered to attack.

Hezbollah has the capability, means, and motive to strike whenever Tehran might command retaliation against Western interests in response to events in Afghanistan, Iraq, or Iran itself. That being the case, any proposals to treat Islamic terrorist groups such Hezbollah as potentially legitimate political players[330] would be folly on our part and viewed by our foes as further signs of weakness, irresolution and submission. Such perceptions invite not only stepped up *dawa*, but violent jihad, as well.

HAMAS

"Israel will arise and continue to exist until Islam abolishes it, as it abolished what went before." (The words of) the shaheed, Imam Hassan al-Bana, may Allah have mercy upon him."

These words, from the opening of the Hamas Covenant, provide the *raison d'être* of this violent Palestinian offshoot of the

Egyptian Muslim Brotherhood: destruction of the Jewish State of Israel. Established in Gaza in 1988, Hamas arose out of an earlier Brotherhood front group (*Mujama'*) that was founded by Ahmad Yassin in 1973.

Ironically, it was the Israeli administration in Gaza that initially encouraged and even indirectly funded this welfare charity in the belief that it would serve as a useful counterweight to Yasser Arafat's Palestinian Liberation Organization (PLO) in the wake of the 1967 Six-Day War. Most of Hamas' funding, however, came from local *zakat* collections, Gulf Islamic organizations and the Palestinian diaspora.[331]

The 1988 formation of Hamas gave the Brotherhood a way to participate in the first Palestinian Intifada against Israel. Founding members of the organization include: Ahmad Yassin, 'Abd al-Aziz Rantisi, Dr. Mahmud Zahar, Musa Abu Marzook and Khalid Meshaal. Hamas's charter, edited and approved by Yassin (considered the group's founder and leader), makes clear that all of historical Palestine is held to be "sacred space," land endowed by Allah to Muslims in perpetuity because it was once conquered and ruled by Muslims. As noted earlier in this report, waqf is land that can never be relinquished to the control of non-Muslims – much less Jews – and must be reconquered, by violent jihad if necessary, in order to subjugate it to shariah and re-incorporate it into the *Dar al-Islam*.

Hamas was created with three principal wings: (1) a political wing for *dawa*, fundraising, and the takeover of mosques; (2) an intelligence apparatus, known as *al-Majd* (glory); and (3) a military wing, the *'Izz al-Din al-Qassam* brigades.

The political wing created a social infrastructure of clinics, hospitals and schools for the purpose of disbursing welfare and performing the indoctrination and recruitment required for *dawa*. At first, Israel did little to disrupt Hamas activities as the latter's social support network was seen to be a useful means of marginal-izing the PLO.[332]

The intelligence wing was tasked with internal policing, in particular the identification and killing of actual and suspected collaborators, which it did ruthlessly. The intelligence wing later merged with the *'Izz al-Din al-Qassam* brigades.

Despite the unambiguous language of its Covenant,[333] Hamas military operations against Israel did not become a signifi-cant security challenge until after the First Gulf War in 1991, when Arafat's error in supporting Saddam Hussein resulted in a massive shift of support from Gulf sheikhdoms away from the PLO and towards Hamas. Millions in new funding enabled Ha-mas to take over what had been the PLO's social support role among Gazans, whose loyalty shifted accordingly.

The pan-Islamic jihad meetings held in Khartoum in the early 1990s at the invitation of Sudanese president Omar al-Bashir and radical Sunni cleric Hasan Turabi brought Palestinian repre-sentatives from Hamas and the PLO together with Osama bin La-den's emerging al Qaeda group, Hezbollah, and the Shiite Iranian regime. Dedication to jihad and shariah, hatred of Jews and Israel and enmity towards the United States and the West unified this otherwise disparate group in a shared dual purpose: destroying Israel and doing battle with infidels.

Imbued with the zeal of this deadly purpose, Hamas op-posed the Oslo Accords of 1993 and launched a campaign of sui-cide bombing that same year. At about this time, too, Hamas lea-dership began perpetrating an endless and familiar taqiyya cam-paign that persists to the current day. Taking a page from the sha-riah playbook that Arafat successfully employed, Hamas leaders offer statements for Western consumption that sound conciliatory to the intended audiences. Periodic suggestions for a truce (or *hudna*) alternate with demands for territorial concessions from

Israel and protestations of victim status that succeed all too well in demonizing Israel in gullible Western eyes.

At the same time, like Arafat, Mahmoud Abbas and others in the Palestine Liberation Organization/Palestinian Authority leadership, those who run Hamas stake out very different positions in Arabic for the ears of their home constituencies. To such audiences, they explicitly revile Jews and espouse the destruction of their state.

Political antagonism between Hamas and Fatah dominated the relationship from the start, not least due to deliberate encouragement of such tensions by Israel. Hamas' Islamic vision for a Palestinian society based on shariah and derived directly from its Muslim Brotherhood roots, inevitably clashed with the more overtly national, secular image cultivated by Arafat, Fatah and the PLO. As the battle against Israel continued through the 1990s and especially during the al-Aqsa Intifada that broke out in September 2000, the rivalry for the hearts and minds of Palestinians intensified, eventually evolving into full-blown hostilities.[334]

Israeli reprisals – including the targeted killing of two top Hamas leaders, Ahmad Yassin and Abdul Azziz Rantisi in 2004, the death of Arafat in November 2004 and international condemnation of Hamas, all seemed only to fuel the group's resolve and inexorable rise to preeminence in Gaza. Then, Israeli Prime Minister Ariel Sharon's decision unilaterally to evacuate all Israeli settlers and troops from Gaza in 2005, like the Jewish State's earlier abandonment of South Lebanon to Hezbollah, confirmed for the Hamas leadership that violent jihad is effective.

A critical turning point was reached with the loss of Saudi funding in this period, which provided an opening for Iran to replace and increase that support, despite the Sunni character of Hamas.[335] That support helped assure that Hamas' decision to participate in the January 2006 Palestinian Legislative Council elections translated into a decisive political victory over the PLO and Fatah.

The overwhelming decision by Gazan Palestinians to cast their votes in those elections for the party of violent jihad and shariah should have been predictable in an environment devoid of the building blocks of civil society. But apparently it came as a complete surprise to both American and Israeli policymakers.[336] In the aftermath of the balloting, armed clashes between Fatah and Hamas broke out. They escalated over the following year and, despite a March 2007 agreement to form a national unity government, Hamas launched a military offensive in June that effectively ended the fighting with all of Gaza under its repressive administration of shariah.[337]

Hamas legalized the savage *hudud* punishments of amputation, crucifixion, and flogging. Women were forced into the hijab and men were required to grow beards. Authorities strictly segregated the sexes, enforcing virtual imprisonment of women in the home. The Islamicization of Gazan society by Hamas has been imposed on the courts, educational system, media and social institutions in general. Gaza's tiny remaining Christian population faces incessant, unchecked and violent persecution. An intractable ideological and political crisis – over tactics and power in the pursuit of more-or-less shared goals divides Gaza and the West Bank, and blocks any meaningful progress towards a unified Palestinian nationhood. Palestinian Authority presidential elections have been put on hold indefinitely.[338]

Particularly noteworthy to any discussion of the threat posed by Hamas is the incessant indoctrination of Gazan children aimed at instilling in them a dedication to shariah, jihad, and revering of *shaheed* (martyrs). Such brainwashing begins in preschool and kindergarten and is intended to prepare the next generation of Hamas terrorist operatives and suicide bombers.

A barrage of television programming, videos and video games, formal classes, cultural performances like skits and plays and summer camps inculcate Palestinian youth with Jew-hatred and themes of armed violence against Israel from the earliest ages.[339] As many as 100,000 youngsters attended some 700 Hamas summer camps in 2009 where banners, slogans, and songs glorified suicide bombers as role models. In addition to crafts, hiking, and swimming, boys in these camps train with plastic and wooden rifles on the rudiments of military tactics, such as ambushes and kidnapping.[340]

In the spring of 2010, masked intruders destroyed United Nations Relief and Works Agency (UNRWA) summer camps in Gaza that provided an alternative to the Hamas message and programs. (According to Arab media sources, the An-Nusseriat camp was one of two UNRWA summer camps whose facilities were hit by arson during May and June 2010.[341]) In fact, UNWRA has been fully in bed with the radical Palestinian agenda for many years. A better explanation for the attacks on it may be that Hamas is simply interested in cutting out the middle-man and controlling directly and by itself all of the U.N.'s billions of dollars of humanitarian relief that is allocated to Gaza.

Hamas has eschewed any pretense of nation-building, in favor of a policy of intensified rocket and missile strikes on Israel, coupled with a skillful *taqiyya* campaign to dupe impressionable Westerners with claims of moderation and victimhood. The roughly four-thousand attacks against Israeli villages and towns within range of Gaza finally provoked Israel to launch Operation Cast Lead in December 2008 to deter further rocket fire. Despite the destruction of much of Hamas' military infrastructure in a campaign noted for extraordinary efforts by the Jewish State to minimize civilian casualties in Gaza and a much-condemned naval blockade of Gaza by Israeli naval forces, Hamas continues to re-arm with longer-range and upgraded rockets. As with Hezbollah's overland resupply route, Hamas seems to be relying primarily for its access to arms and other war materiel on relatively secure ground transits, primarily tunnels under Gaza's border with Egypt.

Neither poverty nor economic collapse in Gaza actually seems imminent, especially given the $540 million budget for 2010 that was approved by the Hamas parliament in December 2009. One parliamentarian told reporters that only about $60 million of that would come from Gaza taxes and fees, lending credibility to comments from other Palestinian sources that identified Iran as the source of the bulk of the budget.[342]

HAMAS' SUPPORT FROM HEZBOLLAH AND IRAN

Iranian support for Hamas is indeed "extremely significant," according to Matthew Levitt of the Washington Institute for Near East Affairs. Levitt spent some 18 months working on terror-funding issues at the Treasury Department during the George W. Bush administration and states flatly that "Hamas could not function as it does today were it not for Iranian financial and material support."[343]

That support takes the form of the massive financial infusions cited above, but also includes terror training conducted in Iran that is provided by both the IRGC/Qods Force and also Hezbollah operatives who specialize in bomb-making and explosives techniques. This cooperative relationship can be traced in part to the 1992 Israeli deportation of key Hamas members to Lebanon, which helped establish basic links between Hamas and Hezbollah. As explained above, the Hamas-Iran relationship gives the Shiite regime influence and another terror proxy inside the Gaza-based Muslim Brotherhood.

The February 2009 visit to Iran by Damascus-based Hamas political leader Khaled Mashaal served public notice of the expanding ties between these Sunni and Shia jihadis. While Iran's longstanding relationship with the Sunni al Qaeda terror group dates from the early 1990s, forging informal ties to the Muslim Brotherhood were more problematic, in part due to Iranian silence when Syria's Hafez al-Assad slaughtered his Brotherhood opposition in the early 1980s.

Still, the possibility for Iran to make amends with the Brotherhood seems present in Egypt based on what appears to be a natural affinity arising from Iranian criticism of Hosni Mubarak's regime and support for anti-government Hezbollah operations in the Sinai.[344] For example, comments by Muslim Brotherhood Supreme Guide Mahdi Akif made to Arab language media in 2008 expressed support for direct contact channels between Iran and the Muslim Brotherhood.[345] The deepening convergence of anti-West and anti-Israel operational objectives among Hamas, Hezbollah, and Iran marks what is, at its base, an ideological congruence founded on mutual dedication to shariah.

HAMAS AND AL QAEDA

The worrisome increase in the presence and activities of Qaeda-affiliated jihadis in Gaza has prompted some Western analysts to take comfort in what they perceive as a fundamental ideological animosity between bin Laden's group and Hamas. This is understandable, given the desire of U.S. policymakers intent upon opening a dialogue with Hamas. Unfortunately, the facts do not support this thesis.

Indeed, according to their own published documents and statements, Hamas and al Qaeda pursue exactly the same agenda: Jihad in the way of Allah to impose shariah and re-establish the caliphate. Osama bin Laden was educated in the late 1970s in Saudi Arabia by Mohammed Qutb, the exiled brother of key Muslim Brotherhood ideologue Sayyid Qutb, as well as by Abdullah Azzam of the Jordanian Muslim Brotherhood. Azzam preceded bin Laden and his deputy, Ayman al-Zawahiri, to Afghanistan in the 1980s, where they all would subsequently work closely together. And al-Zawahiri was leader of Egyptian Islamic Jihad, a Brotherhood offshoot, when he joined forces with al Qaeda in the early 1990s.

The Hamas leadership has been at pains to deny a relationship with al Qaeda, but Palestinian Authority Chairman Mahmoud Abbas told the Arab language *al-Hayat* (a London-based newspaper) on February 26, 2008, that "Al Qaeda is present in Gaza and I'm convinced that they [Hamas] are their allies." He added, "I can say without doubt that al Qaeda is present in the Palestinian territories and that this presence, especially in Gaza, is facilitated by Hamas."[346] While Abbas' claims may be questionable given that he has his own reasons for vilifying Hamas, Israeli intelligence has also reported that that al Qaeda members have been infiltrating Gaza through breaches in the border with Egypt.

What is undeniable is that groups claiming affiliations with al Qaeda and using names such as the al Qaeda in Palestine Organization, Army of Believers, Army of Islam (*Jaish al-Islam*) and the Swords of Righteousness have attacked Christian facilities in Gaza and claimed responsibility for the 2007 kidnapping of Alan Johnston, a BBC reporter.[347] The Army of Islam joined forces with Hamas in the 2006 kidnapping of Israeli soldier Gilad Shalit and the Egyptians have complained that al Qaeda leaders in Egypt fled across the border and sought refuge in Gaza.[348]

In a 2007 web posting, Osama bin Laden spoke to the doctrine of Islamic Sacred Space: "We will not recognize a state for the Jews, not even one inch of the land of Palestine." Seen in this light, Gaza is merely the latest of al Qaeda's chosen jihad fronts. Seeking new battlefields in which to bloody Jewish and Western armies and new safe havens from which to train and operate, al Qaeda has proven adept at inserting itself into local conflicts around the world.

Viewed properly as the jihadist, shariah-adherent terror organization that it is, Hamas can be seen to pose a dangerous threat not only to Israel, but to U.S. national security. Its expanding operational affiliation with fellow jihadis, both Sunni and Shia, at the national and sub-national levels, should be serious cause for concern to U.S. defense and security officials.

Such considerations should, most especially, preclude U.S. government outreach to Hamas terror representatives – whose hands are, after all, stained with the blood of Americans, Israelis and Palestinians alike. Hamas control of the levers of power in Gaza, achieved by brute force in compliance with Islamic doctrine, history and law, does not make it a moderate or reformist entity deserving of recognition.

To the contrary, all available evidence, including that presented in this volume, indicates that Hamas has never deviated, nor is it likely *ever* to deviate, from the jihadist declarations of its foundational Covenant. Instead, it may be expected that Hamas will continue to strengthen its ties to fellow jihadis in the Iranian regime and among other terror organizations such as al Qaeda and Hezbollah. *Any policy based on a scenario in which infidel Westerners influence shariah-compliant jihadis like Hamas to make concessions to Jews is beyond absurd: It is suicidal.*

HIZB UT-TAHRIR

Hizb ut-Tahrir (HT) is an Islamic political movement, present in over 40 countries across the globe, whose openly-stated objective is the destruction of Western civilization, democracy and the capitalist system. Frankly supremacist, if not – for the moment – overtly violent, Hizb ut-Tahrir members view themselves as the ideologically pure vanguard of Islam, dedicated to re-establishment of the caliphate and replacement of capitalism with shariah.

In the words of Zeyno Baran, a Turkish-American scholar at the Hudson Institute, in espousing a policy for the redistribution of wealth (specifically Muslim oil wealth) away from current Arab/Muslim regimes deemed corrupt and toward the Muslim *ummah*, HT "effectively combines Marxist-Leninist methodology and Western slogans with reactionary Islamic theology."[349] Hizb ut-Tahrir's advocacy for refutation of "non-Islamic ideals" (like capitalism), and their replacement with "Islamic solutions," finds practical expression in the spread of shariah-compliant finance programs throughout the West, including in the United States.

Hizb-ut-Tahrir (HT) was founded in 1952 by Taqiuddin Nabhani, a Palestinian member of the Muslim Brotherhood, to advance the cause of a global Islamic State ruled by a reestablished caliphate. After completing his studies at al-Azhar in Cairo, Nabhani attempted to form an Islamist party in Jordan and eventually ran candidates in Jordanian elections.[350] Frustrated with his party's poor performance, Nabhani later urged a rejection of elections as a means of achieving the re-Islamization of society.

Instead, Taqiuddin Nabhani advocated an underground organizational structure based on ideologically rigorous cells, operating at a remove from the group's leadership. This methodology would permit targeted societies to be infiltrated in a three-stage process which mirrors that outlined by Muslim Brotherhood ideologue and strategist Sayyid Qutb: The first stage is dedicated to building a vanguard through propaganda and recruitment. In the second stage, followers embed themselves in major social institutions to subvert society from within. In the final stage, the organization will impose a top-down revolution on society through these positions of influence and infiltration.[351] Nabhani even authored a proposed constitution composed of 187 articles for his envisioned Islamic State, detailing rules for governing virtually all elements of life in accordance with Islamic law.

To realize its goals, Hizb ut-Tahrir seeks to liberate Islamic countries from Western thoughts, systems and laws. Through its program of infiltration and subversion in the West, HT also strives eventually to bring infidel lands into the orbit of the borderless *ummah*.[352] Until then, as Nabhani explained in a 2001 publication, it will be the duty of the Caliph to spread Islam through both *dawa* and violent jihad.[353] A more recent manifesto, *Methodology of Hizb ut-Tahrir for Change,* explicitly emphasizes the use of violence: "Jihad is a war against anyone who stands against the call of Islam, whether he is an aggressor or not."[354]

Despite such statements, Hizb ut-Tahrir cadres operating in the West profess a commitment to pursuing the organization's goal of reestablishing a global caliphate through peaceful means. Many HT members have nonetheless embraced violent methods, prompting Hudson's Zeyno Baran to describe the group as an enabler of terror-wielding jihadists:

> HT is not itself a terrorist organization, but it can usefully be thought of as a conveyor belt for terrorists. It indoctrinates individuals with radical ideology, priming them for recruitment by more extreme organizations where they can take part in actual operations. By combining fascist rhetoric, Leninist strategy, and Western sloganeering with Wahhabi ideology, HT has made itself into a very real and potent threat that is extremely difficult for liberal societies to counter.[355]

Hizb ut-Tahrir's targeted recruits for this ideological program are males aged 18-30. Also targeted for recruitment are law enforcement personnel and local government representatives who can shield the group from surveillance and prosecution.

Potential candidates are examined on religious knowledge and each new member, called *Dorises*, is charged with recruiting at least five others. In the initial stage, new members are instructed on a wide range of topics, including religious education and world affairs. After another set of examinations, they will move to the next stage of membership, *Khizbi*, at which time they will pledge an oath to follow the goals and leadership of Hizb ut-Tahrir. At this point they are given responsibility for training new members and continue to undergo rigorous ideological training. The third stage of membership, *Naquib*, is reserved for those who have demonstrated extraordinary commitment and leadership within the organization.[356]

HIZB UT-TAHRIR IN BRITAIN

Numerous documented terror connections with Hizb ut-Tahrir validate Baran's "conveyor belt" theory. For example, prior to September 11, 2001, Hizb ut-Tahrir leader Omar Bakri Mohammed was part of a select group of Muslim leaders who in 1998 received a faxed letter from Osama bin Laden laying out several tactics for attacking the United States. "Bring down their airliners. Prevent the safe passage of their ships. Occupy their embassies. Force the closure of their companies and banks," bin Laden's letter urged.[357] In the run-up to 9/11, the FBI was tracking Hizb ut-Tahrir members training at U.S. aviation schools.[358] Intelligence sources have confirmed that al Qaeda in Iraq leader Abu Musab al-Zarqawi was a "graduate" of the Jordanian branch of Hizb ut-Tahrir.[359]

What is more, two British-born members of Al-Muhajiroun, the U.K. Hizb ut-Tahrir affiliate, were responsible in 2003 for Britain's first documented case of suicide bombing by British citizens. Three people were killed and more than fifty injured when Asif Mohammed Hanif detonated his bomb inside Mike's Place in Tel Aviv, Israel. Both Hanif and his accomplice, Omar Khan Sharif, were disciples of U.K. Hizb ut-Tahrir leader Omar Bakri Mohammed, and had been recruited through the group in Britain to conduct the suicide bombing for Hamas.[360]

Just days before his scheduled April 2010 trial on charges of providing material support for terrorism, Syed Hashmi, a

Brooklyn College graduate who grew up in Queens and had become actively involved in Hizb ut-Tahrir there, entered a guilty plea. Hashmi admitted that when he was arrested in June 2006 at London's Heathrow Airport, he was carrying cash and military gear intended for al Qaeda forces fighting U.S. troops in Afghanistan.[361]

One of Hashmi's comrades in Hizb ut-Tahrir, Mohammed Junaid Babar, also from New York, pled guilty in 2004 of smuggling money and military supplies to al Qaeda and helping to set up a training camp for jihad.[362]

What draws these young recruits to Hizb ut-Tahrir's cause is not just a toxic, triumphalist theology, but also the group's savvy exploitation of alternative media and advanced technology to purvey their message and to network their followers internationally. As counterterrorism analyst Madeleine Gruen explains:

> The younger generation's pioneering spirit has made [Hizb-ut-Tahrir America] one of the most innovative extremist groups in terms of its use of new media as a means of marketing its ideology. Some of the marketing schemes have included hip hop fashion boutiques, hip hop bands, use of online social networks, use of video sharing networks, chat forums and blogs."[363]

HIZB UT-TAHRIR IN AMERICA

That Hizb ut-Tahrir is a growing presence in the United States is evidenced by the group's July 2009 conference, "The Fall of Capitalism and the Rise of Islam," held in at a Hilton Hotel in the Chicago suburb of Oak Lawn, Illinois. Conference topics included "Capitalism is Doomed to Fail," "The Global Rise of Islam," "Life under the Islamic Economic System," and the "Role of Muslims in America."

The general manager of the hotel defended hosting the conference, saying "We're United States citizens and an American business – if it's legal, we're able to host it, as long as it's nothing that disrupts our other guests' privacy and security."[364] The event had originally been scheduled to be held at the al-Aqsa Islamic school in Bridgeview, Illinois, but the school canceled the reservation after national media exposure of the event and Hizb ut-Tahrir's ideology.[365] Hizb ut-Tahrir faced similar difficulties as it attempted to find a Chicago-area venue for its 2010 conference.[366]

The future direction of Hizb ut-Tahrir in America may be seen in the experience of Britain, the Western country in which the group has the largest and most visible presence. For instance, in the U.K., Hizb ut-Tahrir is now sufficiently well established that it has gone from recruiting students to actually *teaching* them in some of the country's most prominent universities, including the London School of Economics.[367]

Based on the British experience, we should anticipate the infiltration of Hizb ut-Tahrir members into other key institutions besides academia. In keeping with the group's methodology, HT members have been identified working in major U.K. media organizations and corporations. In 2005, *The Guardian* newspaper hired Dilpazier Aslam, a Hizb ut-Tahrir member who used his position to write on the 7/7 London bombings and justify the terror attacks.[368] An investigation by *The Independent* newspaper found Hizb ut-Tahrir members working for Reuters and a number of blue-chip companies.[369]

If the HT playbook in the U.K. is any guide, Hizb ut-Tahrir operatives will be working to penetrate the U.S. government, as well. Perhaps the most serious case of infiltration by Hizb ut-Tahrir in the United Kingdom involved Abid Javaid, who works for the Immigration and Nationality Directorate that is responsible for processing visa and asylum applications. An investigation by the BBC discovered Javaid's leadership in the organization, prompting the Home Secretary John Reid to launch an inquiry into his ties to Hizb ut-Tahrir.[370] Javaid retained his position, however, because the government said it was powerless to fire him since the government had not officially banned the organization.[371]

The claims by Hizb ut-Tahrir leaders in the West that their group's aims are entirely peaceful are belied by their own publications and statements made by HT members in their more candid moments. This is what reporter James Brandon of the *Christian Science Monitor* discovered when he interviewed three Hizb ut-Tahrir activists in Amman, Jordan. One member explained in frank terms the progressive stages to accomplish Islamic rule, culminating in violence directed at anyone opposing their program:

> Islam obliges Muslims to possess power so that they can intimidate – I would not say terrorize – the enemies of Islam. In the beginning, the caliphate would strengthen itself internally and it wouldn't initiate jihad. But after that we would carry Islam as an intellectual call to all the world. And we will make people bordering the caliphate believe in Islam. Or if they refuse then we'll ask them to be ruled by Islam. And if after all discussions and negotiations they still refuse, then the last resort will be a jihad to spread the spirit of Islam and the rule of Islam. This is done in the interests of all people to get them out of darkness and into light.[372]

TABLIGHI JAMAAT

Formed in 1927, just a few years after the dissolution of the Ottoman caliphate and barely predating the establishment of the Muslim Brotherhood, the highly secretive Tablighi Jamaat (TJ) has grown into one of the largest Islamic revivalist movements in the world. Based in Pakistan and rooted in the Deobandi school of Islam, TJ's goal is to revive the *ummah* through *dawa* missionary activity. Its purpose is to call Muslims back to the "true faith" as practiced by Mohammed and his companions in the "Golden Age" of Islam. Like its counterparts in other shariah-adherent organizations, Tablighi Jamaat calls for the establishment of a global Islamic State, the imposition of shariah and separation of the faithful from non-Muslims. The group runs major mosques in at least ten states and has an estimated U.S. membership of 50,000.[373]

Adherents of the group engage in what they call "the Effort," which initially entails traveling to mosques in their own country in small groups for three-to-ten days at a time, encouraging Muslims to live their lives in imitation of Mohammed and his companions. More dedicated followers will later undertake a 40-day missionary trip. After completing those stages, members will be invited to take a four-month trip to Pakistan or India.[374]

What concerns intelligence and law enforcement authorities is that *individuals associated with Tablighi Jamaat have been repeatedly tied to terrorist plots around the world.* Their missionary activity has provided travel cover for terrorist operatives and their adherence to shariah makes the group a perfect incubator for terrorist recruiters, prompting one Western diplomat to call Tablighi Jamaat a "honey pot" for Pakistani-based jihadist groups.[375] French intelligence officers describe the group as an "antechamber of fundamentalism."[376]

TABLIGHI JAMAAT AND VIOLENT JIHAD

Dozens of detainees at Guantanamo Bay have been held based on evidence of their involvement with the Tablighi Jamaat.[377] A classified April 2004 Defense Intelligence Agency analysis said that TJ members "have the capability to conduct a terrorist attack in the U.S.," noting that seven members in America were then under investigation and that a Tablighi official at major Midwestern mosque "has associations with several al Qaeda supporters."[378]

That DIA memo echoed the assessment of Michael Heimbach, deputy chief of the FBI's international terrorism section, who in 2003 told the *New York Times*, "We have a significant presence of Tablighi Jamaat in the United States, and we have found that al Qaeda used them for recruiting, now and in the past."[379] Heimbach was referencing the case of Ohio al Qaeda member Iyman Faris, who used Tablighi Jamaat as a cover while traveling in Pakistan.

Tablighi Jamaat was also the path that led "American Taliban" John Walker Lindh to fighting with the Taliban against U.S. troops in Afghanistan, where he was captured. Lindh joined a missionary tour with Tablighi Jamaat after encountering them at his California mosque, and a group official enrolled him in a Pakistani madrassa, where he was encouraged to join the Taliban.[380]

Faris and Lindh are not the only Americans who have turned to terrorism through their involvement in Tablighi Jamaat. Six Yemeni-Americans, who were arrested in 2002 for traveling to Pakistan and Afghanistan to train in an al Qaeda terrorist camp, had been recruited at their Lackawanna, New York, mosque by a Tablighi Jamaat preacher.[381] And Jeffrey Battle, a member of a Portland, Oregon, terror cell who wanted to launch attacks on synagogues, sought the aid of Tablighi Jamaat officials in Bangladesh to help him train and join the Taliban.[382]

The Department of Homeland Security cited an Arizona doctor's leadership position in Tablighi Jamaat as grounds for denying his application for U.S. permanent residency. He was detained and eventually deported for failing to acknowledge his role with the group, which Homeland Security officials described as "a terrorist organization (that)...provides material support...to members of a designated terrorist organization – al Qaeda; and provides the same types of material support...to an undesignated terrorist organization – the Taliban."[383] This precedent should be applied more generally to those who seek to immigrate to the United States for the purpose of promoting shariah in this country or elsewhere.

More recently, American-born al Qaeda member Bryant Neal Vinas, who helped plot a terror bombing campaign directed at the New York City subway, became an adherent to shariah at the Al-Falah mosque in Corona, Queens – the U.S. headquarters of the Tablighi Jamaat movement.[384]

Tablighi members have also been tied to terrorist plots in Europe and the Middle East. For example, the leader of the 7/7 London bombing attack, Mohammed Sidique Khan, and another plotter, Shehazad Tanweer, both attended the mosque in Dewsbury, West Yorkshire, which serves as the European headquarters for the group.[385]

Another former member of the same TJ mosque was would-be shoe-bomber Richard Reid, who attempted to blow up a Miami-bound airplane.[386] Several members of a UK-based plot to blow up seven planes from Heathrow airport bound for the U.S. and Canada arrested in August 2006 had attended Tablighi Jamaat meetings.[387]

Two German terror suspects arrested in Pakistan in 2007 were studying at the Tablighi Jamaat mosque in Raiwind, Pakistan, according to a report in *Der Spiegel*.[388] Fourteen members were arrested in Spain for plotting a terror attack on Barcelona.[389]

It is not just American and European authorities that have expressed concerns about Tablighi Jamaat's recurring connection to international terror. In a 2008 article in the Saudi newspaper *Al-Jazirah*, reporter Khalid al-Fadil described Tablighi Jamaat as "One of the recruitment gateways of the Al Qaeda organization in our country and in several other Arab and Muslim countries." It further claimed that one member, Muslih Al-Shamrani, was part of a group that carried out a car bombing of a Saudi National Guard building in Riyadh in 1995 that killed five Americans, as was Muhammad Ja'far al-Kahtani, a leading al Qaeda commander in Afghanistan who escaped from the Bagram Prison in July 2005.[390]

In short, there is ample reason to treat Tablighi Jamaat as an integral part of the shariah-directed jihad. Like the Muslim Brotherhood and Hizb ut-Tahrir, TJ's identity as a "non-violent" organization reflects, at best, a tactical determination to use stealthy techniques to advance the goals it shares with other adherents to shariah. At worst, it is simply providing cover to those within its own group and associated with other like-minded jihadists to prepare and execute murderous and terrifying attacks.

JAMAAT UL-FUQRA

One Islamic group operating in the United States that has exhibited no hesitation about turning to violence is Jamaat ul-Fuqra (JUF). JUF operates as many as 30 rural compounds across the United States and Canada and has several thousand followers. The group also uses the names "Muslims of America" and the "International Quranic Open University."

Founded by Pakistani Sheikh Mubarak Ali Gilani in Brooklyn in 1980, JUF actively recruited members to participate in the jihad in Afghanistan against the Soviets. But during the 1980s, it was also the most active terrorist group in the United States, conducting 17 bombings and assassinations, and 12 murders targeting non-Muslims and moderate Muslims alike.[391]

Jamaat ul-Fuqra gained particular national attention when the only American-born member of the cell responsible for the 1993 World Trade Center bombing, Clement Rodney Hampton-El, was found to be part of JUF.[392] During the investigation into that terror attack, it was discovered that Hampton-El had conducted military training exercises with the other bombing cell members at a farm outside Harrisburg, Pennsylvania, which included testing for the bomb that would eventually be used.[393] As a 2005 Stratfor analysis observes, members of Jamaat ul-Fuqra worked closely with the Al-Kifah Refugee Center, known as the

Brooklyn Jihad Office, which was the primary fundraising and co-ordination center for what eventually became al Qaeda.[394]

Because of its violent domestic activities and its connection to international terrorist organizations, Jamaat ul-Fuqra was listed in several State Department terrorism reports until 1999. One report described the group's ideology and methods as follows:

> Jamaat ul-Fuqra is an Islamic sect that seeks to purify Islam by violence. Fuqra is led by Pakistani cleric Shaykh Mubarik Ali Gilani, who established the organization in the 1980s. Gilani now lives in Pakistan, but most Fuqra cells are located in North America. Fuqra members have purchased isolated rural compounds in North America to live communally, practice their faith and insulate themselves from Western culture."[395]

The obvious question was put to the State Department press spokesman in the daily press briefing on January 31, 2002: "The group headed by Shaykh Gilani used to be designated by the State Department as a terrorist group but it was taken off the list. Why?" The answer read as follows: "Jamaat ul-Fuqra has never been designated as a Foreign Terrorist Organization. It was included in several recent annual terrorism reports under 'Other Terrorist Groups,' i.e., groups that had carried out acts of terrorism but that were not formally designated by the Secretary of State. However, because of the group's inactivity during 2000, it was not included in the most recent terrorism report covering that calendar year."

In other words, an organization that had engaged in myriad terrorist attacks was no longer treated as a terrorist organization because it had been "inactive" in one year. This treatment by the State Department – and, therefore, by other federal agencies that follow its lead – is all the more appalling when one considers both what is known about the abiding intentions of Jamaat ul-

Fuqra's founder and the fact that his organization has been anything but "inactive" in preparing for violent jihad.

Sheikh Gilani's supremacist vision for the group is expressed in his book, *Mohammedian Revelations*, in which he explains that "the mission of this Jamaat ul-Fuqra is to lead Muslims to their final victory over Communists, Zionists, Hindus (and) deviators."[396]

Gilani participated in an international terror conference held in Khartoum, Sudan, in December 1993 and described elsewhere in this report in connection with the presence there of representatives from al Qaeda, Egyptian Jihad, Hamas, Hezbollah and the Iranian regime. Osama bin Laden was also present. A video obtained by the Canadian Broadcasting Corporation of the Khartoum conference recorded the attendees chanting, "Down, down USA! Down, down CIA" and "Death to the Jews."[397]

CBS News reported in 2002 that bin Laden and Gilani had in common a close mutual friend, a former Pakistani air force officer and member of his nation's Islamist-sympathizing intelligence service, the ISI. Interestingly, this friend, Khalid Khawaja, was murdered in May 2010 under mysterious circumstances.[398] Gilani is also believed to have been responsible for luring *Wall Street Journal* reporter Daniel Pearl to his death by beheading in Pakistan on the pretext of meeting with the terrorist leader.[399]

The paramilitary nature of Jamaat ul-Fuqra can be seen in a recruiting video recorded in the early 1990s and subsequently obtained by U.S. law enforcement authorities. Entitled "Soldiers of Allah," it features Sheikh Gilani and others teaching how to employ firearms, explosives, carjackings, ambushes and assassinations.[400] In the video, Gilani encourages potential recruits to contact the group's headquarters in Hancock, New York where they are promised "advanced training courses in Islamic Military Warfare."

A 2009 documentary film entitled "Homegrown Jihad"[401] provided chilling details about: the Jamaat ul-Fuqra; its founder; its members (a number of whom are released convicts who embraced shariah while in prison – a fact that further underscores the folly of allowing Muslim Brotherhood operatives to minister in the U.S. penal system); their goals; and JUF training programs and infrastructure.

Among other noteworthy highlights of the video documentary, Gilani brags of having established with his compounds a modern terrorist training infrastructure in America. While many of these JUF camps are typically in areas that are remote, they often are within striking distance of dams, power plants, military installations and other strategic targets. For example, the group's headquarters is near Hancock, New York, close by the watershed for New York City's water supply.

Particularly alarming was the video's footage showing the fear and frustration of local law enforcement and private citizens in communities outside a number of JUF compounds as they reported that that their appeals for help from the FBI and other federal authorities have been consistently rebuffed. Here again, no official explanation has been forthcoming as to why such refusals continue to this day.

A new JUF video[402] features, along with poor quality footage of hand-to-hand combat training and guerilla-style military maneuvers, a statement read by the self-described Secretary General of "the Muslims of the Americas" [sic], Muhammed Patik Shaheed (phonetic spelling). Shaheed declares that – on the basis of "a fact-finding mission" and "nationwide census" – "We are one-hundred percent certain that Muslims are the majority in America" and that, as a result, "America is our country."

Shaheed goes on to warn that "We will not let people bring false accusations against peace-loving Muslims. We will defend our country against all these enemies, foreign and domestic." Unfortunately, the enemies they have in mind are the non-Muslim Americans who may think the United States is *not* the JUF's country, or that of any others who would supplant the Constitution with shariah.

THE JAMAAT UL-FUQRA THREAT TO NORTH AMERICA

The U.S. government is not the only one to express concern about Jamaat ul-Fuqra. A classified report from the Canadian Integrated Threat Assessment Center obtained by the *National Post* describes JUF as "a Muslim criminal extremist group that seeks to purify Islam and defend it against perceived enemies using violence where necessary."[403] The report goes on to state that, "Fuqra members frequently travel to Pakistan for religious indoctrination and paramilitary training. There have been uncorroborated reports that members attended training camps in the Sudan."

Another April 2003 report by the Royal Canadian Mounted Police entitled, *Strategic Assessment of the Nature and Extent of Criminal Extremism/Terrorism*, discusses the ideology that inspires the group's violence: "Members of the Fuqra are taught there is a Satanist-Zionist conspiracy to destroy Islam and that Fuqra is God's chosen instrument to defeat the enemies of Islam."[404]

The concerns expressed about Jamaat ul-Fuqra by Canadian authorities have been validated by news of a potential plot by a cell composed of two Canadian and three American JUF members who reportedly wanted to target an Indian-owned theater in Toronto and a Hindu temple in York.[405] The cell members were arrested in October 1991 while attempting to cross the U.S.-Canadian border at Niagara Falls, New York.

Documents recovered from the two vehicles included aerial photographs of both locations, floor plans, a shopping list for bomb components, and assignments for a "hit team," a "guard team" and "recon team." Videos recovered also showed the cell members had conducted surveillance of both sites. The three Americans – all from the Dallas, Texas area – were convicted in the case.

As the trial of Jamaat ul-Fuqra members was underway in Canada, the group's activities came under scrutiny by U.S. authorities in Colorado. The case began in September 1989 with the discovery of a storage locker rented by JUF members in Colorado Springs. The locker contained 30 pounds of explosives, three large functional pipe bombs, ten handguns, silencers, military training manuals and bomb-making instructions.[406] Also found were "targeting packages," including surveillance notes and photographs of numerous military installations and electrical facilities.

That investigation later led to the discovery of a 100-acre compound outside of Buena Vista, Colorado. According to a statement published on the Colorado Attorney General's website,[407] five members of that compound were indicted in September 1992 for worker compensation fraud amounting to $350,000, some of which was used to purchase the Buena Vista compound. Additional indictments for conspiracy to commit murder and arson were filed six months later. One of the convicted Colorado cell members, Vicente Rafael Pierre, would be arrested again just days after the 9/11 attacks, along with two other leaders of the group's Red House, Virginia compound, for illegally purchasing weapons.[408]

During the Colorado trial, the chief investigator in the case, Susan Fenger, described the ideological danger from Jamaat ul-Fuqra: "They believe that true Islam will take over the world in the next few years and that they are carrying out the will of Allah by helping this transformation by force and violence. They are often armed and highly dangerous."[409]

The question occurs: Given what is known about Jamaat ul-Fuqra, its intentions and capacity for violent jihad, why is it allowed to maintain an infrastructure across America from which its violence can be mounted at will? Whatever the rationale, the unavoidable fact is that it is reckless in the extreme for the United States government to be ignoring the clear and present danger posed by Jamaat ul-Fuqra inside the United States and across our northern border in Canada.

The combined capacity for jihad present in the array of organizations (including many necessarily beyond the scope of this study) that are promoting shariah – both here and abroad, both through violent means and stealthy ones – is great and growing. The nature of America's open, tolerant society greatly increases the danger. That is especially true at a moment like today, when interpretations of constitutional protections for religion combine with deeply problematic elite and, to some extent, popular attitudes (the subjects of the following sections that make up Part II of this report) to leave much latitude for these shariah-adherent enemies to accomplish our destruction.

PART II

THE UNITED STATES AND SHARIAH

THE ANTI-CONSTITUTIONAL
CHARACTER OF SHARIAH

As a nation, we have lost our understanding of America's founding principles and as a result have become increasingly ill-prepared to defend the superiority of those principles. This puts us at a distinct disadvantage in being able to identify, understand and confront hostile doctrines – both foreign and domestic – that are in conflict with our own. The result of this combination of confusion and lassitude is that, in the face of shariah's violent and stealthy jihadist assaults, our peace and prosperity are at risk to the point where the core tenets of our nation – and ultimately its very existence – are in jeopardy.

In this context, it is worth reexamining America's founding principles and their incompatibility with the doctrines of Islam, especially those political, military and judicial doctrines embodied in shariah.

THE FOUNDING DOCUMENTS

The authoritative statement of America's founding principles is the Declaration of Independence. The Declaration defines the most fundamental of these in this brief, yet sweepingly comprehensive, passage: "We hold these truths to be self-evident, that all men are created equal, that they are endowed by their Creator with certain inalienable Rights ... That to secure these rights, Governments are instituted among Men, deriving their just powers from the consent of the governed."

In conformity with the Declaration, the U.S. Constitution's Preamble is similarly clear in the declaration of its purpose: "[To] secure the Blessings of Liberty to ourselves and our Posterity, do ordain and establish this Constitution."

Note that "We the people" create the Constitution; the Constitution does not create "the people." "The people" as a founding entity were constituted through the voluntary act of consenting to the principles of the Declaration. In creating the Constitution to secure natural rights and liberties, the people acted in their sovereign capacity.

Such is the basis of American government, rooted in "the laws of nature and nature's laws." Noted historian Harry Jaffa explained how the principles of the American founding were derived from a combination of reason and revelation:

> What we call Western civilization is to be found primarily and essentially in the confluence of the autonomous rationalism of classical philosophy and the faith of biblical religion....The unprecedented character of the American Founding is that it provided for the coexistence of the claims of reason and of revelation in all their forms, without requiring or permitting any political decisions concerning them. It refused to make unassisted human reason the arbiter of the claims of revelation, and it refused to make revelation the judge of the claims of reason. It is the first regime in Western civilization to do this, and for that reason it is, in its principles

or speech (leaving aside the question of its practice or deeds), the best regime.[410]

SEPARATION OF CHURCH AND STATE

America's doctrine of separation of church and state, which constitutionalists define more narrowly as a ban on a government-established or official state religion, exemplifies this balance. Popularly viewed as a secular doctrine, it actually has its basis firmly rooted in Judeo-Christian biblical scriptures such as "Submit yourselves for the Lord's sake to every authority instituted among men"[411] and "Render unto to Caesar that which is Caesar's."[412]

Thomas Jefferson's Virginia Statute for Religious Liberty, adopted by the Virginia General Assembly in 1786, exemplifies this concept:

> Whereas, Almighty God hath created the mind free; that all attempts to influence it by temporal punishments or burdens, or by civil incapacitations tend only to beget habits of hypocrisy and meanness, and are a departure from the plan of the Holy Author of our Religion, who being Lord, both of body and mind yet chose not to propagate it by coercions on either, as was in His Almighty power to do.

As the Virginia Historical Society explains:

> Jefferson considered the Virginia Statute for Religious Freedom as one of his three greatest achievements, ranking it with the drafting of the Declaration of Independence and the founding of the University of Virginia. According to the Virginia History and Government Textbook Commission, which was created by a resolution adopted by the General Assembly in its 1950 session, "Virginia was the first sovereign commonwealth, state, or nation in all the world to proclaim by law entire freedom of religious belief or unbelief."[413]

TOLERANCE IN AMERICA VERSUS THE QURAN

This brief examination establishes that American principles are principles of liberty that are rooted in *mutual* toleration. It follows that, in the United States, liberty was never intended to tolerate the intolerant and its citizens were never intended to tolerate totalitarian doctrines. Put differently, intolerant, totalitarian doctrines are in direct conflict with the stated purpose of American government "to secure these rights [endowed by their Creator]."

Even a fairly superficial reading of the Quran and other primary source documents of shariah reveals that it is a political-military-legal doctrine, rather than a religion as defined by the American standards mentioned above. The prominent Islamic scholar Abdul Maududi concurs with this assessment, saying: "But the truth is that Islam is not the name of a 'Religion,' nor is 'Muslim' the title of a 'Nation.' In reality, Islam is a revolutionary ideology and programme which seeks to alter the social order of the whole world and rebuild it in conformity with its own tenets and ideals."[414]

Shariah is, moreover, a doctrine that mandates the rule of Allah over all aspects of society. Specifically, in contrast – and fundamentally at odds – with the Jeffersonian principle of religious freedom, shariah holds that God did not create the mind free, but in subservience to the will of Allah (as detailed in shariah). The condition of human beings is submission to Allah, not freedom.

INTOLERANCE TOWARDS APOSTATES

As noted elsewhere in this report, one particularly clear-cut inconsistency of shariah with the rule of law pursuant to the U.S. Constitution is shariah's requirement that apostates be killed. Quran 4:89 says, "Those who reject Islam must be killed. If they turn back (from Islam), take hold of them and kill them wherever you find them." According to Hadith Sahih al-Bukhari, Mohammed declared, "Whoever changes his Islamic religion, kill him."[415] Clearly, such direction is incompatible with the Constitution's First, Fifth and Sixth Amendment protections.

Virtually every provision of the U.S. Constitution can be juxtaposed with shariah practices that are in violent conflict with America's foundational laws.

As noted in the next chapter of this report, a minimum standard of professional competency for America's political elites and national security professionals demands that they understand the enemy's threat doctrine. To the extent that that doctrine is wholly incompatible with the Constitution, it is, moreover, a violation of their oaths of office if they fail to defend the latter.

THE FOUNDERS AND ISLAM

America's earliest presidents best understood our founding principles. They were not only deeply involved with their formal adoption. They were professionally competent. When confronted with an Islamic threat, they took the effort to consult primary sources and to conduct competent analysis of that threat.

The first Muslim member of the House of Representatives recently made a spectacle of being sworn in on a copy of the Quran, rather than the Bible. He deflected some criticism by using one owned by Thomas Jefferson. Unremarked in all the controversy that ensued was the reason *why* our third President came to own a Quran.

In 1786, Thomas Jefferson, ambassador to France, and John Adams, ambassador to England, met with the emissary of the Islamic potentates of Tripoli to Britain, Sidi Haji Abdul Rahman Adja, regarding the demands for tribute being made at the time by the so-called Barbary Pirates.

Afterwards, Jefferson and Adams sent a four-page report to the Congress describing this meeting. The relevant portion of their report reads:

> We took the liberty to make some inquiries concerning the Grounds of their pretentions to make war upon Nations who had done them no Injury, and observed that we considered all mankind as our friends who had done us no wrong, nor had given us any provocation.

> The Ambassador answered us that it was founded on the Laws of their prophet, that it was written in their Qur'an, that all nations who should not have acknowledged their authority were sinners, that it was their right and duty to make war upon them wherever they could be found, and to make slaves of all they could take as Prisoners, and that every Musselman who should be slain in battle was sure to go to Paradise.

After this, Jefferson read the Quran in order to know his enemy. That knowledge of his adversary led to his doctrine of "Millions for defense, but not one cent for tribute."

John Adams' son, John Quincy Adams, whose formative years coincided with the founding of the republic, offers further insights into the early presidents' views on this subject. Like many Americans, he took an oath to uphold and defend the U.S. Constitution from all enemies, foreign and domestic. And, when faced with an Islamic enemy, he understood his obligation to be educated on the factual aspects of the principles, doctrines, objectives, jurisprudence and theology of shariah that comprised his enemy's threat doctrine.

John Quincy Adams' 136-page series of essays on Islam displayed a clear understanding of the threat facing America then – and now, especially from the permanent Islamic institutions of jihad and *dhimmitude*.[416] Regarding these two topics, Adams states:

... [Mohammed] declared undistinguishing and exterminating war, as a part of his religion, against all the rest of mankind....The precept of the Quran is, perpetual war against all who deny, that [Mohammed] is the prophet of God.

The vanquished [*dhimmi*] may purchase their lives, by the payment of tribute."

As the essential principle of [Mohammed's] faith is the subjugation of others by the sword; it is only by force, that his false doctrines can be dispelled, and his power annihilated.

The commands of the prophet may be performed alike, by fraud, or by force.

This appeal to the natural hatred of the Mussulmen towards the infidels is in just accordance with the precepts of the Quran. The document [the Quran] does not attempt to disguise it, nor even pretend that the enmity of those whom it styles the infidels, is any other than the necessary consequence of the hatred borne by the Mussulmen to them – the paragraph itself, is a forcible example of the contrasted character of the two religions.

The fundamental doctrine of the Christian religion is the extirpation of hatred from the human heart. It forbids the exercise of it, even towards enemies. There is no denomination of Christians, which denies or misunderstands this doctrine. All understand it alike – all acknowledge its obligations; and however imperfectly, in the purposes of Divine Providence, its efficacy has been shown in the practice of Christians, it has not been wholly inoperative upon them. Its effect has been upon the manners of nations. It has mitigated the horrors of war – it has softened the features of slavery – it has humanized the intercourse of social life.

The unqualified acknowledgement of a duty does not, indeed, suffice to insure its performance. Hatred is yet a passion, but too powerful upon the hearts of Christians. Yet they cannot indulge it, except by the sacrifice of their principles, and the conscious violation of their duties. No state paper from a Christian hand, could, without trampling the precepts of its Lord and Master, have commenced by an open proclamation of hatred to any portion of the human race. The Ottoman lays it down as the foundation of his discourse.[417]

As we have seen in chapter two, Adams' analysis of the meaning of jihad is validated in the English-language translation of the authoritative 14th Century text, *Reliance of the Traveller – A Classic Manual of Islamic Sacred Law*.[418] This book reveals in its opening chapter on Jihad:

> o9.0 – Jihad. *Jihad* means to wage war against non-Muslims, and is etymologically derived from the word *mujahada*, signifying warfare to establish the religion. ... The scriptural basis for jihad, prior to scholarly consensus (def: b7) is such Quranic verses as: (1) "Fighting is prescribed for you" (Quran 2:216); (2) "Slay them wherever you find them" (Quran 4:89); (3) "Fight the idolaters utterly" (Quran 9:36); ... I have been commanded to fight people until they testify that there is no god but Allah and that Mohammed is the messenger of Allah, and perform the prayer, and pay *zakat*. If they say it, they have saved their blood and possessions from me, except for rights of Islam over them.

In conclusion, it is clear from the writings of several of our earliest presidents, as well as the texts of the nation's founding documents, that American principles are not at odds with – and imperiled by – some "radical" or "extreme" version of Islam. Rather, it is the mainstream doctrine of shariah that constitutes the threat to the U.S. Constitution and the freedoms it enshrines.

That incompatibility has several practical implications: For one thing, the shariah legal code cannot be insinuated into America – even through stealthy means or democratic processes – without violating the Constitution's Article VI Supremacy Clause, which requires that the Constitution "shall be the supreme Law of the land."

For another, those who advocate the imposition of shariah in America must be considered ineligible to serve in the military, or hold state or federal office, insofar as Article VI requires them to swear an "oath...to support this Constitution" – *not* any other legal code, like shariah. The same disqualifier would appear to govern with respect to immigrants or would-be naturalized citizens.

Lastly, advocacy of and engagement in jihad, of even the *dawa* variety, for the purpose of imposing shariah, supplanting the Constitution and overthrowing the government it mandates would – as a practical matter – constitute a felony violation of the U.S. Code's prohibitions on treason, sedition and subversive activities.

From its founding, America has had a great tradition of tolerance and inclusion, on a mutual basis. Our latter day tendencies, however, for cultural diversity, political correctness and unreciprocated ecumenism – all seen by our enemies as submission and the subject of the following chapter – must not be allowed to create vehicles for our national destruction at the hands of those all-too-willing to use our civil liberties against us toward that end. In World War II, Americans would never have proposed that fascist or Nazi doctrine had some political or moral equivalency with American principles. We rightly identified the two as being completely and unalterably at odds. Today's mortal peril, shariah, must be viewed and treated the same way.

As is discussed at greater length below, the relevant, seminal texts concerning shariah are available *in English* from online booksellers and in mosque bookstores across America. It is, consequently, inexcusable for our political elites to be ignorant of the doctrines that guide shariah-adherent organizations like the Muslim Brotherhood's Islamic Society of North America, the Council on American Islamic Relations, the North American Islamic Trust, etc. as well as al Qaeda, Hezbollah, Hamas, and their ideological cousins.

Even more reprehensible is the willingness of some among America's elites, and it would appear even a subset of its elected leaders, to accede to these groups' increasingly insistent contention that shariah is compatible with the U.S. Constitution. In fact, based on shariah's tenets, its core attributes – especially its intolerance of other faiths and disfavored populations and its bid for supremacy over all other legal or political systems, there can be no confusion on this score: As the Framers fully understood, shariah is an enemy of the United States Constitution. The two are incompatible.[419]

7

THE U.S. AND WESTERN
VULNERABILITIES TO A THREAT
MASQUERADING AS A RELIGION

It is not simply inaccurate, incomplete or bowdlerized information about the threat posed by shariah that has left the United States floundering in its response particularly to the civilization jihad since 9/11. There is another reason. It takes the form of a collective block on reality that serves to prevent facts from influencing our reasoning – or, more specifically, to prevent facts about Islamic doctrine from influencing our strategy to defend ourselves against jihad and the advance of shariah.

POST-MODERNISM AT WORK

Truth – as supported by facts, history and logic – has been vanquished by "politically correct" efforts to impose on this country and its institutions an understanding of Islam that hides the centrality of shariah, jihad, and Islamic supremacism, even though these are defining imperatives that pose an existential threat to Western-style liberty. The Islamist networks and their modus operandi are described in great detail elsewhere in this study. This chapter will explain the reasons why these networks and their agents have been so effective and what are the civilizational vulnerabilities that are laying liberal, democratic society open to conquest.

Our society has come to prize unquestioning acceptance as the highest possible virtue of the "post-modern" Western world. This makes boundaries and taboos, limits and definitions – anything that closes the door on anything else – the lowest of possible sins. Judgment, no matter how discerning, is now tarred as "prejudice" and, therefore, a neo-barbarous act to be repressed and suspended altogether. Patriotism has been caricatured out of polite society as jingoistic war-mongering. Western civilization itself, which may be understood as the product of both judgment and patriotism, has been roundly condemned for being both prejudiced and war-mongering. Weakened by a kind of cultural anemia, we now regard transformation of America the Western into America the Multicultural as a good, or necessary, or even just inevitable thing.

Americans, increasingly, are acting as their own enforcers, promoting adherence to the new ethical mandate of multiculturalism by means of self-censorship. It is one thing not to be well-versed enough to define the enemy; it is another thing to be unwilling or effectively incapable of articulating precise and descriptive words to do so.

Such self-censorship has been a problem for years, distinct and pre-dating the modern Islamic threat. As Western society consciously sought to move beyond its own brutal past, the mistake it made was to assume and expect that other societies naturally would do the same. Further, it was somehow believed that by setting the example of eschewing even the mention of historical *or still-extant* savagery, such restraint would encourage mirroring.

It is this sort of thinking that accounts, at least in part, for the general unwillingness to discuss – and thereby acknowledge –

shariah and particularly its stealth jihad against the West. There is, however, another, deeper motivation at work as well, one that is born of an acute consciousness of our own fortune and success – which, paradoxically, spawns an entirely misplaced guilt.

Unexamined emotions like these are prompting a misguided quest to identify with the "victim," who seems to be just about anyone who opposes the United States and the West. Such responses, already based on emotion rather than reason, are easily magnified, and considerably so, by feelings of intimidation. Taken together, this kind of muddled mentality has induced a widespread moral paralysis rooted in our conditioned reflex to suspend judgment.

JIHADISTS AS 'VICTIMS'

Our national lack of moral certitude – often couched in the language of "neutrality" – reserves a crucial moral space for the possibility of sympathetic judgment, perpetuating the notion that blamelessness for terrorism is just as possible as blame. This implies that terrorism is not beyond the pale.

In a civilized society, though, such a "neutral" position amounts actually to taking sides. Treating terrorism with the same even-handedness accorded to competing tax plans, for example, creates an atmosphere that is amoral to a point of immorality. Besides leaving room for approval, the act of suspending judgment – and this is what may be most significant – delivers terrorism and terrorists from the nether-realm that all civilizations reserve for taboo, anathema and abomination. This begins to explain why the practice is so dangerous.

On some level, such behavior is the latest incarnation of the age-old encounter between the West and the rest – specifically, the non-Western "Other" encountered during various periods of Western exploration, conquest and colonization. Age-of-Exploration Europeans created the image of the noble savage, projecting a nobility onto the primitive peoples of the New World that canceled out, or at least compensated for, their obvious savagery.

Contemporary analysis of the shariah-enslaved jihadi and his assault on Western civilization reprises that mischaracterization. Just as apologists have seen in the barbaric conduct of some indigenous peoples the desperation of the primitive in the face of an advanced and encroaching civilization, apologists today see in the suicide bomber a similar desperation – a plight in which weaponization of a terrorist's life and limbs is presented as his only option for dealing with a technologically superior and encroaching civilization. What sounds like an apology for Islamic terrorism against American, Israeli, and other Western targets also sounds like a variation on the traditional theme: Enlightened society meets primal scream; enlightened society cringes with guilt – and fear.

THE ENEMY WITHIN

There is a crucial difference in the contemporary incarnation of this "Noble Savage Other," however: Where the Other of yesteryear used to live vividly imagined, if dimly understood, in the Western imagination, the contemporary Other now lives, quite literally, in the West itself.

Indeed, a massive demographic shift has brought adherents to shariah – a doctrine that, by definition, opposes all others – deep into the non-Islamic world. The Other is still vividly imagined, if dimly understood. But where he once provided intellectuals with a theoretical foil against modernity, the Other – in this century, in the collective form of practitioners of shariah – now manifests itself as a concrete bloc.

The historical, Other-inspired tradition of self-criticism is no longer deemed adequate in these circumstances. Instead, the Other demands and receives a kind of cultural accommodation – submission – that is the 21st Century echo of the centuries-long subjugation of our European ancestors to Islamic conquest and domination. In the real-life endgame of multicultural "inclusion," left unchecked, this impulse would seem to make the West's renewed dismantlement inevitable.

Such a fate could only happen in an era of Western identity-decline, a time in which cultural relativism has wedged itself between the West and its original and defining beliefs. The spreading contagion of Western self-excoriation leads inexorably to a willing suspension of critical thinking that encourages – indeed, *demands* – that value-based distinctions between Western and non-Western civilizations be abolished.

In other words, "diversity" is automatically "good," as long as the "diversity" being embraced is non-Western and the distinction being denied is Western. But it is "bad" when discrimination of the intellectually honest kind concludes that shariah-inspired savagery is actually savage. Western society is left in a state of moral, cultural, and political paralysis.

Under sway of the multiculturalist credo, notions of the superiority of Western culture are heretical, an imminent threat to the leveling arrangement that makes the European Union's so-called "meeting of different civilizations" possible. As the bureaucrats in Brussels see it, the "values of Europe" disallow consideration of Western civilization as superior to another. In other words, any tendency that threatens to restore the traditional hierarchy that put Western civilization at the pinnacle for having enshrined liberty and human rights must be disavowed, shamed and rejected outright.

IN DENIAL

Such submission abounds in the media and in politics, where discussion of doctrinal links between Islam's shariah and terrorism has been considered out of bounds at least since the George W. Bush years. This logic blackout is now reaching levels of absurdity as "rage over the health care bill" was seriously debated by reporters as a potential motivation for the Times Square bomber, Faisal Shahzad, and as Attorney General Eric Holder balked repeatedly at considering even "radical Islam" as a possible rationale for such terrorist attacks.

The unmistakable trend is to deny shariah's doctrinal association with terrorism in a strange public display of "sensitivity." The collective striving to be sensitive has, paradoxically, deadened our senses and blunted our logic – a condition resembling not just appeasement, but surrender.

As charges of "religious defamation," "racism," "bigotry," and "blasphemy" have become, like Pavlovian gongs, instant conversation-enders, Islam has become in the West increasingly insulated not just from criticism, but also from the poking and prodding of analysis – from reality itself. This may be precisely the kind of "protection" from secular "blasphemy" (read, criticism) that shariah has long maintained it requires, and, indeed, is pursuing in the international arena with anti-blasphemy resolutions at the United Nations. The more challenging question is, Why are non-Muslims so obsessively doing everything they can to help suppress debate about shariah and related subjects?

DHIMMITUDE

The answer is complicated. Certainly one of the forces at work is the West's crisis of confidence in its own value, which indeed, defines the identity crisis of the West itself. But there is something else, as well. That something else is the age-old relationship, not between the West and the rest, but between shariah and the rest – namely, the relationship between its adherents and the *dhimmi,* the millions of non-Muslims through the centuries who have lived in Islamized societies.

To live as a *dhimmi* is to have an inferior legal status under shariah, a codified condition as old as the first Islamic conquests of non-Islamic peoples. The Muslim-to-*dhimmi* relationship is, at best, a master-servant relationship, pitting an identifiable authority figure against an identifiable supplicant.

This was often literally the case since, in many historical contexts, *dhimmis* were required by shariah to be recognizably inferior as evidenced by their clothes, the size and color of their homes, modes of transportation and overall public subservience to Muslims. The relationship's "core element," explains Bat Ye'or, the leading modern scholar of the *dhimmis,* "pertains to the premise of Muslim superiority over all other religious groups."[420]

Made explicitly clear in shariah, and to those conquered by its adherents, was the abject reality that *permission to continue living* rested completely in the hands of the Muslim overlords, whose slightest displeasure could result at any moment in withdrawal of that permission. Fear thus formed the essence of the *dhimmi* system.

Bat Ye'or has introduced a term to the lexicon to describe a mode of behavior or state of mind fostered by shariah-sanctioned religious inferiority: *dhimmitude.* Forbidden to possess arms, own land, criticize shariah or defend themselves either in a fight or in court against a Muslim (among many, many other prohibitions), *dhimmis* developed cross-cultural, cross-continental survival strategies that ensured survival not of the fittest, but rather of the most deferential – self-abasement as self-preservation.

A good example of this phenomenon can be found in the fact that, since criticism of shariah was severely punished, *dhimmis* "adopted a servile language and obsequious demeanor for fear of retaliation and for their self-preservation."[421] In this struggle to survive were lost precious markers of the self: history and identity, truth and tradition. What was left were self-censoring societies, stunted by fear, compromised by fearfulness.

'POLITICAL CORRECTNESS' AS DHIMMITUDE

Certain similarities between *dhimmi* life under Islam and "politically correct" life in a multicultural world are striking. We have long lived in such a self-censoring society, stunted by a kind of fear that political *incorrectness* would result in opprobrium, ostracism or professional failure. Traditionally (because multiculturalism, as noted above, has been with us long enough to be characterized as a tradition), this has had nothing to do with Islam or the *dhimmi*. But this now-well-established practice does help explain the seamless compatibility between *dhimmitude* and the multicultural mindset that flourishes in our post-modernist world.

Importantly, Bat Ye'or has demonstrated that actual *dhimmi* status under shariah in Islamic societies is by no means a prerequisite of *dhimmitude*. Indeed, definite patterns of *dhimmi* behavior exist not only in the shariah states, but throughout the Free World. In the current context, one aspect has particular resonance, or, rather, non-resonance: the silence of *dhimmitude* regarding shariah. It is the silence of the insecure society.

CONFORMING TO SHARIAH 'BLASPHEMY' CODES

It is easy to see why *dhimmi* populations in Islamic lands would collude in "protecting" Islam from "offense" or criticism; they rightly and understandably fear the consequences under shariah. But why do *Westerners*, in academia, the media, Congress, the White House, or the United Nations collude in these same "protections"?

For that matter, why the reluctance to acknowledge patent differences between shariah and the West? Why the refusal to examine whether shariah plays a central role in the so-called "war on terror" – now even more euphemistically known as a fight against "extremism"? Why the failure to study whether the "war on terror" is a defensive response to the latest manifestation of 13 centuries of jihad? Why the cold-sweating fear over even asking the questions?

Bat Ye'or has described Western silence on Islam – today's gruesome human rights violations, yesterday's bloody conquests – as "the politics of *dhimmitude*."[422] The term is provocative, describing a framework of concessions to Islam that goes far beyond multicultural theorizing in a lecture hall or PC politesse in the public arena.

Indeed, the whole concept of *dhimmitude* – predicated on the historic abasement of non-Muslims in Islamic society – envisions a conception of world affairs that pre-dates the Cold War, let alone the post-modern era, by many centuries. Gone are the paradigms of the great powers and bipolar rivalries familiar to recent generations. In their place, a complex power struggle between the West and shariah plays out on a deeply psychological level where Western strengths are checkmated by the machinations of an enemy at once more determined to prevail than we, and more confident in its own superiority.

Whether characterized as a courtesy, a favor or appeasement, every Western wince – from, to cite but a few examples, Margaret Thatcher's concessions to the ayatollahs, to George W. Bush's retreat on "crusade," to Barack Obama's pledge to free *zakat* from the prohibitions on material support for terror – are seen by our enemies as a form of *dhimmitude*. They are, after all, clear manifestations of shariah's influence over the West. Such behavior indicates, as Bat Ye'or writes, an "implicit submission to the shariah prohibitions of blasphemy."[423]

FEAR AS THE NEW REASON

Shariah demands that Islam must not be "disrespected." And Islam is *not* "disrespected," according to Western practice. There is more than etiquette at work here; there is fear. And where there is fear, there is silence. Of this silence – this tacit, non-comprehended acceptance of shariah's dictates – Bat Ye'or writes: It "puts the Western public sphere in the position of conforming to one of the basic rules of *dhimmitude*: the express prohibition of Christians and Jews to criticize Islamic history and doctrine."[424]

That inescapable fear is the fear of confronting the reality that some belief systems and some cultures prey atavistically on others. It would mean admitting that there are others out there who are not like us – and that no adjustment to our own behavior will change their determination to subjugate or kill us. And that is a terrifying reality. Fear has become the new reason.

We fear more fatwas, more rage, protests, assassinations, and boycotts. We are afraid of more violence, more burning flags, more gutted embassies. Afraid of more bomb threats. Afraid of more bombs. And so we close our eyes and close our circle, pretending ourselves into a status quo of our own imagination, a condition dependent on our own delusions: Moderate Islam is emerging as an antidote to shariah. Democracy is the answer. And don't ask any questions. Because there is something else our culture fears more than anything else. We are afraid to *do* anything about our fears – even to name them.

The growth of Muslim populations in the West augurs the inexorable spread of shariah into Western societies – less by violence than by dint of natural procreation, unchecked immigration, and the incessant demands of an aggressive minority that refuses to assimilate. Logic should tell us, then, that the growth of shariah in the West threatens Western-style liberty: threatens freedom of expression, freedom of conscience and upends religious and sexual equality. But we are at a point where we, the children of Athens, fear and deny that logic.

We do so because logic would lead ineluctably to the perception that the beliefs of shariah Islam and the beliefs of the West are at irreconcilable odds. It is not just shariah's place in the West that would then become an acknowledged threat to the survival of the West. The multicultural mirage of interchangeable diversity and "universal values" necessarily vanishes as well.

In its place would arise an inevitable hierarchy of differentiation: Not all religions are equally benign; not all religions are equal. Not all cultures have made equal contributions; not all cultures are equal. To our elites, this would be a bad thing because it would set into motion a rite of passage – a painful, difficult awakening from a dream world of sunny universalism and pale indecision into a stark reality of black and white, good and evil, win or lose, do or die.

Thus, our continued inaction – the Muslim Brotherhood's near-term, tactical goal – depends on our continued silence, just as avoiding clashes depends on our own self-censorship. As a culture, we ignored Ibn Warraq's plea in 2006 for "unashamed, noisy, public solidarity"[425] with the Danish cartoonists as a means of safeguarding freedom of expression. We also ignored his warning that from our silence, "the Islamization of Europe will have begun in earnest."[426]

We have comforted and deluded ourselves by calling our self-censorship the silence of respect. In reality, it is the silence of *fear*. We have called it the silence of tolerance; actually, it is the silence of cultural acquiescence. There has been no clamor to defend the public square from religious tyranny. There is only shame, a shame without justification in reality, but a smothering shame all the same.

STANDING UP FOR THE WEST

The West is the source of the liberating ideas of individual liberty, political democracy, the rule of man-made law, human rights and cultural freedom. It is the West that has raised the status of women, fought against slavery and defended freedom of inquiry, expression, and conscience. The West needs no lectures on the superior values of societies that keep their women in subjugation, cut off their clitorises, stone them to death for alleged adultery, throw acid on their faces, or deny the human rights of those considered unacceptable to a savage, omnipotent deity.[427]

Ibn Warraq's catalogue of Western treasure – onto which an American appendix might include the Founding Fathers, Mark Twain, Thomas Edison, Irving Berlin, Ella Fitzgerald, Watson and Crick, Laurel and Hardy, Ted Williams, Jonas Salk and the 82nd Airborne – is indeed something to be proud of, to derive strength from, and guidance, too. It gives the lie to wishful notions about non-existent "universal values." The end of shariah denial in the West points the way to the end of multiculturalism in the West, too, iconoclastic though that prospect may be to some.

We need to come to grips with the dread reality that ours is not only a time of transformative modernization and heretofore unimaginable affluence, but also a time of supreme, even ultimate struggle. Ours is an age marked by the startling confluence of devalued Western models faced with the unthinkable threat of cultural obliteration via Islamization that is all-too-familiar to those who know history. Arrayed against this looming fate stands but a thin line of courageous Americans and their counterparts in Europe and elsewhere – non-Muslims, former Muslims and a few courageous practicing Muslims whose ranks are much weakened by the cowering *dhimmis* and their willingness to submit to shariah.

There is only one thing that can begin to save us, without which even the rich trove of information and revelation in this study will be of little use: Free speech. Free, unfettered, politically incorrect, informed and precise speech about shariah and the threat it poses to America.

U.S. LEADERSHIP FAILURES IN
THE FACE OF SHARIAH

Our shariah-adherent enemies understand that – given the vast military and economic advantages enjoyed by the West – achieving the goal of forcing the United States and other freedom-loving peoples to submit to their program requires them, of necessity, to exploit the vulnerabilities described in the previous chapter. Specifically, these foes must control our perceptions of the threat they pose and, thereby, our responses to them.

In fact, by manipulating perceptions at the national strategic level about the nature of shariah, the enemy can actually exercise profound influence over the nature and adequacy of the defense mounted. That is most especially true of actions needed to contend with the Muslim Brotherhood's stealth jihad – even though we know its avowed purpose is aimed at "eliminating and destroying the Western civilization from within and 'sabotaging' its miserable house by their hands."

To fully understand America's peril in the face of such enemies, we must carefully consider our collective failure to contend with their successful pursuit of information dominance and psychological strategy, critical ingredients in information warfare. We must come to grips with, and correct, the control they have come to enjoy over what Americans, and most especially the U.S. civilian, intelligence, and military leadership, understand about shariah and its proponents.

WILLFUL BLINDNESS

Information dominance can be advanced by the simple act of concealing relevant information, the "denial" component of the military concept of "denial and deception." As this report makes clear, however, our shariah-adherent enemies provide to each other – and, therefore, make available (at least indirectly) to the rest of us – ample data about their intentions, motivations and capabilities. The problem is that too many in this country and, again, especially those in positions of responsibility for our security, are failing to acquaint themselves with such data, to say nothing of being informed by it or acting upon it.

Former federal prosecutor Andrew McCarthy has called the phenomenon "willful blindness," the title of his 2008 book about the first attempt to destroy the World Trade Center in 1993, which was mounted by the "Blind Sheikh," Omar Abdel-Rahman, and other adherents to shariah. McCarthy described the historic *and on-going*, stubborn refusal of America's senior national security officials to acknowledge the linkage between: (1) mainstream, orthodox Islamic doctrine; (2) kinetic terrorism; and (3) the pre-violent efforts of Muslim jihadis to insinuate shariah into the fabric of our society by stealth and subterfuge.

As we have discussed above, such unwillingness to recognize and acknowledge the enemy's battle doctrine emanates directly from the proclivity of Americans, both in and out of public office, to accommodate even troubling conduct in the name of religious tolerance, multiculturalism and political correctness.

This blindness, however it is rationalized, has a predictable effect: It translates into an inability even to gauge accurately how far advanced is the assault, let alone to execute an effective strategy for countering it.

Former Joint Chiefs of Staff analyst Stephen Coughlin wrote his seminal master's thesis for the National Defense Intelligence College on the U.S. refusal to study and internalize *what the enemy himself says* about why he fights jihad. Coughlin concluded that the failure to investigate these sources has left U.S. national security leadership "disarmed in the war of ideas."[428]

VIOLATING AMERICA'S OWN DOCTRINE

This behavior is singularly disabling and potentially deadly in light of the fact that the United States' own war-fighting doctrine is based on a deliberative decision-making process that begins with "intelligence preparation of the battle space." Such preparation is *supposed to start* with an unconstrained analysis of the doctrinal template of the enemy.

If we refuse to pursue a fact-based determination of the nature of the enemy and his doctrinal template, however, we have no basis for accurately predicting enemy courses of action. Without sound predictions, we are reduced to *guessing* what strategies might be effective for countering our foes.

In short, what amounts to a hostile seizure of control of our doctrinal template through information dominance is a powerful technique for defeating this country. There is ample reason to believe that our shariah-adherent enemies feel confident in their ability to wield this weapon against us with decisive effect. Should they do so, the results will only reflect in part their skill and strategic acumen. In part, it will also be due to our own contributions to such a defeat.

The truth is that there is plenty of blame to go around for this sorry state of affairs and for our national failure to date to develop a correct enemy doctrinal template that is rooted in shariah. In order for the urgently needed corrective action to be taken, it is essential to map where the responsibility for such failure lies.

Deficient Professional Training: It is evident that within the academic halls of U.S. war colleges and training institutions, there is a failure to comprehend and teach shariah as the enemy's ideological wellspring. That shortfall leaves students uninformed about the warfighting principles of the key U.S. global opponent of the 21st Century.

William Gawthrop, the former head of the Joint Terrorism Task Force of the Defense Department's Counterintelligence Field Activity, warned in a military intelligence journal about the dangers of this trend in 2006:

> As late as early 2006, the senior service colleges of the Department of Defense had not incorporated into their curriculum a systematic study of Mohammed as a military or political leader. As a consequence, we *still* do not have an in-depth understanding of the war-fighting doctrine laid down by Mohammed, how it might be applied today by an increasing number of Islamic groups, or how it might be countered.[429] (Emphasis added.)

The U.S. Army Training and Doctrine Command has invested in the cultural and social education of personnel deploying to places like Iraq and Afghanistan, and to officers of all services who have chosen to become regional experts in the Af/Pak Hands program established by the Chairman of the Joint Chiefs of Staff. The study of Islam is an important component of the training. However, the Army-sponsored training program, carried out by the Leader Development and Education for a Sustained Peace (LDESP) program through the Naval Postgraduate School, does not teach enemy threat doctrine. Until security concerns by an LDESP faculty member were raised after the Fort Hood shootings of November 2009, Muslim Brotherhood member Louay Safi of the Islamic Society of North America (ISNA) taught the Islam component to thousands of Army senior enlisted men and officers. LDESP unofficially suspended Safi from teaching, but it also retaliated against the faculty member who gave the warning by dropping him from further instructing the troops.[430]

Self-Censored Guidance: As noted in the previous chapter, self-censorship is a serious contributor to, and manifestation of, America's willful blindness about shariah. This behavior has been expressed most egregiously in various national security documents that have institutionalized U.S. conceptual failure on Islamic jihadist ideology. By issuing such documents, successive administrations of both political parties have locked in a set of self-imposed strategic handicaps that doom any short-term successes on tactical battlefields – to say nothing of victory at a strategic level.

Of particular concern are the 2010 versions of the Pentagon's Quadrennial Defense Review, the Homeland Security Department's Quadrennial Review[431] and the White House-issued National Security Strategy.[432] All hew to the same troubling language guidelines promulgated by DHS,[433] the FBI's Counterterrorism Analytical Lexicon[434] and the National Counterterrorism Center's vocabulary regulations[435] – to the effect that no reference to Islam, jihad or shariah may be made when discussing the threat. This is not simply incompetence. It amounts to malfeasance and it places the U.S. government demonstrably and officially in compliance with Islamic law on slander – a posture that puts the nation in grave peril.

Relying on the Enemy: The terminological constraints now in effect inside the U.S. government come from the Muslim Brotherhood. The immediate provenance may be the Society of Professional Journalists,[436] but the Society in turn apparently obtained the guidelines from sources that critics say got their ideas about vocabulary from Muslim Brotherhood affiliates and associates.[437] Ikhwan operatives have also played important roles in defining what can, and cannot, be said about shariah and the jihadism it requires.

To cite but one example, on May 8, 2007, then-Homeland Security Secretary Michael Chertoff met with a group of self-styled Muslim Americans "leaders." Not surprisingly, most were drawn from the ranks of Ikhwan front groups. (See in this connection the discussion in chapter four.)

The host's stated purpose was to discuss ways the Department can work with the Muslim-American community in the interest of protecting the country, promoting civic engagement and preventing violent radicalization from taking root in the United States. The Muslim participants, however, used the occasion to inveigh against U.S. officials for using terminology the Ikhwan finds offensive – even though, indeed *precisely because*, it accurately describes terrorists who invoke Islamic theology in planning, carrying out and justifying their attacks. As has been discussed above, the Brotherhood routinely dissembles about the validity of this connection and darkly warns that even discussing that possibility will insult and provoke Muslims.

On March 14, 2008, the National Counterterrorism Center (NCTC) conformed to this demand for compliance with shariah slander codes. It issued brief guidelines on jihad terminology in "Words that Work and Words that Don't: A Guide for Counterterrorism Communication."[438] In it, the authors declare:

> We are also attaching an excellent Homeland Security paper entitled *Terminology to Define the Terrorists: Recommendations from American Muslims,* a guide for U.S. government officials to use to describe terrorists who invoke Islamic theology in planning, carrying out, and justifying their attacks.[439]

The NCTC adopted these recommendations uncritically, just as the Department of Homeland Security did theirs. Among the resulting NCTC recommendations were the following:

Try to limit the number of non-English terms you use if you are speaking in English. Mispronunciation could make your statement incomprehensible and/or sound ill-informed. If you must use such a word, make sure your pronunciation is validated by an expert. Don't use words that require use of consonants that do not exist in English and whose nearest English approximation has a totally different meaning.

In national security matters involving threats as grave as those posed by the forces of shariah, the potential risks associated with mispronouncing a term are far outweighed by the *necessity* of accurately understanding – and appropriately drawing upon – the enemy's own, stated rationales for his actions. And we have no better sources for such terminology than the words of authoritative shariah-adherent scholars, jihadists and political figures involving their communications intended for consumption by Muslim audiences (as opposed to *taqiyya* aimed at non-Muslim Western ones). *Such terminology is valid to the enemy and needs to be properly understood and incorporated into our own strategic doctrine.*

Should we persist in policies that exclude such insights, the United States government can only serve to advance the Muslim Brotherhood's mission of "destroying Western civilization from within ... by their own hand." However unintended, the practical effect of conforming to what amounts to an Ikhwan-approved lexicon designed explicitly for *dawa* against the West is to promote our misunderstanding, mischaracterizing and otherwise underestimating the forces of shariah and jihad.

The slow drift toward what is often called a "politically correct" version of threat analysis within the ranks of U.S. intelligence and security agencies actually translates to our enemies as our "submission" – precisely the goal of denying America information dominance as part of the grand jihad.

One further issue that arises when a lexicon, such as that now in force within the Intelligence Community, is obtained from outside the official U.S. national security apparatus, and then imposed by leadership upon subordinates. Under such circumstances, a highly-improper form of "prior restraint" tends to operate.

Today, analysts jeopardize their careers if they try to use accurate language to define the enemy threat doctrine. Undue command influence that effectively calls on professionals *not* to perform their duties to professional standards is, in fact, dereliction of duty in time of war.

Put differently, it would be bad enough if this practice of acquiescing to such intimidation and conforming to the MB's shariah slander/blasphemy dictates simply meant that the Department of Homeland Security and other U.S. agencies have allowed their strategic threat characterization to be dictated by individuals without acceptable national security credentials. As made clear in chapter four, however, the latter are actually – with rare exceptions – agents of influence or actual jihadist operatives who work for the enemy.

This, at a minimum, is tantamount to malpractice and professional incompetence. Comparable breaches of codes of conduct would result in lawyers being disbarred and physicians losing their licenses to practice. To the extent that it involves in this profession turning-a-blind-eye to and probably enabling of *sedition*, it would appear to be a felony offense known as "misprision of treason" in the U.S. Code.[440]

Failing the 'Duty to Know': The case for treating harshly such misconduct is further justified by in cases where our most senior government officials fail to practice due diligence in their execution of their duties. Culpability for that particular failure is a function of the "knowabilty of relevant facts," which reflects the legal standard embodied in the phrase "either knew or should have known." Once a professional is on notice that he does not know something that is material, he is obligated to find it out.

Yet, in numerous cases at very senior levels, that responsibility has not been fulfilled. National security officials must be, above all else, professionals – and the rules of professionalism must apply to them. According to the very first rule of *The Model Rules of Professional Conduct*: "Professionals [in this case, lawyers] have a duty to be competent that includes the requirement to inform oneself of the subject matter by taking the necessary time to prepare oneself to a standard of preparedness necessary to provide successful representation."[441]

"Taking the necessary time to prepare oneself" means that a professional never has the right to claim that he did not have time to know something he was professionally obligated to know.

For all professionals in the national security community, their duty – "duty" being a legally-defined term – requires, at a minimum, that they conform to professional standards. And one of the professional standards is Rule 1.1, "the duty to be competent," which includes the "duty to know." The duty to know, in turn, includes the "duty to take all time necessary to learn." That duty is not just an inherent responsibility for U.S. government officials. They have *sworn* to fulfill it.

The Constitution's Article II, Section 1 that says "The executive power shall be vested in the President" goes on to require the President to swear an oath:

> Before he enters on the Execution of his Office, he shall take the following Oath or Affirmation: "I do solemnly swear (or affirm) that I will faithfully execute the Office of President of the United States, and will *to the best of my Ability preserve, protect and defend the Constitution* of the United States. (Emphasis added.)

Pursuant to the Constitution's Article VI, other officials of the government must take a similar oath, which is specified in Title V § 3331 of the United States Code:

> I do solemnly swear (or affirm) that I will *support and defend the Constitution of the United States* against all enemies, foreign and domestic; that I will bear true faith and allegiance to the same; that I take this obligation freely, without any mental reservation or purpose of evasion; and that I will well and faithfully discharge the duties of the office on which I am about to enter. So help me God." (Emphasis added.)

It is, therefore, fair to ask of U.S. officials with national security responsibilities whether the failure to know an enemy violates not only professional rules of competency but their solemn oath of office? After all, if an officeholder must "protect and defend against all enemies" (N.B. the Constitution uses the word "enemy," not "violent extremists"), this implies that he has to *know* all enemies, or at least undertake the due diligence effort to learn about them.

In short, this report makes clear that the "knowabilty of relevant facts" – reflected in the legal standard established by the phrase "either knew or should have known" – is not in serious dispute. *The true character of shariah is eminently knowable* and, as noted above, once a professional is on notice that he does not know something that is material, he is obligated to find it out. Those in high office who have failed to fulfill these responsibilities must be held accountable.

A CASE STUDY

There is, arguably, no more dramatic example of a senior U.S. government official failing to perform his duty to know – and, seemingly, to fulfill his oath of office – than that of John Brennan, Homeland Security Advisor and Counter-terrorism Advisor to President Obama. To be sure, Brennan is not alone in such a failing; senior officials in previous administrations of both parties, as well as others in the present one, should be held to account, as well.

That said, John Brennan has taken the "failure to know" to new extremes. Unfortunately, the full extent and implications of his doing so can only be surmised at this time, given the nature of his responsibilities, without access to highly classified information.

On the basis of information that *is* in the public domain, though, we can safely say that Brennan epitomizes what is wrong with today's official understanding and characterization of the enemy and his threat doctrine. Brennan is also a prime contributor to the environment characterized by submission to shariah's dictates in which the rest of the U.S. government's national security apparatus increasingly is required to operate. The following are illustrative examples taken from Brennan's relatively few public appearances and statements.

In a May 2010 speech at the Center for Strategic and International Studies, Brennan exhibited his ignorance of shariah by arguing that the "violent extremists" attacking the United States are victims of "political, economic and social forces" and should not be described in "religious terms": "Nor do we describe our enemy as 'jihadists' or 'Islamists' because jihad is a holy struggle, a legitimate tenet of Islam, meaning to purify oneself or one's community, and there is nothing holy or legitimate or Islamic about murdering innocent men, women and children."[442]

Brennan also declared in his remarks at CSIS that "Describing our enemy in religious terms would lend credence to the lie propagated by al Qaeda and its affiliates to justify terrorism, that the United States is somehow at war against Islam. The reality, of course, is that we have never been and will never be at war with Islam. After all, Islam, like so many faiths, is part of America."

The evidence shows that these statements are wholly disconnected from the true nature and requirements of shariah. Those who adhere to shariah are not lying when they say it not only justifies terroristic jihad, but actually *requires* them to engage in it. That is deemed to be true even against "innocents" in the ordinary sense of the word, since, if those targeted do not adhere to shariah, they are – by definition – *not* innocents. What is more, shariah is absolutely and unalterably "at war" with the *Dar al-Harb*, including notably the United States and Western civilization more generally.

In an op-ed published in *USA Today* on February 9, 2010, Brennan defended the Obama administration's handling of the brief interrogation and swift lawyering-up of Umar Farook Abdulmutallab, the Christmas day bomber. In response to a damning editorial by the paper entitled, "National security team fails to inspire confidence; Officials, handling of Christmas Day attack looks like amateur hour," Brennan defensively claimed the critics were "misrepresenting the facts to score political points, instead of coming together to keep us safe." He asserted that, "Politically motivated criticism and unfounded fear-mongering only serve the goals of al Qaeda. Terrorists are not 100 feet tall."[443]

The point is not that the critics are exaggerating the gravity of the threat from adherents to shariah. It is that Brennan and his colleagues are systematically underestimating and mischaracterizing it, and attempting to discredit or marginalize those who attempt to estimate and characterize the threat.

John Brennan called Hezbollah a "very interesting organization" in remarks at the Washington-based Nixon Center in May 2010. Despite the fact that the State Department long has designated this jihadist group as a Foreign Terrorist Organization, Brennan opined that: "There certainly [are] the elements of Hezbollah that are truly a concern to us – what they're doing. And what we need to do is to find ways to diminish their influence within the organization and to try to build up the more moderate elements within Hezbollah."[444]

The claim that there are actually true "moderates" in any conventional meaning of the word within the shariah-adherent community – to say nothing of within one of its most virulently jihadist organizations, Hezbollah – is unsubstantiated by the facts. Such statements bespeak not only "willful blindness." They are suggestive of the sort of top-level guidance that can only subvert efforts within the U.S. government to defeat this and other terrorist groups.

In a February 13, 2010 speech at NYU's Islamic Center,[445] Brennan referred to Jerusalem as "Al Quds," an Arabic name for the city used only by Muslims that translates literally as "The Holy." No top U.S. policymaker had ever used that term before in such a public address.

For shariah-adherent Muslims, "Al Quds" or "Al Qods" is a rallying cry. In August of 1979, Ayatollah Khomeini designated the last Friday of Ramadan as Al Quds Day, during which Muslims around the world should protest Israel's control of Jerusalem, saying in part: "I ask all the Muslims of the world and the Muslim governments to join together to sever the hand of this usurper [Israel] and its supporters....I ask God Almighty for the victory of the Muslims over the infidels."[446]

Al Quds has other well-known jihadist connotations. For example, the Al-Quds Brigades (in Arabic, Saraya al-Quds) is the armed wing of the Palestinian terrorist organization Palestinian Islamic Jihad (PIJ). The Al-Qods Force is an Iranian military organization and intelligence arm of the Islamic Revolutionary Guard Corps. (For more on the IRGC, see chapter six.)

Brennan's deliberate choice of the term Al-Quds obviously represents pandering to the aspirations of those who are determined to "liberate" what they consider to be "infidel-occupied" Jerusalem. Whether intended as such or not, it can only be perceived as a further indication of the ominous distancing of the United States under President Obama from America's most important strategic ally in the region, Israel, and of submission to the shariah's inexorably rising tide.

In the NYU speech, Brennan also enthused about the very heart of the shariah enterprise, Saudi Arabia, where he had once served as the CIA station chief: "In Saudi Arabia, I saw how our Saudi partners fulfilled their duty as custodians of the two holy mosques at Mecca and Medina. I marveled at the majesty of the Hajj and the devotion of those who fulfilled their duty as Muslims by making that pilgrimage."[447]

The only way Brennan could literally have seen how the Saudis "fulfilled their duty as custodians of Mecca and Medina" and "marvel at the Hajj" is if he himself were a Muslim. That is because non-Muslims are not allowed to set foot in either place. Assuming he was speaking figuratively in this effusive way, the message of pandering – read, once again, submission – was as unmistakable to the intended audience, namely the House of Saud, as was President Obama's notorious bow to the Saudi king.

At NYU, Brennan went beyond pandering towards the custodians of shariah to propound a classic bit of MB *taqiyya*: "Whatever our differences in nationality, or race, or religion or language, there are certain aspirations that we all share. To get an education. To provide for our family. To practice our faith freely."

No one with even passing familiarity with Saudi Arabia, let alone the head of CIA operations there, could possibly think that those who adhere to shariah – whether in the Kingdom or elsewhere – have any mutual respect for the free practice of other faiths. In fact, the Saudis will not allow anyone to wear a cross in public, let alone build or attend a Christian church. It is increasingly dangerous to try to practice faiths other than Islam in much of the rest of the "Muslim world" (notably, Egypt, Lebanon, Iraq and Malaysia) as well, thanks to the Saudi-led and – underwritten promotion of shariah around the globe.

On the occasion of his speech to New York University, Brennan was introduced by Ingrid Mattson, president of the Islamic Society of North America. As we have seen, ISNA is not only the largest Muslim Brotherhood front in the United States. It was an unindicted co-conspirator in America's largest terror funding trial, U.S. vs. Holy Land Foundation. Recall that the HLF prosecution resulted in the conviction of all of the defendants on a total of 108 charges, and proved that the Foundation had funneled over $12 million to the Brotherhood's Palestinian franchise: the State Department-designated terrorist organization, Hamas.

Brennan, nonetheless, enthused about Mattson, expressing appreciation "For your leadership as an academic whose research continues the rich tradition of Islamic scholarship, and as the president of the Islamic Society of North America, where you have been a voice for the tolerance and diversity which defines Islam."[448]

The characterization of a top Muslim Brotherhood operative in these terms and the embrace of MB disinformation about what "defines" Islam would be a problem in an entry-level CIA analyst. Coming from the top White House official with responsibility for counter-terrorism and homeland security – who is also reputed to be the most influential figure in U.S. intelligence – such deferential treatment is appalling.

Indeed, it is hard to overstate the danger associated with the President of the United States having as his top advisor in these sensitive portfolios someone so severely compromised with respect to shariah and the threat it poses. Corrective actions of the sort outlined in the following chapter must begin with the installation of a leadership that is under no illusion about these topics, and that is both determined *and allowed* to replace willful blindness and susceptibility to Muslim Brotherhood influence operations with vigilance and fact-based guidance.

CONCLUSION

Under successive presidencies, the United States has failed to understand, let alone counter successfully, the threat posed to its constitutional form of government and free society by shariah. In the past, such failures were reckless. Today, they are intolerable.

The preceding pages document shariah's true supremacist and totalitarian character. They make clear its incompatibility with the Constitution as the only source of law for this country. As we have seen, shariah explicitly seeks to replace representative governance with an Islamic State, to destroy sovereign and national polities with a global caliphate.

If shariah is thus viewed as an alien legal system hostile to and in contravention of the U.S. Constitution, and as one which dictates both violent and non-violent means to a capable audience ready to act imminently, then logically, those who seek to establish shariah in America – whether by violent means or by stealth – can be said to be engaged in criminal sedition, not the protected practice of a religion.

Ignoring this reality does nothing to mitigate the danger posed by shariah. Rather, its adherents regard their accommodation – even in the name of religious tolerance – as "submission" to their doctrine. The unavoidable result is a further emboldening of those who seek to impose their agenda on the rest of us, quite possibly by using force instead of stealthy, non-violent techniques.

After all, in accordance with Muhammad's example, violence is only supposed to be eschewed when it is impracticable. Evidence that civilization jihad is no longer needed – that submission is being achieved and can be accelerated by terror – can only result in more, and more terrifying, jihadist attacks.

In addition, this behavior, which is often justified as necessary to prevent the alienation of "moderate Muslims," generally has the opposite result: As with bullies and thugs of other stripes, efforts to appease the Islamists *reinforces* their determination to dominate co-religionists and to compel their conformity to shariah. In mosques, the workplace, financial institutions, courtrooms and government, concessions to shariah actually have the practical effect of denying law-abiding, tolerant Muslims who cherish this country the latitude to enjoy and uphold a free society.

As has been shown in this study (notably in the Appendix), there is arguably no better example of this syndrome than the West's embrace of the stealthy jihadist practice of shariah-compliant finance. In the absence of options to conduct their financial affairs in a "shariah-compliant" fashion, Muslims in America are – pursuant to the shariah doctrine of "necessity" – able to engage in transactions the shariah-adherent consider *haram* (impure).

Once such arrangements *are* available, however, theretofore non-adherent Muslims are subjected to intense pressure to conform to shariah. This can result, among other problematic implications, in the latters' tithing through shariah-compliant financial mechanisms that wind up underwriting jihad.

Particularly problematic have been the concerted efforts made by successive U.S. administrations to embrace the Muslim Brotherhood, both here and abroad. As established above, this organization has as its mission "the destruction of Western civilization from within…by its own miserable hand and that of the Brothers."

Relying on Brotherhood operatives for "outreach to the Muslim community," let alone appointing them to influential government jobs, is a formula for disaster. It gives prominence and legitimacy to enemy agents engaged in covert and not-so-covert acts of sedition. It facilitates their penetration and influence over the intelligence, law enforcement and national and homeland security agencies responsible for discerning and defeating such threats.

Importantly, official embrace of MB front organizations and their personnel also has the counterproductive effect of signaling to Muslims who are not shariah-adherent – and therefore, for the moment at least – not the problem, that they should follow and conform to the dictates of those who unalterably *are*. It is hard to imagine a more self-defeating course of action when the best, and possibly only, hope for the survival of Western civilization is to enlist natural allies in the fight against shariah, namely, Muslims who want no more than the rest of us to live under its repression, against their enemies *and ours*: jihadis on a mission to impose shariah.

While detailed recommendations for adopting a more prudential and effective strategy for surviving shariah's onslaught are beyond the scope of this study, several policy and programmatic changes are clearly in order. These include:

- U.S. policy-makers, financiers, businessmen, judges, journalists, community leaders and the public at large must be equipped with an accurate understanding of the nature of shariah and the necessity of keeping America shariah-free. At a minimum, this will entail resisting – rather than acquiescing to – the concerted efforts now being made to allow that alien and barbaric legal code to become established in this country as an alternate, parallel system to the Constitution and the laws enacted pursuant to it. Arguably, this is already in effect for those who have taken an oath to "support and defend" the Constitution, because the requirement is subsumed in that oath.

- U.S. government agencies and organizations should cease their outreach to Muslim communities through Muslim Brotherhood fronts whose mission is to destroy our country from within as such practices are both reckless and counterproductive. Indeed, these activities serve to legitimate, protect and expand the influence of our enemies. They conduce to no successful legal outcome that cannot be better advanced via aggressive prosecution of terrorists, terror-funders and other lawbreakers. They also discourage patriotic Muslims from providing actual assistance to the U.S. government lest they be marked for ostracism or worse by the Brothers and other shariah-adherent members of their communities.

- In keeping with Article VI of the Constitution, extend bans currently in effect that bar members of hate groups such as the Ku Klux Klan from holding positions of trust in federal, state, or local governments or the armed forces of the United States to those who espouse or support shariah. Instead, every effort should be made to identify and empower Muslims who are willing publicly to denounce shariah.

- Practices that promote shariah – notably, shariah-compliant finance and the establishment or promotion in public spaces or with public funds of facilities and activities that give preferential treatment to shariah's adherents – are incompatible with the Constitution and the freedoms it enshrines and must be proscribed.

- Sedition is prohibited by law in the United States. To the extent that imams and mosques are being used to advocate shariah in America, they are promoting seditious activity and should be warned that they will not be immune from prosecution.

- Textbooks used in both secular educational systems and Islamic schools must not promote shariah, its tenets, or the notion that America must submit to its dictates.

- Compounds and communities that seek to segregate themselves on the basis of shariah law, apply it alongside or in lieu of the law of the land or otherwise establish themselves as "no-go" zones for law enforcement and other authorities must be thwarted in such efforts. In this connection, assertion of claims to territory around mosques should be proscribed.

- Immigration of those who adhere to shariah must be precluded, as was previously done with adherents to the seditious ideology of communism.

Such measures will, of course, be controversial in some quarters. They will certainly be contested by shariah-adherent Muslims committed to jihad and others who, in the name of exercising or protecting civil liberties, are enabling the destruction of those liberties in furtherance of shariah.

Far from being dispositive, their opposition should be seen as an opportunity – a chance, at a minimum, for a long-overdue debate about the sorts of policies that have brought the West in general and the United States in particular to the present, parlous state of affairs. If this study catalyzes and usefully informs that debate, it will have succeeded.

APPENDIX I:
SHARIAH-COMPLIANT FINANCE

Shariah-complaint finance (SCF) is a category of investment or financial transactions that is conducted or structured in such a way as to be considered by Islamic authorities to be "legal," "authorized" or "pure" (*halal*) pursuant to shariah. Whether a given transaction is deemed "compliant" depends on the approval of one or more Islamic scholars – men who are recognized by such authorities as possessing the requisite knowledge of shariah and who are engaged to serve on a shariah advisory board for the purpose of vetting each deal.[449]

Proponents of shariah-compliant finance often convey the impression that SCF is an "ethical" financial system whose roots and practice are to be found in the Quran, *hadiths* and traditions of early Islam. In fact, it was invented out of whole cloth in the mid-20th Century by Muslim Brotherhood figures like Sayyid Qutb and Sayyid Abul A'la al-Mawdudi. Its purpose was to provide yet another method to penetrate and undermine Western societies by stealthily insinuating shariah into their capitalist free markets. To this end, the Ikhwan seized upon what was, in fact, a biblical injunction against usury and transformed it into a prohibition on charging or earning *any* interest.

According to the SCF industry, other "impure" activities that must not be allowed to sully financial transactions involve pork, gambling, tobacco, music, drugs, pornography and *Western* defense. (N.B. Transactions involving *Muslim* militaries are not considered *haram*, just those of the United States and its allies, unless they benefit Muslims.)

The shariah-compliant finance industry did not amount to much until the beginning of the present century, when – thanks to the increased price of oil – vast foreign reserves created leverage for the oil-exporting nations, their ruling elites and sovereign wealth funds to demand increasingly SCF options in exchange for recycling their petrodollars. Meanwhile, Western capital market managers and government officials saw an opportunity to repatriate those funds. A number of the most skilled among them set about devising various ingenious gambits that simply *obscured*, rather than actually dispensed with, compensation for the time-value of money.

As long as some shariah authority can be persuaded to bless the construct, it can be marketed as shariah-compliant. Since, without exception, such authorities seek to promote shariah's triumph, they have every incentive to allow the maximum penetration of Western capital markets and have approved an array of mortgages and other lending mechanisms, bonds and investment vehicles that, on close inspection, are artifices for concealing what amounts to interest by any other name.

SHARIAH-COMPLIANT FINANCE'S BENEFITS FOR THE JIHADISTS

The shariah-compliant finance industry provides multiple benefits to the stealth jihadists. For starters, it has created a new instrument for forcing non-shariah-adherent Muslims to conform to their program. Once Western capital markets and governments began accommodating themselves to shariah-compliant finance, such Muslims would be denied the excuse that they previously had to utilize, of "necessity," interest-related finance (for mortgages, bonds, investments, etc.) – namely, simply because no other option existed.

Another benefit to the Ikhwan and its allies: SCF enables the "shariah advisors" to penetrate Western companies that retain their services, often essentially at board level. Once installed as the arbiters of what is *halal* and what is *haram* (impure), these champions of shariah are able to gain insights into investments under consideration, shape deals, and discourage those of which they do not approve.

It stands to reason that from such influential positions, the advisors may be able to have a say not only over transactions involving Muslims, but others, as well. At some point, the mere threat to withdraw approval of large pieces of a bank's lending portfolio, for example, because another part of the enterprise is doing business with, say, Israel, may be sufficient to enforce what amounts to a boycott of the Jewish State. Needless to say, playing such a role would greatly magnify the opportunities shariah-compliant finance provides, in the words of Muslim Brotherhood spiritual leader Yousuf al-Qaradawi, to wage "jihad with money."

That is especially so since SCF affords at least two other ways to advance the stealth jihad, besides directly or indirectly influencing Western financial transactions. In accordance with the Islamic obligation to perform *zakat*, promoters of shariah-compliant finance seek to facilitate and control such charitable donations. Qaradawi and other Muslim Brotherhood operatives calculated that by building automatically deducted *zakat* into their various deals, the advisors could obtain and channel vast sums to approved "charities" in accordance with shariah.

Since three of the eight causes that shariah approves for philanthropy indirectly involve supporting jihad and its perpetrators and another one explicitly does so, SCF amounts to a way to dress up substantial opportunities for illegal material support for terror as a protected religious practice of tithing.

The same can be said of funds derived from the "purification" of financial transactions initially deemed to be shariah-compliant but subsequently determined to be *haram*, instead. By sluicing the profits in this way from investments, financial instruments, etc., that were once deemed acceptable, the shariah advisors are able at their discretion to increase still further the sums available for their favorite charities. The latter tend to be shariah-compliant, stealthy – and at least in some cases, actually *violently* – jihadist "charitable organizations."

'AGENTS OF INFLUENCE'

For some time now, despite the aforementioned, serious problems, Wall Street has been marketing SCF as little more than a kind of "hot," "new" product for American pension funds, insurance companies and corporations. Investment banks and other financial institutions have been hiring Muslim religious authorities to sit on corporate SCF advisory boards that directly influence the investment of billions of U.S. dollars.

By so doing, Wall Street has welcomed Islamic Law into the American financial sector. Among major international firms with a presence on Wall Street that now offer SCF products are: AIG, Bank of America, Citicorp, Goldman Sachs, J.P. Morgan Chase, Merrill Lynch, Morgan Stanley Capital, and Wachovia/Wells Fargo.

What is even worse, the U.S. Department of the Treasury also has been officially promoting SCF throughout the U.S. banking and financial system. For example, in November 2008, Treasury featured a training class for U.S. government employees in association with the Islamic Finance Project at Harvard Law School. Dubbed "Islamic Finance 101," the one-day seminar was intended to familiarize officials from "U.S. banking regulatory agencies, Congress, Department of Treasury and other parts of the Executive Branch" with what the Treasury termed "an increasingly important part of the global financial industry.[450]

The Treasury Department and other agencies of the U.S. government have been warned repeatedly and in detail that – whether it is called "Islamic Finance" or the more clear "Shariah-Compliant-Finance" – SCF is used to legitimate and facilitate the penetration of Shariah. As such, it is inherently antithetical to American law.

Unfortunately, to date, neither Treasury, the Securities and Exchange Commission, the Federal Reserve Board, nor the rest of the federal government has recognized this reality about either shariah or SCF, the financial component of jihad. In fact, in response to a brief, a senior official actually had the temerity to say to a critic of SCF, "I don't know what shariah law is, but it can't possibly be what you say it is."[451] The willful blindness of Treasury officials regarding the threat to U.S. national security posed by Islamic Law constitutes professional malpractice, at a minimum.

AIG: A CASE STUDY

In September 2008, at the height of the U.S. financial crisis, the U.S. government used more than $180 billion of taxpayer funds to buy 79.9 percent of the preferred shares of American International Group (AIG) – a massive insurance company deemed "too big to fail." That purchase made every American taxpayer a part-owner in a company that aggressively promotes SCF. Indeed, AIG is the largest purveyor of shariah-compliant insurance products in the world, thanks to its so-called *Takaful* (or SCF) division that has sold such shariah-based insurance products since 2006. Its Sun America, AIG Financial Services Corp. and other divisions also deal in shariah financial instruments.[452]

In December 2008, the Michigan-based Thomas More Law Center and attorney David Yerushalmi, a litigator expert in security transactions and shariah-compliant financing, filed a lawsuit against the Treasury Department and the Federal Reserve Board alleging that AIG is promoting Islam in violation of the First Amendment's Establishment clause.[453] This constitutional provision requires the separation of church and state.

Clearly, in the case of AIG, the state is actively *promoting* a religious program: shariah. For example, AIG's division for SCF products (which changed its name from AIG Takaful to CHARTIS Takaful (a.k.a. Enaya) in November 2009 and scrubbed its website of shariah references) has explicitly promoted shariah, not just its SCF products.[454]

In addition, in accordance with Islamic Law, AIG's Shariah-compliant business units must not invest funds in any enterprise that does business with religious entities that are *not* Muslim. As noted above, AIG's Shariah-compliant business units may invest in a Muslim-owned arms factory that sells exclusively to Muslim armies – but not one that is owned by Christians or Jews, or that sells weapons to Christians or Jews.

In these and myriad other ways, the U.S. government and taxpayers are effectively made participants by their ownership of AIG in a global campaign to subjugate the world to shariah Islam. While most U.S. taxpayers are completely unaware that they have been embroiled in such activities, officials at the Department of the Treasury, Federal Reserve and Security Exchange Commission have a professional obligation to know. So, too, do those charged with oversight of these agencies on Capitol Hill.

Closely related to the objectionable U.S. ownership of a shariah compliant entity is the fact that the Islamic legal authorities that sit on AIG's board of advisors for shariah compliance are themselves either advocates of jihad in the name of shariah or are the students and disciples of such authorities. Specifically, AIG's takaful advisors include Mufti Imran Usmani, who is the "son, student, and disciple" of Mufti Taqi Usmani.[455] The elder Usmani sat on the Dow Jones Islamic Index shariah advisory board for some 10 years beginning in 1999 during which time, he called on Western Muslims to rise up in violent jihad.[456]

In short, it is clear that the U.S. government, and in particular the U.S. Department of the Treasury, is engaged – wittingly or unwittingly – in conduct calculated to introduce shariah not just into the U.S. banking and financial system, but into the society more generally. Given the wealth of information available to these officials (and explicated throughout this report) about the critical threat posed by shariah to the existing U.S. system of law, their behavior that as the effect of promoting a legal system demonstrably antithetical to the Constitution can only be described as reckless and malfeasant.

Whether reckless out of ignorance or willfully malfeasant, these officials must be held to their oaths of office and, in particular, their sworn obligation to defend, uphold and protect the American legal system as established by the Constitution. (See chapter eight.)

APPENDIX II:
"AN EXPLANATORY MEMORANDUM ON THE GENERAL STRATEGIC GOAL FOR THE GROUP IN NORTH AMERICA"

The following Muslim Brotherhood document was entered into evidence in the *U.S. v Holy Land Foundation* trial, and is a primary source threat document that provides new insights into global jihad organizations like the Muslim Brotherhood. These documents (covered extensively in chapter four) define the structure and outline of domestic jihad threat entities, associated non-governmental organizations and potential terrorist or insurgent support systems. The Memorandum also describes aspects of the global jihad's strategic information warfare campaign and indications of its structure, reach and activities. It met evidentiary standards to be admissible as evidence in a Federal Court of law.

In the original document, the first 16 pages are in the original Arabic and the second are English translations of the same. It is dated May 22, 1991 and titled "An Explanatory Memorandum on the General Strategic Goal for the Group in North America" (Memorandum). The document includes an Attachment 1 that contains *"a list of our organizations and the organizations of our friends."*

The Memorandum expressly recognizes the Muslim Brotherhood (Ikkwan) as the controlling element of these organizations and expressly identifies the Muslim Brotherhood as the leadership element in implementing the strategic goals. The Memorandum is reproduced here in its official Federal Court translation, as Government Exhibit 003-0085 3:04-CR-240-G in *U.S. v Holy Land Foundation, et al.* with punctuation, line spacing and spelling intact.

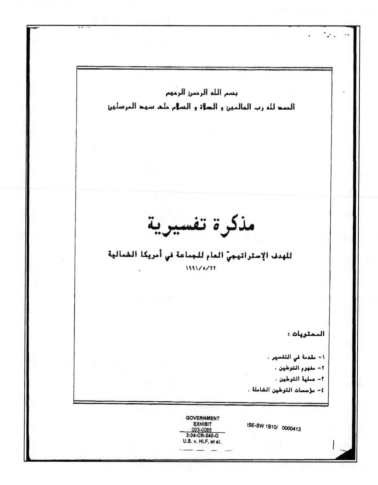

AN EXPLANATORY MEMORANDUM ON THE GENERAL STRATEGIC GOAL FOR THE GROUP IN NORTH AMERICA—5/22/1991

In the name of God, the Beneficent, the Merciful
Thanks be to God, Lord of the Two Worlds
And Blessed are the Pious
The beloved brother/The General Masul, may God keep him
The beloved brother/secretary of the Shura Council, may God keep him
The beloved brothers/Mernbers of the Shura Council, may God keep them
God's peace, mercy and blessings be upon you. ... To proceed,

I ask Almighty God that you, your families and those whom you love around you are in the best of conditions, pleasing to God, glorified His name be.

I send this letter of mine to you hoping that it would seize your attention and receive your good care as you are the people of responsibility and those to whom trust is given. Between your hands is an "Explanatory Memorandum" which I put effort in writing down so that it is not locked in the chest and the mind, and so that I can share with you a portion of the responsibility in leading the Group in this country.

What might have encouraged me to submit the memorandum in this time in particular is my feeling of a "glimpse of hope" and the beginning of good tidings which bring the good news that we have embarked on a new stage of Islamic activism stages in this continent.

The papers which are between your hands are not abundant extravagance, imaginations or hallucinations which passed in the mind of one of your brothers, but they are rather hopes, ambitions and challenges that I hope that you share some or most of which with me. I do not claim their infallibility or absolute correctness, but they are an attempt which requires study, outlook, detailing and rooting from you.

My request to my brothers is to read the memorandum and to write what they wanted of comments and corrections, keeping in mind that what is between your hands is not strange or a new submission without a root, but rather an attempt to interpret and explain some of what came in the long-term plan which we approved and adopted in our council and our conference in the year (1987).

So, my honorable brother, do not rush to throw these papers away due to your many occupations and worries, All what I'm asking of you is to read them and to comment on them hoping that we might continue together the project of our plan and our Islamic work in this part of the world. Should you do that, I would be thankful and grateful to you.

I also ask my honorable brother, the Secretary of the Council, to add the subject of the memorandum on the Council agenda in its coming meeting.

May God reward you good and keep you for His Daw'a

Your brother Moharned Akrarn

In the name of God, the Beneficent, the Merciful
Thanks be to God, Lord of the Two Worlds
And Blessed are the Pious

SUBJECT: A PROJECT FOR AN EXPLANATORY MEMORANDUM FOR THE GENERAL STRATEGIC GOAL FOR THE GROUP IN NORTH AMERICA MENTIONED IN THE LONG-TERM PLAN

One: The Memorandum is derived from:

1. The general strategic goal of the Group in America which was approved by the Shura Council and the Organizational Confer-

ence for the year [1987] is "Enablement of Islam in North America, meaning: establishing an effective and a stable Islamic Movement led by the Muslim Brotherhood which adopts Muslims' causes domestically and globally, and which works to expand the observant Muslim base, aims at unifying and directing Muslims' efforts, presents Islam as a civilization alternative, and supports the global Islamic State wherever it is".

2. The priority that is approved by the Shura Council for the work of the Group in its current and former session which is "Settlement".

3. The positive development with the brothers in the Islamic Circle in an attempt to reach a unity of merger.

4. The constant need for thinking and future planning, an attempt to read it and working to "shape" the present to comply and suit the needs and challenges of the future.

5. The paper of his eminence, the General Masul, may God keep him, which he recently sent to the members of the Council.

Two: An Introduction to the Explanatory Memorandum:

In order to begin with the explanation, we must "summon" the following question and place it in front of our eyes as its relationship is important and necessary with the strategic goal and the explanation project we are embarking on. The question we are facing is: "How do you like to see the Islam Movement in North America in ten years?", or "taking along" the following sentence when planning and working, "Islamic Work in North America in the year (2000): A Strategic Vision".

Also, we must summon and take along "elements" of the general strategic goal of the Group in North America and I will intentionally repeat them in numbers. They are:

[1 - Establishing an effective and stable Islamic Movement led by the Muslim Brotherhood.

2 - Adopting Muslims' causes domestically and globally.

3 - Expanding the observant Muslim base.

4- Unifying and directing Muslims' efforts.

5 - Presenting Islam as a civilization alternative

6 - Supporting the establishment of the global Islamic State wherever it is].

- It must be stressed that it has become clear and emphatically known that all is in agreement that we must "settle" or "enable" Islam and its Movement in this part of the world.

- Therefore, a joint understanding of the meaning of settlement or enablement must be adopted, through which and on whose basis we explain the general strategic goal with its six elements for the Group in North America.

Three: The Concept of Settlement:

This term was mentioned in the Group's "dictionary" and documents with various meanings in spite of the fact that everyone meant one thing with it. We believe that the understanding of the essence is the same and we will attempt here to give the word and its "meanings" a practical explanation with a practical Movement tone, and not a philosophical linguistic explanation, while stressing that this explanation of ours is not complete until our explanation of "the process" of settlement itself is understood which is mentioned in the following paragraph. We briefly say the following:

Settlement: "That Islam and its Movement become a part of the homeland it lives in".

Establishment:	"That Islam turns into firmly-rooted organizations on whose bases civilization, structure and testimony are built".
Stability:	"That Islam is stable in the land on which its people move".
Enablement:	"That Islam is enabled within the souls, minds and the lives of the people of the country in which it moves".
Rooting:	"That Islam is resident and not a passing thing, or rooted "entrenched" in the soil of the spot where it moves and not a strange plant to it".

Four: The Process of Settlement:

- In order for Islam and its Movement to become "a part of the homeland" in which it lives, "stable" in its land, "rooted" in the spirits and minds of its people, "enabled" in the live of its society and has firmly-established "organizations" on which the Islamic structure is built and with which the testimony of civilization is achieved, the Movement must plan and struggle to obtain "the keys" and the tools of this process in carry out this grand mission as a "Civilization Jihadist" responsibility which lies on the shoulders of Muslims and - on top of them - the Muslim Brotherhood in this country. Among these keys and tools are the following:

1- Adopting the concept of settlement and understanding its practical meanings:

The Explanatory Memorandum focused on the Movement and the realistic dimension of the process of settlement and its practical meanings without paying attention to the difference in understanding between the resident and the non-resident, or who is the settled and the non-settled and we believe that what was mentioned in the long-term plan in that regards suffices.

2 - Making a fundamental shift in our thinking and mentality in order to suit the challenges of the settlement mission.

What is meant with the shift - which is a positive expression - is responding to the grand challenges of the settlement issues. We believe that any transforming response begins with the method of thinking and its center, the brain, first. In order to clarify what is meant with the shift as a key to qualify us to enter the field of settlement, we say very briefly that the following must be accomplished:

- A shift from the "amputated" partial thinking mentality to the "continuous" comprehensive mentality.
- A shift from the mentality of caution and reservation to the mentality of risk and controlled liberation.
- A shift from the mentality of the elite Movement to the mentality of the popular Movement.
- A shift from the mentality of preaching and guidance to the mentality of building and testimony
- A shift from the single opinion mentality to the multiple opinion mentality.
- A shift from the collision mentality to the absorption mentality.
- A shift from the individual mentality to the team mentality.
- A shift from the anticipation mentality to the initiative mentality.
- A shift from the hesitation mentality to the decisiveness mentality.
- A shift from the principles mentality to the programs mentality.
- A shift from the abstract ideas mentality the true organizations mentality
[This is the core point and the essence of the memorandum].

3- Understanding the historical stages in which the Islamic Ikhwani activism went through in this country:

The writer of the memorandum believes that understanding and comprehending the historical stages of the Islamic activism which was led and being led by the Muslim Brotherhood in this continent is a very important key in working towards settlement, through which the Group observes its march, the direction of its movement and the curves and turns of its road. We will suffice here with mentioning the title for each of these stages [The title expresses the prevalent characteristic of the stage] [Details maybe mentioned in another future study]. Most likely, the stages are:

A - The stage of searching for self and determining the identity.

B - The stage of inner build-up and tightening the organization.

C - The stage of mosques and the Islamic centers.

D - The stage of building the Islamic organizations - the first phase.

E - The stage of building the Islamic schools - the first phase.

F - The stage of thinking about the overt Islamic Movement - the first phase.

G - The stage of openness to the other Islamic movements and attempting to reach a formula for dealing with them - the first phase.

H - The stage of reviving and establishing the Islamic organizations - the second phase.

We believe that the Group is embarking on this stage in its second phase as it has to open the door and enter as it did the first time.

4- Understanding the role of the Muslim Brother in North America:

The process of settlement is a "Civilization-Jihadist Process" with all the word means. The Ikhwan must understand that their work in America is a kind of grand Jihad in eliminating and destroying the Western civilization from within and "sabotaging" its miserable house by their hands and the hands of the believers so that it is eliminated and God's religion is made victorious over all other religions. Without this level of understanding, we are not up to this challenge and have not prepared ourselves for Jihad yet. It is a Muslim's destiny to perform Jihad and work wherever he is and wherever he lands until the final hour comes, and there is no escape from that destiny except for those who chose to slack. But, would the slackers and the Mujahedeen be equal.

5- Understanding that we cannot perform the settlement mission by ourselves or away from people:

A mission as significant and as huge as the settlement mission needs magnificent and exhausting efforts. With their capabilities, human, financial and scientific resources, the Ikhwan will not be able to carry out this mission alone or away from people and he who believes that is wrong, and God knows best. As for the role of the Ikhwan, it is the initiative, pioneering, leadership, raising the banner and pushing people in that direction. They are then to work to employ, direct and unify Muslims' efforts and powers for this process. In order to do that, we must possess a mastery of the art of "coalitions", the art of "absorption" and the principles of "cooperation".

6- The necessity of achieving a union and balanced gradual merger between private work and public work:

We believe that what was written about this subject is many and is enough. But, it needs a time and a practical frame so that what is needed is achieved in a gradual and a balanced way that is compatible with the process of settlement.

7- The conviction that the success of the settlement of Islam and its Movement in this country is a success to the global Islamic Movement and a true support for the sought-after state, God willing:

There is a conviction - with which this memorandum disagrees - that our focus in attempting to settle Islam in this country will lead to negligence in our duty towards the global Islamic Movement in supporting its project to establish the state. We believe that the reply is in two segments: One - The success of the Movement in America in establishing an observant Islamic base with power and effectiveness will be the best support and aid to the global Movement project.

And the second - is the global Movement has not succeeded yet in "distributing roles" to its branches, stating what is the needed from them as one of the participants or contributors to the project to establish the global Islamic state. The day this happens, the children of the American Ikhwani branch will have far-reaching impact and positions that make the ancestors proud.

8- Absorbing Muslims and winning them with all of their factions and colors in America and Canada for the settlement project, and making it their cause, future and the basis of their Islamic life in this part of the world:

This issues requires from us to learn "the art of dealing with the others", as people are different and people in many colors. We need to adopt the principle which says, "Take from people ... the best they have", their best specializations, experiences, arts, energies and abilities. By people here we mean those within or without the ranks of individuals and organizations. The policy of "taking" should be with what achieves the strategic goal and the settlement process. But the big challenge in front of us is: how to connect them all in "the orbit" of our plan and "the circle" of our Movement in order to achieve "the core" of our interest. To me, there is no choice for us other than alliance and mutual understanding of those who desire from our religion and those who agree from our belief in work. And the U.S. Islamic arena is full of those waiting..., the pioneers.

What matters is bringing people to the level of comprehension of the challenge that is facing us as Muslims in this country, conviction of our settlement project, and understanding the benefit of agreement, cooperation and alliance. At that time, if we ask for money, a lot of it would come, and if we ask for men, they would come in lines, What matters is that our plan is "the criterion and the balance" in our relationship with others.

Here, two points must be noted; the first one: we need to comprehend and understand the balance of the Islamic powers in the U.S. arena [and this might be the subject of a future study]. The second point: what we reached with the brothers in "ICNA" is considered a step in the right direction, the beginning of good and the first drop that requires growing and guidance.

9- Re-examining our organizational and administrative bodies, the type of leadership and the method of selecting it with what suits the challenges of the settlement mission:

The memorandum will be silent about details regarding this item even though it is logical and there is a lot to be said about it.

10- Growing and developing our resources and capabilities, our financial and human resources with what suits the magnitude of the grand mission:

If we examined the human and the financial resources the Ikhwan alone own in this country, we and others would feel proud and glorious. And if we add to them the resources of our friends and allies, those who circle in our orbit and those waiting on our banner, we would realize that we are able to open the door to settlement and walk through it seeking to make Almighty God's word the highest.

11- Utilizing the scientific method in planning, thinking and preparation of studies needed for the process of settlement:

Yes, we need this method, and we need many studies which aid in this civilization Jihadist operation. We will mention some of them briefly:

- The history of the Islamic presence in America.
- The history of the Islamic Ikhwani presence in America.
- Islamic movements, organizations and organizations: analysis and criticism.
- The phenomenon of the Islamic centers and schools: challenges, needs and statistics.
- Islamic minorities.
- Muslim and Arab communities.
- The U.S. society: make-up and politics.
- The U.S. society's view of Islam and Muslims ... And many other studies which we can direct our brothers and allies to prepare, either through their academic studies or through their educational centers or organizational tasking. What is important is that we start.

12- Agreeing on a flexible, balanced and a clear "mechanism" to implement the process of settlement within a specific, gradual and balanced "time frame" that is in-line with the demands and challenges of the process of settlement.

13- Understanding the U.S. society from its different aspects an understanding that "qualifies" us to perform the mission of settling our Dawa' in its country "and growing it" on its land.

14- Adopting a written "jurisprudence" that includes legal and movement bases, principles, policies and interpretations which are suitable for the needs and challenges of the process of settlement.

15- Agreeing on "criteria" and balances to be a sort of "antennas" or "the watch tower" in order to make sure that all of our priorities, plans, programs, bodies, leadership, monies and activities march towards the process of the settlement.

16- Adopting a practical, flexible formula through which our central work complements our domestic work.

[Items 12 through 16 will be detailed later].

17- Understanding the role and the nature of work of "The Islamic Center" in every city with what achieves the goal of the process of settlement:

The center we seek is the one which constitutes the "axis" of our Movement, the "perimeter" of the circle of our work, our "balance center", the "base" for our rise and our "Dar al-Arqam" to educate us, prepare us and supply our battalions in addition to being the "niche" of our prayers.

This is in order for the Islamic center to turn - in action not in words - into a seed "for a small Islamic society" which is a reflection and a mirror to our central organizations. The center ought to turn into a "beehive" which produces sweet honey. Thus, the Islamic center would turn into a place for study, family, battalion, course, seminar, visit, sport, school, social club, women gathering, kindergarten for male and female youngsters, the office of the domestic political resolution, and the center for distributing our newspapers, magazines, books and our audio and visual tapes.

In brief we say: we would like for the Islamic center to become "The House of Dawa'" and "the general center" in deeds first before name. As much as we own and direct these centers at the continent level, we can say we are marching successfully towards the settlement of Dawa' in this country.

Meaning that the "center's" role should be the same as the "mosque's" role during the time of God's prophet, God's prayers and peace be upon him, when he marched to "settle" the Dawa' in its first generation in Madina. from the mosque, he drew the Islamic life and provided to the world the most magnificent and fabulous civilization humanity knew.

This mandates that, eventually, the region, the branch and the Usra turn into "operations rooms" for planning, direction, monitoring and leadership for the Islamic center in order to be a role model to be followed.

18- Adopting a system that is based on "selecting" workers, "role distribution" and "assigning" positions and responsibilities is based on specialization, desire and need with what achieves the process of settlement and contributes to its success.

19- Turning the principle of dedication for the Masuls of main positions within the Group into a rule, a basis and a policy in work. Without it, the process of settlement might be stalled [Talking about this point requires more details and discussion].

20- Understanding the importance of the "Organizational" shift in our Movement work, and doing Jihad in order to achieve it in the real world with what serves the process of settlement and expedites its results, God Almighty's willing:

The reason this paragraph was delayed is to stress its utmost importance as it constitutes the heart and the core of this memorandum. It also constitutes the practical aspect and the true measure of our success or failure in our march towards settlement. The talk about the organizations and the "organizational" mentality or phenomenon does not require much details. It suffices to say that the first pioneer of this phenomenon was our prophet Mohamed, God's peace, mercy and blessings be upon him, as he placed the foundation for the first civilized organization which is the mosque, which truly became "the comprehensive organization". And this was done by the pioneer of the contemporary Islamic Dawa',

Imam martyr Hasan al-Banna, may God have mercy on him, when he and his brothers felt the need to "re-establish" Islam and its movement anew, leading him to establish organizations with all their kinds: economic, social, media, scouting, professional and even the military ones. We must say that we are in a country which understands no language other than the language of the organizations, and one which does not respect or give weight to any group without effective, functional and strong organizations.

It is good fortune that there are brothers among us who have this "trend", mentality or inclination to build the organizations who have beat us by action and words which leads us to dare say honestly what Sadat in Egypt once said, "We want to build a country of organizations" - a word of right he meant wrong with. I say to my brothers, let us raise the banner of truth to establish right "We want to establish the Group of organizations", as without it we will not able to put our feet on the true path.

- And in order for the process of settlement to be completed, we must plan and work from now to equip and prepare ourselves, our brothers, our apparatuses, our sections and our committees in order to turn into comprehensive organizations in a gradual and balanced way that is suitable with the need and the reality. What encourages us to do that - in addition to the aforementioned - is that we possess "seeds" for each organization from the organization we call for [See attachment number (1)].

- All we need is to tweak them, coordinate their work, collect their elements and merge their efforts with others and then connect them with the comprehensive plan we seek. For instance, We have a seed for a "comprehensive media and art" organization: we own a print + advanced typesetting machine + audio and visual center + art production office + magazines in Arabic and English [The Horizons, The Hope, The Politicians, Ila Falastine, Press Clips, al-Zaytouna, Palestine Monitor, Social Sciences Magazines...] + art band + photographers + producers + programs anchors +journalists + in addition to other media and art experiences".

Another example:

We have a seed for a "comprehensive Dawa' educational" organization: We have the Daw'a section in ISNA + Dr. Jamal Badawi Foundation + the center run by brother Harned al-Ghazali + the Dawa' center the Dawa' Committee and brother Shaker al-Sayyed are seeking to establish now + in addition to other Daw'a efforts here and there...".

And this applies to all the organizations we call on establishing.

- The big challenge that is ahead of us is how to turn these seeds or "scattered" elements into comprehensive, stable, "settled" organizations that are connected with our Movement and which fly in our orbit and take orders from ow guidance. This does not prevent - but calls for - each central organization to have its local branches but its connection with the Islamic center in the city is a must.

- What is needed is to seek to prepare the atmosphere and the means to achieve "the merger" so that the sections, the committees, the regions, the branches and the Usras are eventually the heart and the core of these organizations.

Or, for the shift and the change to occur as follows:

1 - The Movement Department + The Secretariat Department	- The Organizational & Administrative Organization - The General Center
2- Education Department + Dawa'a Com.	- Dawa' and Educational Organization
3- Sisters Department	- The Women's Organization
4- The Financial Department + Investment Committee + The Endowment	- The Economic Organization
5- Youth Department + Youths Organizations Department	- Youth Organizations
6- The Social Committee + Matrimony Committee + Mercy Foundation	- The Social Organization
7- The Security Committee	- The Security Organization

8- The Political Depart. + Palestine Com.	- The Political Organization
9- The Group's Court + The Legal Com.	- The Judicial Organization
10- Domestic Work Department	Its work is to be distributed to the rest of the organizations
1 1 - Our magazines + the print + our art band	- The Media and Art Organization
12- The Studies Association + The Publication House + Dar al-Kitab	- The Intellectual & Cultural Organization
13- Scientific and Medial societies	- Scientific, Educational & Professional Organization
14- The Organizational Conference	- The Islamic-American Founding Conference
15- The Shura Council + Planning Com.	- The Shura Council for the Islamic-American Movement
16- The Executive Office	- The Executive Office of the Islamic-American Movement
17- The General Masul	- Chairman of the Islamic Movement and its official Spokesman
18- The regions, branches & Usras	- Field leaders of organizations & Islamic centers

Five: Comprehensive Settlement Organization:

- We would then seek and struggle in order to make each one of these above-mentioned organizations a "comprehensive organization" throughout the days and the years, and as long as we are destined to be in this country. What is important is that we put the foundation and we will be followed by peoples and generations that would finish the march and the road but with a clearly-defined guidance.

And, in order for us to clarify what we mean with the comprehensive, specialized organization, we mention here the characteristics and traits of each organization of the "promising" organizations.

1- From the Dawa' and educational aspect [The Dawa' and Educational Organization]: to include:

- The Organization to spread the Dawa' (Central and local branches).

- An institute to graduate Callers and Educators.

- Scholars, Callers, Educators, Preachers and Program Anchors,

- Art and communication technology, Conveyance and Dawa'.

- A television station.

- A specialized Dawa' magazine.

- A radio station.

- The Higher Islamic Council for Callers and Educators.

- The Higher Council for Mosques and Islamic Centers.

- Friendship Societies with the other religions... and things like that.

2- Politically [The Political Organization]: to include:

- A central political party.

- Local political offices.

- Political symbols.

- Relationships and alliances.

- The American Organization for Islamic Political Action

- Advanced Information Centers ... .and things like that.

3- Media [The Media and Art Organization]: to include:

- A daily newspaper.

- Weekly, monthly and seasonal magazines.

- Radio stations.

- Television programs.

- Audio and visual centers.

- A magazine for the Muslim child.

- A magazine for the Muslim woman.

- A print and typesetting machines.

- A production office.

- A photography and recording studio

- Art bands for acting, chanting and theater.

- A marketing and art production office... and things like that.

4- Economically [The Economic Organization]: to include:

- An Islamic Central bank.
- Islamic endowments.
- Investment projects.
- An organization for interest-free loans... and things like that.

5- Scientifically and Professionally [The Scientific, Educational and Professional Organization]: to include:

- Scientific research centers.
- Technical organizations and vocational training.
- An Islamic university.
- Islamic schools.
- A council for education and scientific research.
- Centers to train teachers.
- Scientific societies in schools.
- An office for academic guidance.
- A body for authorship and Islamic curricula....and things like that.

6- Culturally and Intellectually [The Cultural and Intellectual Organization]: to include:

- A center for studies and research.
- Cultural and intellectual foundations such as [The Social Scientists Society - Scientists and Engineers Society....]
- An organization for Islamic thought and culture.
- A publication, translation and distribution house for Islamic books.
- An office for archiving, history and authentication
- The project to translate the Noble Quran, the Noble Sayings... and things like that.

7- Socially [The Social-Charitable Organization]: to include:

- Social clubs for the youths and the community's sons and daughters

- Local societies for social welfare and the services are tied to the Islamic centers

- The Islamic Organization to Combat the Social Ills of the U.S. Society

- Islamic houses project

- Matrimony and family cases office... and things like that.

8- Youths [The Youth Organization]: to include:

- Central and local youths foundations.

- Sports teams and clubs

- Scouting teams... and things like that.

9- Women [The Women Organization]: to include:

- Central and local women societies.

- Organizations of training, vocational and housekeeping.

- An organization to train female preachers.

- Islamic kindergartens... and things like that.

10- Organizationally and Administratively [The Administrative and Organizational Organization]: to include:

- An institute for training, growth, development and planning

- Prominent experts in this field

- Work systems, bylaws and charters fit for running the most complicated bodies and organizations

- A periodic magazine in Islamic development and administration.

- Owning camps and halls for the various activities.

- A data, polling and census bank.

- An advanced communication network.

- An advanced archive for our heritage and production... and things like that.

11- Security [The Security Organization]: to include:

- Clubs for training and learning self-defense techniques.
- A center which is concerned with the security issues [Technical, intellectual, technological and human]....and things like that.

12- Legally [The Legal Organization]: to include:

- A Central Jurisprudence Council.
- A Central Islamic Court.
- Muslim Attorneys Society.
- The Islamic Foundation for Defense of Muslims' Rights... and things like that.

And success is by God.

A list of our organizations and the organizations of our friends
[Imagine if t they all march according to one plan!!!]

1- ISNA	ISLAMIC SOCIETY OF NORTH AMERICA
2- MSA	MUSLIM STUDENTS' ASSOCIATION
3- MCA	THE MUSLIM COMMUNITIES ASSOCIATION
4- AMSS	THE ASSOCIATION OF MUSLIM SOCIAL SCIENTISTS
5- AMSE	THE ASSOCIATION OF MUSLIM SCIENTISTS AND ENGINEERS
6- IMA	ISLAMIC MEDICAL ASSOCIATION
7- ITC	SLAMIC TEACHING CENTER
8- NAIT	NORTH AMERICAN ISLAMIC TRUST
9- FID	FOUNDATION FOR INTERNATIONAL DEVELOPMENT
10- IHC	ISLAMIC HOUSING COOPERATIVE
11- ICD	ISLAMIC CENTERS DIVISION
12- ATP	AMERICAN TRUST PUBLICATIONS
13- AVC	AUDIO-VISUAL CENTER
14- IBS	ISLAMIC BOOK SERVICE
15- MBA	MUSLIM BUSINESSMEN ASSOCIATION
16- MYNA	MUSLIM YOUTH OF NORTH AMERICA
17- IFC	ISNA FIQH COMMITTEE
18- IPAC	ISNA POLITICAL AWARENESS COMMITTEE
19- IED	ISLAMIC EDUCATION DEPARTMENT
20- MAYA	MUSLIM ARAB YOUTH ASSOCIATION
21- MISG	MALASIAN [sic] ISLAMIC STUDY GROUP
22- IAP	ISLAMIC ASSOCIATION FOR PALESTINE
23- UASR	UNITED ASSOCIATION FOR STUDIES AND RESEARCH
24- OLF	OCCUPIED LAND FUND

25- MIA	MERCY INTERNATIONAL ASSOCIATION
26- ISNA	ISLAMIC CIRCLE OF NORTH AMERICA
27- BMI	BAITUL MAL INC
28- IIIT	INTERNATIONAL INSTITUTE FOR ISLAMIC THOUGHT
29- IIC	ISLAMIC INFORMATION CENTER

ABOUT THE AUTHORS

 Lieutenant General William G. "Jerry" Boykin
US Army (Ret.) served primarily in Delta Force
and Special Forces assignments during his 36-year
career in the Army, which culminated with ap-
pointment as Deputy Undersecretary of Defense
for Intelligence in the Pentagon, overseeing the gathering and exploitation of intelligence during the wars in Afghanistan and Iraq.
He is an original member of the Army's elite Delta Force and participated in almost all of the U.S.'s special operations since 1979,
including the Desert One hostage-rescue attempt in Iran in 1980,
Panama in 1989, and the invasion of Grenada in 1983, where he
was wounded by a .50 caliber machine-gun round through the
chest. Gen. Boykin attended the Armed Forces Staff College,
Army War College and received his Masters Degree at Shippens-
burg University. His badges include the Master Parachutist Badge,
Military Freefall Badge, Ranger Tab and Special Forces Tab.
Medals and awards include: the Service Medal, Defense Superior
Service Medal (with 3 Oak Leaf Clusters), Legion of Merit (with
Oak Leaf Cluster), Bronze Star Medal, Air Medal, and two Purple
Hearts (with Oak Leaf Cluster).

Lieutenant General Edward Soyster, US Army (Ret.) was a career Army officer with staff and command assignments at all levels. All of his assignments as a general officer were in intelligence culminating as Director, Defense Intelligence Agency during Panama Invasion and Desert Shield/Storm.

 Christine Brim is the Chief Operating Officer, Center for Security Policy. She has over twenty years experience in risk management, business continuity planning and disaster recovery planning. She has published in the areas of communications and logistics. She received her MBA from George Mason University with a focus on decision support systems.

 Ambassador Henry F. Cooper is Chairman of the Board of Directors of High Frontier and Chairman Emeritus of Applied Research Associates. Ambassador Cooper was appointed by the President to serve as Deputy Assistant Secretary of the Air Force with oversight responsibility for Air Force strategic and space systems and has served as Assistant Director of the Arms Control and Disarmament Agency, Ambassador and Chief U.S. Negotiator at the Geneva Defense and Space Talks with the Soviet Union, and Director of the Strategic Defense Initiative (SDI). In the private sector, he taught Engineering Mechanics at Clemson University, and worked at Bell Telephone Laboratories, R&D Associates, JAYCOR and Applied Research Associates. He served in the U.S. Air Force and as Scientific Advisor to the Air Force Weapons Laboratory. Throughout his career, he served on numerous technical and policy working groups and advisory boards—including the Defense Science Board, the Air Force Scientific Advisory

Board, U.S. Strategic Command's Strategic Advisory Group, the Defense Nuclear Agency's Scientific Advisory Group on Effects, and a Congressional Commission to assess the U.S. government's organization and programs to combat the proliferation of weapons of mass destruction. He holds BS and MS degrees from Clemson University and a PhD from New York University, all in Mechanical Engineering.

Stephen C. Coughlin, Esq. is an attorney and holds the rank of Major in the U.S. Army Reserves. He is a specialist on Islamic Sharia Law, Islamic doctrine and ideology, and the strategic information/War of Ideas with experience in international law, intelligence, strategic communications and project management. He holds a Masters degree in Strategic Intelligence, with a focus on global terrorism and Jihadist movements; his JD is from the William Mitchell School of Law.

Michael del Rosso is an accomplished technology executive whose career spans 30 years. He has served as CEO and CTO of large public companies and early stage companies. He is a Senior Member of the Institute of Electrical and Electronics Engineers (IEEE), past Chairman of the IEEE-USA Critical Infrastructure Protection Committee (CIPC), a 2006 Lincoln Fellow at The Claremont Institute where he is presently Research Fellow in National Security Policy, Senior Fellow for Homeland and National Security at the Center for Security Policy, and has been a Certified Information Systems Security Professional (CISSP).

Frank Gaffney is the Founder and President of the Center for Security Policy in Washington, D.C., a not-for-profit, non-partisan educational corporation established in 1988. Mr. Gaffney is the host of Secure Freedom Radio, a nationally-syndicated radio program heard weeknights throughout the country that addresses current and emerging threats to national security, sovereignty and our ways of life. Mr. Gaffney is the lead-author of *War Footing: Ten Steps America Must Take to Prevail in the War for the Free World* (Naval Institute Press, 2005), a highly acclaimed volume that constitutes an "owner's manual" for the new global conflict in which America finds itself engaged - the War for the Free World. Mr. Gaffney also contributes actively to the security policy debate in his capacity as a weekly columnist and contributor to National Review Online and other nationally syndicated columns and radio programs. In 1987, Mr. Gaffney was nominated by President Reagan to become the Assistant Secretary of Defense for International Security Policy, the senior position in the Defense Department with responsibility for policies involving nuclear forces, arms control and U.S.-European defense relations. Previously, from August 1983 until November 1987, Mr. Gaffney was the Deputy Assistant Secretary of Defense for Nuclear Forces and Arms Control Policy under Assistant Secretary Richard Perle. Mr. Gaffney holds a Master of Arts degree in International Studies from the Johns Hopkins University School of Advanced International Studies and a Bachelor of Science in Foreign Service from the Georgetown University School of Foreign Service.

John Guandolo is a 1989 graduate of the U.S. Naval Academy, who took a commission as an Officer in the United States Marine Corps. He served with 2d Battalion 2d Marines as an Infantry Platoon Commander in combat in Operations Desert Shield/Storm. Mr. Guandolo was a combat diver, a military freefall parachutist, and is a graduate of U.S. Army Ranger School. In 1996, Mr. Guandolo resigned his commission in the Marine Corps to join the Federal Bureau of Investigation, serving at the Washington Field Office where he conducted narcotics investigations domestically and overseas; in 2001, he served for one year as the FBI Liaison to the U.S. Capitol Police investigating threats against the President, Vice-President, Members of Congress, and other high-level government officials. Shortly after 9/11, Mr. Guandolo began an assignment to the Counterterrorism Division of the Washington Field Office working there for over five years and developing an expertise in the Muslim Brotherhood, Islamic Doctrine, the global Islamic Movement, and myriad terrorist organizations to include Hamas, Al Qaeda, and others. In 2006, Mr. Guandolo created and implemented the FBI's first Counterterrorism Training/Education Course focusing on the Muslim Brotherhood and their subversive movement in the United States, Islamic Doctrine, and the global Islamic Movement. Mr. Guandolo currently works advising governments— U.S. and others—on matters related to National Security, specifically the threat from the Global Islamic Movement. He actively educates members of law enforcement, the intelligence community, military, national guard, key community leaders.

Brian T. Kennedy is President of the Claremont Institute. Mr. Kennedy has been with the Institute since 1989. He became the fourth president of the Claremont Institute in 2002. During his tenure he has directed the Institute's Golden State Center in Sacramento and also the Institute's National Security Project. In addition to his duties as president, Mr. Kennedy serves as publisher of the Claremont Review of Books and is a member of the Independent Working Group on Missile Defense. His articles on national security affairs and public policy issues have appeared in The Wall Street Journal, National Review, and Investor's Business Daily. Mr. Kennedy is a native Californian and a graduate of Claremont McKenna College.

 **Clare M. Lopez** is a strategic policy and intelligence expert with a focus on Middle East, national defense, and counterterrorism issues. Currently a senior fellow at the Center for Security Policy and vice president of the Intelligence Summit, she formerly was a career operations officer with the Central Intelligence Agency and Executive Director of the Iran Policy Committee from 2005-2006. Ms. Lopez is deputy director of the U.S. Counterterrorism Advisory Team for the Military Department of the South Carolina National Guard and serves as a member of the Board of Advisors for the Center for Democracy and Human Rights in Saudi Arabia, the Institute of World Affairs, and the Intelligence Analysis and Research program at her undergraduate alma mater, Notre Dame College of Ohio. She has been a Visiting Researcher and guest lecturer at Georgetown University. Ms. Lopez is a regular contributor to print and broadcast media on subjects related to Iran and the Middle East and the co-author of two published books on Iran. She is the author of an acclaimed paper for the Center, The Rise of the Iran Lobby. Ms. Lopez received a B.A. in Communications and French from Notre Dame College of Ohio and an M.A. in International Relations from the Maxwell School of Syracuse University. She completed Marine Corps Officer Candidate School (OCS) in Quantico, Virginia before declining a commission to join the CIA.

Admiral James A. "Ace" Lyons, Jr. (U.S. Navy, Ret.), is President/CEO of LION Associates LLC. As an Officer of the U.S. Navy for thirty-six years, most recently as Commander in Chief of the U.S. Pacific Fleet, the largest single military command in the world, Admiral Lyons' initiatives contributed directly to the economic stability and humanitarian understanding in the Pacific and Indian Ocean regions and brought the U.S. Navy Fleet back to China. He also served as Senior U.S. Military Representative to the United Nations. As the Deputy Chief of Naval Operations from 1983–1985, he was principal advisor on all Joint Chiefs of Staff matters and was the father of the Navy Red Cell, an anti-terrorism group comprised of Navy Seals he established in response to the Marine Barracks bombing in Beirut. Admiral Lyons was also Commander of the U.S. Second Fleet and Commander of the NATO Striking Fleet, which were the principal fleets for implementing the Maritime Strategy. As Fleet Commander he managed a budget of over $5 billion and controlled a force of 250,000 personnel. He is a graduate of the U.S. Naval Academy and has received post graduate degrees from the U.S. Naval War College and the U.S. National Defense University.

Andrew C. McCarthy is the author of two *New York Times* bestsellers, *Willful Blindness* (2008) and, most recently, *The Grand Jihad*. He is a senior fellow at the National Review Institute, and a contributing editor at *National Review*. For 18 years he was an assistant United States attorney in the Southern District of New York, and in 1995 he led the terrorism prosecution against the "Blind Sheikh" (Omar Abdel Rahman) and the jihadist cell that carried out the World Trade

Center bombing and plotted to attack New York City landmarks. After the 9/11 attacks, he supervised the U.S. attorney's command post near Ground Zero.

Patrick Poole is one of the nation's leading analysts on issues related to the Muslim Brotherhood and terrorist activities in the United States. He is a primary presenter at the U.S. Army Counterterrorism conference, and has briefed numerous law enforcement and intelligence units throughout America. Mr. Poole is a journalist writing for several think tanks, publications, and blog sites regarding national security issues, specifically pertaining to the Muslim Brotherhood Movement, and has done international work involving Eastern Europe, Latin America, and Asia. His articles on jihadist ideology and Islamic radicalization have appeared in the *Journal of International Security Affairs*, the *Journal on Counterterrorism and Homeland Security* and the *Middle East Review of International Affairs*.

 **Joseph E. Schmitz** served as the fifth Senate-confirmed Inspector General of the Department of Defense from April 2002 to September 2005. As such, he was agency head of the most expansive Inspector General organization in the world, with statutory policy oversight responsibility for roughly 60,000 auditors, investigators, inspectors, law enforcement officers, and oversight professionals throughout the Department of Defense. Prior to that, he was a Partner in the international law firm of Patton Boggs LLP, and at the same time, as a Naval Reservist, served as Inspector General of the Naval Reserve Intelligence Command. Mr. Schmitz currently serves as CEO of JOSEPH E. SCHMITZ, PLLC, the core values of which are integrity, transparent accountability, disciplined teamwork, and independ-

ence. He graduated with distinction from the U.S. Naval Academy and earned his J.D. degree from Stanford Law School.

 **Tom Trento** is the Director of the Florida Security Council, an organization specializing in international terrorism research and grassroots activism. Trento works to alert the public about the growing threat of Islamic terrorism, its legal system known as shariah, and its intent to destroy Western culture. A dynamic speaker with degrees in Law Enforcement, Theology, and Philosophy, Tom communicates the menace of shariah, organize grassroots action, and produce advocacy videos challenging any Islamic effort to undermine the US Constitution.

 **J. Michael Waller,** Vice President for Information Operations, Center for Security Policy. A journalist and author, Dr. Waller brings expertise in terrorism, intelligence, the former Soviet Union and the Americas. He has covered wars and political violence in five countries, has written for Insight magazine, Reader's Digest, the Washington Times and the Wall Street Journal and has served as a consultant to the U.S. Department of State. He holds a Ph.D. in international security affairs from Boston University, and is a former staff member of the United States Senate. He holds the Walter and Leonore Annenberg Chair in International Communication at the Institute of World Politics, a graduate school of national security.

 **Diana West** is the author of *The Death of the Grown-Up: How America's Arrested Development Is Bringing Down Western Civilization* (St Martin's Press). She writes a weekly column that ap-

pears in about 120 newspapers, including the Washington Examiner on Sundays. Her work has appeared in many publications including The Wall Street Journal, The Washington Times, The New Criterion, The Public interest, The Weekly Standard, In Character, and The Washington Post Magazine, and her fiction has appeared in the Atlantic Monthly. She has made numerous television appearances as a CNN contributor to "Lou Dobbs Tonight" and "Lou Dobbs This Week." She is now at work on her second book for St Martin's Press, *The Hollow Center*.

 R. James Woolsey, Chairman, Woolsey Partners LLC is also a Venture Partner and Senior Advisor to VantagePoint Venture Partners, of Counsel to the law firm of Goodwin Procter, and chairman of the Strategic Advisory Group of Paladin Capital Corporation. In 2009 he was the Annenberg Distinguished Visiting Fellow at the Hoover Institution at Stanford University. Before he joined VantagePoint, Mr. Woolsey was a partner with Booz Allen Hamilton and previously a partner with Shea & Gardner law firm. He also held Presidential appointments in four administrations -- two Democratic, two Republican -- serving as Director of Central Intelligence (1993-95).

 **David Yerushalmi**, Esq., General Counsel to the Center for Security Policy. Mr. Yerushalmi is a lawyer specializing in litigation and risk analysis, especially as it relates to geo-strategic policy, national security, international business relations, securities law, disclosure, and due diligence requirements for domestic and international concerns. David Yerushalmi has been involved in international legal and constitutional matters for over 25 years. David Yerushalmi is today considered an expert on Is-

lamic law and its intersection with Islamic terrorism and national security. In this capacity, he has published widely on the subject including the principal critical scholarship on Shariah-compliant finance published in the Utah Law Review (2008, Issue 3). This work and the empirical investigation known as the Mapping Shariah project in America was the focus of a recent monograph published by the McCormack Foundation and the Center for Security Policy.

NOTES

---

1 See, e.g., "Muslim Public Opinion on US Policy, Attacks on Civilians and al Qaeda," University of Maryland Program on International Policy Attitudes, April 24, 2007, http://www.worldpublicopinion.org

2 See in this regard, Andrew McCarthy, "Which Islam Will Prevail in America," August 20, 2010, http://www.nationalreview.com/articles/244349/which-islam-will-prevail-america-andrew-c-mccarthy.

3 Mohamad Akram, *An Explanatory Memorandum: On the General Strategic Goal for the Group,* May 22, 1991, Government Exhibit 003-0085/3:04-CR-240-G U.S. v. HLF, et al., United States District Court, Northern District of Texas, http://www.txnd.uscourts.gov/judges/hlf2/09-25-08/Elbarasse%20Search%203.pdf, 18. Hereafter cited as *Explanatory Memorandum.*

4 Paragraph 1, §§ 1 and 2, *Explanatory Memorandum*, 18. Reads:

One: The Memorandum is
derived from:

1 - The general strategic goal of the Group in America which was approved by the *Shura* Council and the Organizational Conference for the year [1987] is "Enablement of Islam in North America, meaning: establishing an effective and a stable Islamic Movement led by the Muslim Brotherhood which adopts Muslims' causes domestically and globally, and which works to expand the observant Muslim base, aims at unifying and directing Muslims'

efforts, presents Islam as a civilization alternative, and supports the global Islamic State wherever it is".

Two: An Introduction to the Explanatory Memorandum:
In order to begin with the explanation, we must "summon" the following question and place it in front of our eyes as its relationship is important and necessary with the strategic goal and the explanation project we are embarking on. The question we are facing is: "How do you like to see the Islam Movement in North America in ten years?", or "taking along" the following sentence when planning and working, "Islamic Work in North America in the year (2000): A Strategic Vision". Also, we must summon and take along "elements" of the general strategic goal of the Group in North America and I will intentionally repeat them in numbers. They are: 1- Establishing an effective and stable *Islamic Movement led by the Muslim Brotherhood.*

5 Paragraph 4, *Explanatory Memorandum*, 20. Reads:

Four: The Process of Settlement:

In order for Islam and its Movement to become "a part of the homeland" in which it lives, "stable" in its land, "rooted" in the spirits and minds of its people, "enabled" in the lives of its society and has firmly-established "organizations" on which the Islamic structure is built and with which the testimony of civilization is achieved, the Movement must plan and struggle to obtain "the keys" and the tools of this process in carry out this grand mission as a "Civilization Jihadist" responsibility which lies on the shoulders of Muslims and - on top of them - the Muslim Brotherhood in this country. Among these keys and tools are the following ...

6 Paragraph 4, § 4, *Explanatory Memorandum*, 21. Reads:

4- Understanding the role of the Muslim Brother in North America:

The process of settlement is a "Civilization-Jihadist Process" with all the word means. The *Ikhwan* must understand that their work in America is a kind of grand Jihad in eliminating and destroying the Western civilization from within and "sabotaging" its miserable house by their hands and the hands of the believers so that it is eliminated and God's religion is made victorious over all other religions. Without this level of understanding, we are not up to this challenge and have not prepared ourselves for Jihad yet. It is a Muslim's destiny to perform Jihad and work wherever he is and wherever he lands until the final hour comes, and there is no escape from that destiny except for those who chose to slack. But, would the slackers and the Mujahedeen be equal.

7 Newt Gingrich, "America at Risk: Camus, National Security and Afghanistan," accessed August 1, 2010, http://www.aei.org/video/101267

8 See, for example, Congressional Muslim Staff Association briefing on Capitol Hill, September 1, 2010.

9 See, for example, http://www.tabletmag.com/news-and-politics/42898/lawless/Lee Smith" September 5th, 2010, http://www.tabletmag.com/news-and-politics/42898/lawless/.

10 Ahmad ibn Naqib al-Misri, Umdat al-Salik (*Reliance of the Traveller: A Classic Manual of Islamic Sacred Law*), rev. ed., trans. Nuh Ha Mim Keller. (Beltsville, Amana Publications, 1994) ', Chapter h8.17, 272.

11 Quran Sura 65:4 describes the waiting period for a divorce to be final: "Such of your women as have passed the age of monthly courses, for them the prescribed period, if ye have any doubts, is three months; and for those who have no courses (it is the same)."

12 al-Misri, *Reliance of the Traveler*, Chapter ol.2, pgs. 583-84 enumerates those categories of Muslims who "are not subject to retaliation" for killing: "(4) a father or mother (or their fathers or mothers) for killing their offspring, or offspring's offspring."

13 al-Misri, *Reliance of the Traveler*, Chapter o4.3: "Circumcision is obligatory (for both men and women.....for women, removing the prepuce of the clitoris...)."

14 Quran Sura 4:3: "...marry women of your choice, two, or three, or four..."

15 Quran Sura 4:34: "....And to those women on whose part ye fear disloyalty and ill-conduct, admonish them (first), (next) refuse to
share their beds, (and last) beat them...."

16 Quran Sura 2:233: "Your wives are as a tilth unto you, so approach your
tilth when or how ye will...."

17 Maxim Lott, "Advocates of Anti-Shariah Measures Alarmed by Judge's
Ruling," *Fox News*, August 5, 2010, accessed August 6, 2010,
http://www.foxnews.com/us/2010/08/05/advocates-anti-
shariah-measures-alarmed-judges-ruling/

18 Shamim A Siddiqi, *Methodology of Dawah Ilallah In American Perspective*, (Brooklyn, NY, 1989). The text in full is available online, accessed July 18, 2010,
http://www.dawahinamericas.com/bookspdf/MethodologyofDa
wah.pdf

19 *Explanatory Memorandum* , 18.

20 Paragraph 1, §§ 1 and 2, *Explanatory Memorandum*, 18. Reads:

One: The Memorandum is derived from:

1 - The general strategic goal of the Group in America which was
approved by the *Shura* Council and the Organizational Conference for the year [1987] is "Enablement of Islam in North America, meaning: establishing an effective and a stable *Islamic Movement led by the Muslim Brotherhood* which adopts Muslims' causes
domestically and globally, and which works to expand the observant Muslim base, aims at unifying and directing Muslims' efforts,
presents Islam as a civilization alternative, and supports the global
Islamic State wherever it is."

Two: An Introduction to the Explanatory Memorandum:
In order to begin with the explanation, we must "summon" the following question and place it in front of our eyes as its relationship
is important and necessary with the strategic goal and the explanation project we are embarking on. The question we are facing is:
"How do you like to see the Islam Movement in North America in
ten years?", or "taking along" the following sentence when planning and working, "Islamic Work in North America in the year

(2000): A Strategic Vision". Also, we must summon and take along "elements" of the general strategic goal of the Group in North America and I will intentionally repeat them in numbers. They are: 1- Establishing an effective and stable *Islamic Movement led by the Muslim Brotherhood.*

21 Paragraph 4, *Explanatory Memorandum*, 20. Reads:

Four: The Process of Settlement:

In order for Islam and its *Movement* to become "a part of the homeland" in which it lives, "stable" in its land, "rooted" in the spirits and minds of its people, "enabled" in the lives of its society and has firmly-established "organizations" on which the Islamic structure is built and with which the testimony of civilization is achieved, the *Movement* must plan and struggle to obtain "the keys" and the tools of this process in carry out this grand mission as a *"Civilization Jihadist"* responsibility which lies on the shoulders of Muslims and - on top of them - the *Muslim Brotherhood* in this country. Among these keys and tools are the following ...

22 Paragraph 4, § 4, *Explanatory Memorandum*, 21. Reads:

4- Understanding the role of the Muslim Brother in North America:

The process of settlement is a "Civilization-Jihadist Process" with all the word means. The *Ikhwan* must understand that their work in America is a kind of grand Jihad in eliminating and destroying the Western civilization from within and "sabotaging" its miserable house by their hands and the hands of the believers so that it is eliminated and God's religion is made victorious over all other religions. Without this level of understanding, we are not up to this challenge and have not prepared ourselves for Jihad yet. It is a Muslim's destiny to perform Jihad and work wherever he is and wherever he lands until the final hour comes, and there is no escape from that destiny except for those who chose to slack. But, would the slackers and the Mujahedeen be equal.

23 Robert Spencer, *Stealth Jihad: How Radical Islam is Subverting America Without Guns or Bombs*, Regnery Publishing, 2008.

24 Sayyid Qutb, *Milestones*, (Salimiah, Kuwait: International Islamic Federation of Student Organizations.1978 [written 1966]), 139.

25 Louay M. Safi, *Peace and the Limits of War: Transcending Classical Conception of Jihad.* (Herndon, VA: IIIT, 2001), 42.

26 U.S. v Holy Land Foundation case, No. 43, Attachment A, List of Unindicted Co-conspirators and/or Joint Ventures, United States of America vs. Holy Land Foundation, United States District Court for Northern District of Texas, Dallas Division, (Case 3:04-cr-00240, Document 656-2), 29 March 2007, at 8, at http://www.websupp.com/data/NDTX/3:04-cr-00240-635-NDTX.pdf or at http://www.nefafoundation.org/miscellaneous/HLF/US_v_HLF_Unindicted_Coconspirators.pdf

27 Government Exhibit: Philly Meeting - 15, 3:04-CR-240-G, U.S. v. HLF, et al., at 2,3, at http://www.txnd.uscourts.gov/judges/hlf2/09-29-08/Philly%20Meeting%2015.pdf

28 Steven Merley, "The Muslim Brotherhood in the United States," *Research Monographs on the Muslim World*, Series No 2, Paper No 3 (Hudson Institute, Washington, DC, April 2009), Appendix II, 52.

29 "List of Unindicted Co-conspirators and/or Joint Venturers," *United States of America v. Holy Land Foundation for Relief and Development, Attachment A*, in the online library of the NEFA Foundation, pp 1-11, accessed September 8, 2010, http://www.nefafoundation.org/miscellaneous/HLF/US_v_HLF_Unindicted_Coconspirators.pdf

30 Andrew C. McCarthy, "The Government's Jihad on *Jihad*," *The National Review Online*, May 13, 2008, accessed September 8, 2010, http://www.nationalreview.com/articles/224461/governments-jihad-i-jihad-i/andrew-c-mccarthy

31 Patrick Poole, "Willful Blindness: Army Unprepared for Another Jihadist Attack," May 3, 2010, http://pajamasmedia.com/blog/willful-blindness-army-unprepared-for-another-jihadist-attack

32 Accessed August 28th, 2010, http://www.defense.gov/news/d20100820FortHoodFollowon.pdf

33 *Ibid.*

34 "Ahmadinejad: Israel must be wiped off map," *Gulf Times* (Qatar), October 27, 2005 (http://www.gulf-times.com/site/topics/article.asp?cu_no=2&item_no=58372&version=1&template_id=37&parent_id=17).

35 The White House, Office of the Press Secretary, Remarks by John O. Brennan, Assistant to the President for Homeland Security and Counterterrorism—As Prepared for Delivery: "A New Approach to Safeguarding Americans," *Center for Strategic and International Studies*, James S. Brady Press Briefing Room, Washington, DC, August 6, 2009.

36 "Counterterror Adviser Defends Jihad as 'Legitimate Tenet of Islam,'" *Fox News*, May 27, 2010.

37 al-Misri, *Reliance of the Traveler,*, (Chapter o9.0), "Jihad," 599.

38 "Backgrounder: The President's Quotes on Islam," *News and Policies/Policies in Focus*, the White House, http://merln.ndu.edu/MERLN/PFIraq/archive/wh/islam1.pdf

39 "Remarks by the President on Strengthening Intelligence and Aviation Security," The White House, Office of the Press Secretary, January 7th, 2010, accessed April 29th, 2010, http://www.whitehouse.gov/the-press-office/remarks-president-strengthening-intelligence-and-aviation-security

40 Gary DeMary, "America's 200-Year War with Islamic Terrorism: The Strange Case of the Treaty of Tripoli" ;2009, http://www.americanvision.org/mediafiles/americas-200-year-old-war-with-islam.pdf

41 See Major Hasan's Power Point presentation at JihadWatch.org: http://www.Jihadwatch.org/images/MAJ%20Hasan%20Slides.pdf

42 Former Joint Chiefs of Staff expert Stephen Coughlin modified an existing briefing to show the fidelity of Major Hasan's presentation to shariah. On Hasan's acceptability as am "acting" substitute for the Fort Hood Imam based on that imam's assessment, see http://abcnews.go.com/video/playerIndex?id=9013819 accessed September 27, 2010.

43 Robert Spencer, "Islamic Radical Tied to New Boston Mosque," *Jihad Watch*, March 9, 2004, accessed August 5, 2010, http://www.jihadwatch.org/2004/03/islamic-radical-tied-to-new-boston-mosque.html

44 Explanatory Memorandum

45 "Criminal Complaint, United States of America vs. Abdurahman Mohammed Alamoudi, United States District Court, Eastern District of Virginia", September 2003, accessed April 29, 2010, http://fl1.findlaw.com/news.findlaw.com/hdocs/docs/terrorism/usalamoudi93003cmp.pdf

46 al-Misri, *Reliance of the Traveler*, h8.17, 272.

47 al-Misri, '*Reliance of the Traveler*, o1.2, 583-84 enumerates those categories of Muslims who "are not subject to retaliation" for killing: "(4) a father or mother (or their fathers or mothers) for killing their offspring, or offspring's offspring."

48 al-Misri, *Reliance of the Traveler*, m10.4, 538. See also Quran Sura 4:34: "....And to those women on whose part ye fear disloyalty and ill-conduct, admonish them (first), (next) refuse to share their beds, (and last) beat them...."

49 al-Misri, *Reliance of the Traveler*, o4.3: "Circumcision is obligatory (for both men and women.....for women, removing the prepuce of the clitoris...)."

50 Quran Sura 4:3: "...marry women of your choice, two, or three, or four..."

51 Mohammed ibn Isma'il Bukhari, *The Translation of the Meaning of Sahih al-Bukhari*, trans. Mohammed Muhsin Khan, 8 vols. (Medina, Dar al-Fikr: 1981) 5:58.234

52 al-Misri, *Reliance of the Traveler*, m3.7, 520.

53 al-Misri, *Reliance of the Traveler*, m5.1, 525.

54 al-Misri, *Reliance of the Traveler*, o1.2, pgs. 583-84 enumerates those categories of Muslims who "are not subject to retaliation" for killing: "(4) a father or mother (or their fathers or mothers) for killing their offspring, or offspring's offspring."

55 Quran Sura 2:233: "Your wives are as a tilth unto you, so approach your tilth when or how ye will...."

56 Maxim Lott, "Advocates of Anti-shariah Measures Alarmed by Judge's Ruling," *Fox News*, August 5, 2010. Accessed August 6, 2010, http://www.foxnews.com/us/2010/08/05/advocates-anti-shariah-measures-alarmed-judges-ruling/

57 Imran Ahsan Khan Nyazee, *Theories of Islamic Law: The Methodology of Ijtihad.*, 2d ed., (Kuala Lumpur: The Other Press, 2002), 50. For example, from a contemporary Pakistani law professor:

> Islam, it is generally acknowledged, is a "complete way of life" and at the core of this code is the law of Islam. This implies that a Muslim through his submission to Islam not only accepts the unity of Allah, the truth of the mission of Mohammed, but also agrees through a contract (*bay'ah*) with the Muslim community that his life be regulated in accordance with the *ahkam* of Allah, and in accordance with these *ahkam* alone. No other sovereign or authority is acceptable to the Muslim, unless it guarantees the application of these laws in their entirety. Any other legal system, howsoever attractive it may appear on the surface, is alien for Muslims and is not likely to succeed in the solution of their problems; it would be doomed from the start. ... A comprehensive application of these laws, which flow directly or indirectly from the decrees (*ahkam*) of Allah, would mean that they should regulate every area of life, from politics to private transactions, from criminal justice to the laws of traffic, from ritual to international law, and from the laws of taxation and finance to embezzlement and white collar crimes.

58 Jerrold M. Post, *Leaders and their Followers in a Dangerous World: The Psychology of Political Behavior,* (Cornell University Press: Ithaca, NY, 2004), 139, citing Amir Taheri, *Holy Terror,* (unknown binding, 1989).

"It is the nature of Islam to dominate, not to be dominated, to impose its law on all nations and to extend its power to the entire planet."

59 Andrew Bostom, "Shiite Iran's Genocidal Jew-Hatred: Part 3," accessed August 6, 2010,
http://www.andrewbostom.org/blog/2008/07/20/390/

60 Jason Burke and Ian Traynor, "Fears of an Islamic Revolt in Europe Begin to Fade," *The Guardian Observer,* July 26, 2009, accessed July 4, 2010,
http://www.guardian.co.uk/world/2009/jul/26/radicalisation-european-muslims

61 Sayyid Qutb, *Milestones,* (Salimiah, Kuwait: International Islamic Federation of Student Organizations, 1978 [written 1966]), 139.

62 Majid Khadduri, *War and Peace in the Law of Islam,* (Baltimore, 2006), 64. See also Andrew Bostom, *The Legacy of Jihad* (Amherst, NY: Prometheus, 2005), 95-6.

63 Siddiqi, Methodology of Dawah Ilallah, 57.

64 See the Mapping Shariah Project at https://www.mappingsharia.us

65 See The Investigative Project on Terrorism, directed by Steven Emerson, for a voluminous collection of the Holy Land Foundation trial documents at http://www.investigativeproject.org

66 Accessed September 9, 2010, http://www.shoebat.com/bio.php

67 Accessed September 9, 2010, http://www.kamalsaleem.com/

68 Accessed September 9, 2010,
http://www.ignatius.com/Products/SOH-H/son-of-hamas.aspx

69 Nyazee, *Theories of Islamic Law: The Methodology of Ijtihad,* 118, 119, 318, 316.

70 Amir Taheri, *Holy Terror: Inside the World of Islamic Terrorism* (Adler & Adler, 1987), 241-3.

71 Yahiya Emerick, Yahiya Emerick. What Islam is all About: A Student Textbook, Grades 7 to 12, 5th rev. ed. (Lebanon, Noorart, 2004), 354.

72 See, for example, Congressional Muslim Staff Association briefing on Capitol Hill, September 1, 2010.

73 See, for example, Lee Smith, accessed September 5th, 2010, http://www.tabletmag.com/news-and-politics/42898/lawless

74 "Sources of Islamic Law," *Legal Service India*, accessed August 16, 2010, http://www.legalserviceindia.com/article/l302-Sources-of-Islamic-Law.html

75 Asaf A.A. Fyzee, *Outlines of Mohammedan Law*, 4th ed. (Delhi, India: Oxford University Press, 1974), 19. Cited hereafter as Fyzee.

76 al-Misri, *Reliance of the Traveler*, vii.

77 David Bukay, "Peace of Jihad? Abrogation in Islam," *Middle East Quarterly*, Fall 2007 (3-11), accessed June 7, 2010, http://www.meforum.org/1754/peace-or-Jihad-abrogation-in-islam

78 Qutb, *Milestones*, 28, 29.

79 Slide 16 "Conclusions," Major Nidal M. Hasan, "Koran," June 2007, first given to fellow psychiatrist/interns at Walter Reed Army Hospital in Washington, D.C., published by the Washington Post as a PowerPoint in PDF format at URL: http://www.washingtonpost.com/wp-dyn/content/gallery/2009/11/10/GA2009111000920.html, 5 November 2009. Cited hereafter as "Slide # "slide title," Major Hasan Briefing."

80 Slide 35 "Example: Jihad-rule of Abrogation," Major Hasan Briefing

81 It is important to note that there is no consensus on the use of the *Sira* to arrive at shariah. The *Sira* is mentioned here merely as the accompanying component of the *Sunna* to the *ahadith* but should in no way be considered their legal equivalent.

82 See, for example, Q 3:103, 3:110, 4:59 and 4:115

83 Abdur Rahman I. Doi, *Shariah: The Islamic Law.* (Kuala Lampur: A.S. Noordeen, 1984), 5. Cited hereafter as Doi, *shariah.*

84 Mohammed Hashim Kamali, *Principles of Islamic Jurisprudence,* 3d rev. ed., (Cambridge, UK, The Islamic Text Society, 2003), 8.

85 Kamali, *Principles,* 8.

86 Nyazee, *Theories of Islamic Law: The Methodology of Ijtihad,* 50.

87 Nyazee, *Ijtihad,* at 50.

88 Doi, *shariah,* 466.

89 al-Misri, *Reliance of the Traveler,* at § b2.1, Reads: b2.0. The Koranic Evidence for Following Scholars, b2.1 (Mohammed Sa'id Buti:) "The first aspect of it is the work of Allah the Majestic, *'Ask those who recall if you know not'* (Qur'an 16:43). By *consensus of all the scholars* (ijma), this verse is an imperative for someone who does not know a ruling in Sacred Law or the evidence for it to follow someone who does. *Virtually all scholars* of fundamental Islamic law have made this verse their principle evidence that it is obligatory for the ordinary person to follow the scholar who is a *mujtahid.*"89 (Emphasis added.)

90 al-Misri, *Reliance of the Traveler* at §§ b7.1 and b7.2:

§ b7.1: ("Abd al-Wahhab Khallaf:) Scholarly consensus *(ijma)* is the agreement of all the *mujtahids* of the Muslims existing at one particular period after the Prophet's death (Allah bless him and give him peace) about a particular ruling regarding a matter or event."
§ b7.2 "When the ... necessary integrals of consensus exist, the ruling agreed upon is an authoritative part of Sacred Law that is obligatory to obey and not lawful to disobey. Nor can *mujtahids* of a succeeding era make the thing an object of new *ijtihad,* because the ruling on it, verified by scholarly consensus, is an absolute ruling which does not admit of being contravened or annulled."

91 Hamdy Al-Husseini & Abdullah Farag, IOL Correspondents, "IAMS Delegation to Visit Darfur: Al-Qaradawi," *IslamOnline.net,* Hamdy

Al-Husseini & Abdullah Farag, September 1, 2006, accessed June 12 2010, http://www.islamonline.net/English/News/2004-09/01/article02.shtml

92 Doi, *shariah*, 465, 466.

93 Emerick. *What Islam is all About*, 381.

94 Emerick, *What Islam is All About*, 377.

95 Emerick, *What Islam is All About*, 376.

96 See Mark Durie, *The Third Choice: Islam, Dhimmitude and Freedom*, (Deror Books, 2009).

97 Douglas E. Streusand, "What Does Jihad Mean?" *Middle East Quarterly*, September 1997. For a listing of all appearances in the Quran of Jihad and related words, see Mohammed Fu'ad 'Abd al-Baqi, *Al-Mu'jam al-Mufahras li-Alfaz al-Quran al-Karim* (Cairo, Matabi' ash-Sha'b, 1278), 182-83; and Hanna E. Kassis, *A Concordance of the Quran* (Berkeley: University of California Press, 1983), 587-88.

98 Bukhari, Hadith, 4:34:204.

99 *Bukhari, Hadith* ,4:196:124

100 al-Misri, *Reliance of the Traveler*.

101 *Ibid.*, § o9.0, "Jihad," 599.

102 *Ibid.*

103 *Ibid.*

104 Burhan al-Din al-Farghani, al-Marghinani, *Al-Hidaya: The Guidance*, 2 vols. Trans. Imran Ahsan Khan Nyazee. (Bristol, England, Amal Press, 2008). As cited in Andrew Bostom, *The Legacy of Jihad*, 27.

105 Abu al-Walid Mohammed ibn Ahmad ibn Rushd, (aka Averroës), *The Distinguished Primer (Bidayat al-Mujtahid wa Nihayat al-Muqtasid)*. 2 vols. Trans. Imran Ahsan Khan Nyazee. (Reading, Garnet Publishing, 2002). As cited in Andrew Bostom, *The Legacy of Jihad* ,147-160.

106 Mohammed ibn al-Hasan al-Shaybani. *The Islamic Law of Nations: Shaybani's Siyar (Kitab al-siyar al-kabir).* Trans. Majid Khadduri. (Baltimore, Johns Hopkins University Press, 1966). As cited in Andrew Bostom, *The Legacy of Jihad,* , 182-3.

107 Streusand.

108 Qutb, *Milestones,*

109 Qutb, *Milestones,* 127.

110 Quran 3:104, 110 commands Muslims to "enjoin the good and forbid the evil." This phrase covers the entire moral content of Islam.

111 Johannes J.G. Jansen, "The Neglected Duty: The Creed of Sadat's Assassins and Islamic Resurgence in the Middle East." (1986), accessed May 4, 2010, http://gertrudebelljar.typepad.com/the_gertrude_belljar/2003/03/the_neglected_d.html

112 Brigadier S. K. Malik, Pakistani Army, *The Quranic Concept of War,* First Indian Reprint, (New Delhi, India, Himalayan Books, 1986).

113 Brigadier S.K. Malik, *The Quranic Concept of War* (with a forward by General Zia-ul-Haq), (Lahore, Pakistan, Wajid Al's Ltd., 1979), (This paper relies on the 1986 First Indian Reprint). Cited hereafter as S.K. Malik, xi.

114 S.K. Malik, xiii.

115 Translating Jihad, March 18, 2010, http://translating-Jihad.blogspot.com/2010/03/moheet-purpose-of-Jihad-is-to-establish.html

116 The Legacy of Jihad, 28
117 Etan Kohlberg, "The Development of the Imami Shi'i Doctrine of Jihad", *Zeitschrift der Deutschen Morgenländischen Gesellschaft,* 1976, 126, 64–86; 80-81.
118 *Ibid.* 80
119 *Ibid.*
120 *Ibid.* 81; also The Legacy of Jihad, 28,88, 213-220, 620-622.
121 *The Legacy of Jihad,* 28.

122 Kohlberg, "The Development of the Imami Shi'i Doctrine of Jihad",
    81-83.

123 Ibid. 83.

124 Quoted from Ibn Warraq, *Why I am Not A Muslim,* (Prometheus
    Books, 1995), 11-12, 381. See also Amir Taheri, *Holy Terror,*
    (London, 1987) 226-227.

125 Andrew Bostom, *The Legacy of Jihad,* 125.

126 "Shariah-Compliant Finance: Benign or Belligerent?" Continuing Le-
    gal Education Course (Law Offices of David Yerushalmi, P.C.
    May 2009), http://www.davidyerushalmi.com/Law-Offices-of-
    David-Yerushalmi-present-shariah-compliant-finance--disclosure-
    -seminar-for-online-viewing-b9-p1.html See also Andrew Bos-
    tom, *The Legacy of Jihad,* 147-160.

127 Ibn Rushd. As cited in Andrew Bostom, *The Legacy of Jihad,* 147-160.

128 Andrew Bostom, *The Legacy of Jihad,* , 182.

129 *Ibid.*

130 *Ibid.*

131 *Ibid.*

132 *The Meaning of the Holy Quran,* 10th ed., trans. 'Abdullah Yusuf 'Ali
    (Beltsville: Amana Publications, 1999). Cited hereafter as Yusuf
    Ali.

133 Bukhari, Hadith 52:269

134 Bukhari, Hadith, 7:67:427

135 al-Misri, *Reliance of the Traveler,* Book O "Justice," at o9.0 "Jihad," at
    o9.16: "Truces."

    (O: As for truces, the author does not mention them. In Sacred
    Law truce means a peace treaty with those hostile to Islam, involv-
    ing a cessation of fighting for a specified period, whether for pay-
    ment or something else. The scriptural basis for them includes
    such Quranic verses as: *"An acquittal from Allah and His Messen-
    ger…"* (9:1) and *"If they incline towards peace, then incline towards
    it also"* (8:61) as well as the truce which the Prophet (Allah bless

him and give him peace) made with the Quraish in the year of Hudaybiyyah, as related by Bukhari and Muslim.

Truces are permissible, not obligatory. The only one who may effect a truce is the Muslim ruler of a region (or his representative) with a segment of the non-Muslims of the region, or the caliph (o22) (or his representative). When made with other than a *portion* of the non-Muslims, or when made with all of them, or with all in a particular region such as India or Asia Minor, then only the caliph (or his representative) may effect it, *for it is a matter of the gravest consequence because it entails the nonperformance of jihad, whether globally or in a given locality, and our interest must be looked after therein,* which is why it is best left to the caliph under any circumstances, or to someone he delegates to see to the interests of the various regions.

136 Nyazee, *Ijtihad,* 172. As cited in Andrew Bostom, *The Legacy of Jihad ,* 182.

137 Al-Shaybani, 182.

138 Khadduri, *War and Peace in the Law of Islam,* , 158-159.

139 Patrick Sookhdeo,*Global Jihad: The Future in the Face of Militant Islam,* (Isaac Publishing, McLean, Virginia, 2007).

140 "Turkey's Charismatic, Pro-Islamic Leader," *BBC News,* November 4, 2002. The 1998 speech in which Erdogan recited these lines from an Islamic poem landed him in jail for inciting religious hatred. Some five years later, in 2003, he became Turkey's Prime Minister. Accessed June 15, 2010, http://news.bbc.co.uk/2/hi/europe/2270642.stm

141 Sookhdeo, *Global Jihad.*

142 Olivier Mandon, *Tableau de bord des zones franches urbaines en Ile-de-France,* éditions IAURIF, (Paris, 2007) (60 pages). See also Daniel Pipes, "The 751 No Go Zones of France," November 14, 2006, accessed August 26, 2010, http://www.danielpipes.org/blog/2006/11/the-751-no-go-zones-of-france

143 al-Misri, *Reliance of the Traveler,* Book O "Justice," § o8.0 "Apostasy from Islam (*RIDDA*)," at §§ o8.0 and o8.1.

144 Alan Wall, Abdul Rahman and the 'New' Afghanistan, NewMax.com, 24 March 2006, URL: http://archive.newsmax.com/ archives/articles/2006/3/23/161702.shtml?s=lh

145 al-Misri, *Reliance of the Traveler,* Book O, "Justice," at o8.0.

146 al-Misri, 'al-Misri, *Reliance of the Traveler,* Book C "The Nature of Legal Rulings," at §c2.5.

147 Safi, *Peace and Limits of War,* at 32.

148 Quran 40:28

149 al-Misri, *Reliance of the Traveler,* at §§r7.0, r7.1.

150 al-Misri, *Reliance of the Traveler,* at §r7.1(1)

151 al-Misri, *Reliance of the Traveler,* at §r8.2

152 al-Misri, *Reliance of the Traveler,* at §r8.2

153 al-Misri, *Reliance of the Traveler,* at § r8.2

154 Quran 66:1

155 Quran 13:27

156 Bukhari, Hadith,7:67:427

157 al-Misri, *Reliance of the Traveler,* at §r10.3

158 Al-Hafiz Abu al-Fida' 'Imad Ad-Din Isma'il bin 'Umar bin Kathir Al-Qurashi Al-Busrawi ibn Kathir, *Tafsir of Ibn Kathir,* Vol. 2, Translated by Abdul-Malik Mujahid. (Riyadh, Darussalam, 2000), 141.

159 Raymond Ibrahim, "Islam's doctrines of deception," *Middle East Forum,* October 2008, accessed July 17, 2010, http://www.meforum.org/2095/islams-doctrines-of-deception

160 William Gawthrop, "Islam's Tools of Penetration," CIFA Working Brief, April 19, 2007, slides 6, 7, 15.

161 No 43, Attachment A, List of Unindicted Co-conspirators and/or Joint Ventures, United States of America vs. Holy Land Founda-

tion, United States District Court for Northern District of Texas, Dallas Division, (Case 3:04-cr-00240, Document 656-2), 29 March 2007, at 8, at http://www.websupp.com/data/NDTX/3:04-cr-00240-635-NDTX.pdf or at http://www.nefafoundation.org/ miscellane-ous/HLF/US_v_HLF_Unindicted_Coconspirators.pdf. Cited hereafter as Attachment A, US v HLF.

162 Government Exhibit: Philly Meeting - 15, 3:04-CR-240-G, U.S. v. HLF, et al., at 2,3, at http://www.txnd.uscourts.gov/judges/hlf2/09-29-08/Philly%20Meeting%2015.pdf

163 Raymond Ibrahim, "War and Peace—and Deceit—in Islam," *Pajamas Media*, February 12, 2009. Accessed July 17, 2010 at http://www.raymondibrahim.com/7347/war-and-peace-and-deceit-in-islam

164 *Ibid.*

165 Al-Qaradawi, Yousuf, "Why is secularism incompatible with Islam?" *Saudi Gazette*, 11 June 2010.

166 "Criticism of Sheikh Al-Qaradhawi's 'Islamist Democracy' Doctrine," *Middle East Media Research Institute* (MEMRI), Special Dispatch No. 740, July 7, 2004, Accessed June 17, 2010 at http://www.memri.org/report/en/0/0/0/0/0/0/1166.htm

167 Tariq Alhomayed, "The Political Activist Yusuf al-Al-Qaradawi," *Asharq Alawsat* (the London-based daily), January 21, 2010, ac-cessed June 12, 2010, http://www.alarabiya.net/views/2010/01/21/98050.html

168 Hamdy Al-Husseini & Abdullah Farag, IOL Correspondents, "IAMS Delegation to Visit Darfur: Al-Qaradawi," *IslamOnline.net*, Sep-tember 1, 2006, accessed June 12, 2010, http://www.islamonline.net/English/News/2004-09/01/article02.shtml

169 al-Misri, *Reliance of the Traveler*, Book R "Holding One's Tongue," r2.0 "Slander," r2.2.

170 *Ibid.,* r2.0 "Slander," r2.1, r2.2.

171 *Ibid.,* r2.0 "Slander," r2.6.

172 *Ibid.,* r3.0 "Talebearing (*Namima*)," r3.1.

173 Authors' Note: This does not mean that the inputs from someone beholden to such a rule should not be heard but rather only that there is risk associated with basing a decision on information that is solely dependent on inputs that may have been filtered to meet requirements that may not accord with national strategic objectives.

174 "The Muslim Brotherhood's Official English Website," accessed August 21, 2010, http://www.ikhwanweb.com. See also "The Muslim Brotherhood Arabic website, accessed August 22, 2010, http://www.ikhwanonline.com (Recommend Google Translator, from Arabic to English, http://www.google.com/language_tools?hl=en)

175 Qutb, *Milestones*, 12.

176 Muslim Brotherhood website, accessed September 9, 2010, http://www.ikhwanweb.com/article.php?id=794

177 Explanatory Memorandum, *ibid.,* 18.

178 Accessed on August 28th, 2010, http://www.ikhwanweb.com/article.php?id=22687

179 "*Selected Government Exhibits & Documents from U.S. v. Holy Land Foundation,*" NEFA Foundation, accessed September 4, 2010, http://www.nefafoundation.org/hlfdocs.html

180 Official Muslim Brotherhood Website, www.ikhwanweb.com

181 Steven Emerson, "Report on the Roots of Violent Islamist Extremism and Efforts to Counter It: The Muslim Brotherhood," *Hearing before the Committee on Homeland Security and Governmental Affairs,* United States Senate, July 10, 2008, accessed September 1, 2010, http://www.gpo.gov/fdsys/pkg/CHRG-110shrg942/html/CHRG-110shrg942.htmReport and http://counterterrorismblog.org/2008/07/steven_emersons_statement_for.php

182 Ehud Rosen, "The Muslim Brotherhood's Concept of Education," *Current Trends in Islamist Ideology*, vol. 7 (Hudson Institute, Washington DC, 2008), 115.

183 Israel Elad Altman, *Strategies of the Muslim Brotherhood Movement, 1928-2007*, Research Monographs on the Muslim World, Series No 2, Paper No 2 (Hudson Institute, Washington DC, February 2009), 7.

184 Encyclopedia Britannica (Turkey/Ataturk)

185 Official Muslim Brotherhood Website, www.ikhwanweb.com

186 Muslim Brotherhood website, accessed September 7, 2010, http://www.ikhwanweb.com/article.php?id=22687

187 US v HLF, Gov't Exhibit, "Ikhwan in America, Zeid." Transcript of Senior Muslim Brother Zeid Noman speaking to Muslim Brothers in the U.S. in 1980's about the settlement of the MB in America.

188 Ziad Munson, "Islamic Mobilization: Social Movement Theory and the Egyptian Muslim Brotherhood," *The Sociological Quarterly* 42(4), January 2002.

189 Accessed on August 21, 2010, http://www.ikhwanweb.com/article.php?id=24152

190 Interview with Ghaleb Himmat by Ian Johnson

191 Ian Johnson, *A Mosque in Munich: Nazis, the CIA, and the Rise of the Muslim Brotherhood in the West* (Houghton Mifflin Harcourt, NY, 2010)

192 *Ibid.*

193 U.S. Customs interview of Soliman Biheri, 6/02/04, Case# DC02PU02DC0005

194 *Ibid.*

195 Michael Whine, "The Advance of the Muslim Brotherhood in the UK," *Current Trens in Islamist Ideology*, vol. 2 (Hudson Institute, Washington DC, 2005), 30.

196 Interview with Ahmed al-Rawi, 7/21/04, Markfield (UK)

197 "Sheik Yusuf al-Qaradawi: Theologian of Terror," Anti-Defamation League Biography, accessed September 5, 2010, http://www.adl.org/main_Arab_World/al_Qaradawi_report_2 0041110.htm

198 UOIF Official website, accessed September 8, 2010, http://www.uoif-online.com/v2/

199 Lorenzo Vidino, "The Muslim Brotherhood's Conquest of Europe," *Middle East Quarterly*, Winter 2005, 25-34.

200 Whine, *ibid.*, 36.

201 Vidino, *ibid.*

202 Press Release, U.S. Department of Treasury, 8/29/02, PO-3380

203 Jean-Charles Brisard, "Al Taqwa, the Ramadan brothers and Pakistani radicals," *JCB, International Expert on Terrorism and Terrorism Financing*, accessed September 10, 2010, http://jcb.blogs.com/jcb_blog/2005/11/ali_ghaleb_himm.html

204 Shiraz Maher, "UK: The Rise of The Muslim Voting Bloc," *Hudson New York Briefing Council*, April 15, 2010, accessed September 8, 2010, http://www.hudson-ny.org/1150/uk-the-rise-of-the-muslim-voting-bloc

205 Declassified CIA Report of July 1953 entitled "Comments on the Islamic Colloquium" in Washington, D.C. CIA RDP83-00423R001300710001

206 Merley, "The Muslim Brotherhood in the United States,", 11.

207 Merley, *ibid.*

208 Sheikh Hisham Kabbani, President, Islamic Supreme Council of America. Speech to U.S. State Department, January 7, 1999.

209 Merley, *ibid.*

210 "Ismail Selim Elbarasse," Case File, The Investigative Project On Terrorism, accessed September 8, 2010, http://www.investigativeproject.org/case/453

211 US v HLF Trial Transcripts. See
    www.nefafoundation.org/hlfdocs2.html for more information.

212 "Federal Jury in Dallas Convicts Holy Land Foundation and Its Lead-
    ers for Providing Material Support to Hamas Terrorist Organiza-
    tion," Department of Justice Press Release, November 24, 2008,
    accessed September 9, 2010,
    http://www.justice.gov/opa/pr/2008/November/08-nsd-
    1046.html

213 "Fight Over Co-Conspirator List Continues," *The Investigative Project
    on Terrorism Blog,* August 30, 2010, accessed September 5, 2010,
    http://www.investigativeproject.org/blog/2010/08/fight-over-
    co-conspirator-list-continues

214 US v HLF, Government Exhibit, "An Explanatory Memorandum,"
    May 1991

215 Steven Emerson, "Fairfax Cop Who Tipped Terror Suspect Helped
    Kill Training Program," *The Investigative Project on Terrorism,* May
    9, 2008, accessed September 5, 2010,
    http://www.investigativeproject.org/664/fairfax-cop-who-
    tipped-terror-suspect-helped-kill-training

216 Statements provided to authors by current and former FBI agents, and
    an agent currently serving with DHS.

217 Unsigned and undated Muslim Brotherhood document known as
    "Phases of World Underground Movement Plan."
    http://www.centerforsecuritypolicy.org/upload/wysiwyg/article
    %20pdfs/Underground%20Movement%20Plan.pdf

218 On the phases of Muslim Brotherhood tactics, see Paul Sperry and
    David Gaubatz, *Muslim Mafia: Inside the Secret Underworld That's
    Conspiring to Islamize America* (WND Books, 2009), 259; also Pa-
    trick Sookhdeo, *Faith, Power, Territory: A Handbook of British Is-
    lam* (Isaac Publishing, 2008), 75; also Zeyno Baran, "The Muslim
    Brotherhood's U.S. Network," *Current Trends in Islamist Ideology
    Vol 6* (Center on Islam, Democracy and the Future of the Modern
    World, Hudson Institute, Washington, DC, 2008), pp 95-122; al-
    so Israel Elad Altman, *Strategies of the Muslim Brotherhood Move-*

ment 1928-2007, Research Monographs on the Muslim World, Series No 2, Paper No 2, (Hudson Institute, Washington DC, February 2009), 16-17.

219 US v Alamoudi, Plea Agreement, Eastern District of Northern Virginia, 7/29/04

220 "Religious Expressions in Public Schools," U.S. Department of Education, April 1995

221 Alamoudi Profile accessed on August 28, 2010, http://www.discoverthenetworks.org/individualProfile.asp?indid =1311 See Also Steven Emerson, "Friends of Hamas in the White House," *Wall Street Journal,* March 13, 1996, accessed September 8, 2010, http://www.investigativeproject.org/349/friends-of-hamas-in-the-white-house

222 United States Senate Committee On The Judiciary Subcommittee on Terrorism, Technology and Homeland Security Staff Report, *Two Years After 9/11: Keeping America Safe,* March 2004, 11; see also "Abdul Rahman Al-Amoudi," *Charlie Rose [Public Television Program],* November 21, 1994, accessed September 8, 2010, http://www.charlierose.com/guest/view/5164

223 "Feds Arrest Va. Man For Libya Ties: Muslim Activist Accused Of Accepting Illegal Funds From Libya" CBS News, September 29, 2003, accessed September 8, 2010 http://www.cbsnews.com/stories/2003/09/29/terror/main575 749.shtml ; see also U.S. SOCOM press release, accessed September 10, 2010, http://www.southcom.mil/AppsSC/files/2UI2I1169400163.pdf

224 Paul E. Sperry, *Infiltration: How Muslim Spies and Subversives Have Penetrated Washington,* (Thomas Nelson Inc. ,NY, 2005), accessed September 8, 2010, canceled checks facsimiles posted at (http://sperryfiles.com/images/8-1a.jpg)

225 Sperry, *ibid.,* Chapter "Penetrating the White House"

226 Kenneth Timmerman, "Islamist's Front Man," *Insight Magazine,* February 24, 2004.

227 "In Difficult Times Muslims Count on Unlikely Advocate," *Wall Street Journal*, June 11, 2003, *accessed* September 8, 2010 http://www.rifailaw.com/wallstreetjournalnorquist.html;see also "Friends in High Places," St. Petersburg Times, March 11, 2003; accessed September 8, 2010 http://www.sptimes.com/2003/03/11/Floridian/Friends_in_hi gh_place.shtml ; see also "Suhail Khan versus Frank Gaffney Debate", audio, accessed September 8, 2010, http://www.archive.org/details/FrankGaffneyVs.SuhailKhan ;see also "Some Reflections on the Rashad Hussain Affair," Global Muslim Brotherhood Daily Report, February 28, 2010, accessed September 8, 2010, http://globalmbreport.org/?p=2350

228 "Rally at Lafayette Park: Alamoudi", October 28, 2000, video and transcript , accessedSeptember 8, 2010, http://www.investigativeproject.org/218/rally-at-lafayette-park-alamoudi.

229 Jerry Markon, "Muslim activist sentenced to 23 years for Libya contacts," *Washington Post*, October 16, 2004, Accessed August 6, 2010, http://www.washingtonpost.com/ac2/wp-dyn/A36718-2004Oct15?language=printer

230 Daniel Pipes, "United States of America vs. Abdurahman Muhammad Alamoudi ", September 29, 2003 (updated through October 27, 2008), accessed September 8, 2010, http://www.danielpipes.org/blog/2003/09/united-states-of-america-vs-abdurahman . A highly detailed and well-sourced history of the Alamoudi case.

231 Patrick Poole, "The Muslim Brotherhood 'Project,'" *Front Page Magazine*, May 11th, 2006, Document text in full may be found at http://www.onthewing.org/user/Islam%20-%20Muslim%20Brotherhood%20Project.pdf

232 Siddiqui, *Methodology of Dawah Ilallah in American Perspective*

233 Explanatory Memorandum, *ibid.*

234 See the ISNA website at
http://www.isna.net/Conferences/pages/Annual-
Convention.aspx for details about its 2010 Annual Convention.

235 See Andrew C. McCarthy's discussion of his experience with this pressure precluding cooperation from patriotic Muslims in the course
of his prosecution of the Blind Sheikh Omar Abdul Rahman,
http://www.nationalreview.com/articles/244349/which-islam-
will-prevail-america-andrew-c-mccarthy, as accessed on August
28, 2010.

236 The Authors have preserved a Screen Save of the earlier version of the
MSA website. [See
http://www.centerforsecuritypolicy.org/teamb]

237 See the MSA website, www.msanational.org

238 Steven Emerson, "Muslim Students Association: The Investigative
Project on Terrorism Dossier," *The Investigative Project on Terrorism,* accessed August 5, 2010,
http://www.investigativeproject.org/documents/misc/84.pdf

239 See http://www.youtube.com/watch?v=zuNva3j12X0 for the video-
taped statement by Jumanah Imad Albahri, an MSA member at
the University of California, San Diego in which she explicitly
called for the rounding up of Jews to be killed.

240 Andrew Elliott, "The Jihadist Next Door," *New York Times,* January
27th, 2010, accessed July 18, 2010,
http://www.nytimes.com/2010/01/31/magazine/31Jihadist-
t.html

241 Emerson, "Muslim Students Association: The Investigative Project on
Terrorism Dossier."

242 US v HLF, Gov't Exhibit, "A Historical Outline and the Main Issue,"
10/25/91

243 Mohamed Elsanousi," The Islamic Society of North America (ISNA)",
accessed July 18, 2010,
http://learningtogive.org/faithgroups/phil_in_america/islam_n
a.asp

244 "Government's Memorandum in Opposition to Council on American Islamic Relations' Motion for Leave to File a Brief *Amicus Curiae Instanter* and *Amicus* Brief in Support of the Unindicted Co-Conspirators' First and Fifth Amendment Rights." Full document text accessed 18 July 2010 at http://www.investigativeproject.org/documents/case_docs/479.pdf

245 See ISNA website, http://www.isna.net. As accessed August 12, 2010.

246 FBI Action Memorandum from FBI Counterterrorism Assistant Director Dale Watson to Director, Office of Foreign Asset Control Richard Newcomb, November 5, 2010.

247 FBI Analysis of Philadelphia Meeting, entered into evidence: US v HLF

248 US v HLF, Gov't Exhibit, "Islamic Action for Palestine," October 1992.

249 *Ibid.*

250 *Ibid.*

251 *Ibid.*

252 "Government's Memorandum in Opposition to Council on American Islamic Relations' Motion for Leave to File a Brief *Amicus Curiae Instanter* and *Amicus* Brief in Support of the Unindicted Co-Conspirators' First and Fifth Amendment Rights." Full document text accessed July 18, 2010, http://www.investigativeproject.org/documents/case_docs/479.pdf

253 *Ibid.*

254 CAIR Action Alert #609, "FBI Visits Prompt Reminder of Muslims' Legal Rights," May 21, 2010, accessed July 18, 2010, http://www.cair.com/ArticleDetails.aspx?mid1=763&&ArticleID=26404&&name=n&&currPage=1

255 Paul Sperry and David Gaubatz, *Muslim Mafia: Inside the Secret Underworld That's Conspiring to Islamize America,* (WND Books, 2009).

256 Paul Sperry's website, Accessed August 28, 2010,
http://www.sperryfiles.com..

257 Letter from Assistant Attorney General for Legislative Affairs Ronald
Weich to Rep. Sue Myrick, February 12, 2010, accessed September 6, 2010,
http://www.investigativeproject.org/documents/misc/360.pdf

258 The Center for Security Policy's website,
http://www.centerforsecuritypolicy.org and
http://www.cairobservatory.org

259 "Grand Jury's CAIR Probe Points to Hamas," *The Investigative Project
on Terrorism*, February 2, 2010, accessed July 18, 2010,
http://www.investigativeproject.org/1772/grand-jurys-cair-
probe-points-to

260 "Muslim American Society Dossier," The Investigative Project on Terrorism, accessed September 9, 2010,
http://www.investigativeproject.org/profile/169

261 US v HLF, Gov't Exhibit, Elbarasse Address Book

262 http://www.investigativeproject.org/1013/mahdi-brays-secret-
checkered-past. Accessed August 21, 2010.

263 "Mahdi Bray: Voting with Conviction," *The Investigative Report on Terrorism*, March 27, 2009, accessed September 6, 2010,
http://www.investigativeproject.org/1015/mahdi-bray-voting-
with-conviction

264 http://mahdibray.net/2010/08/17/mas-freedom-press-conference-
demonstrates-broad-interfaith-support-for-muslim-religious-
freedoms-mosque-construction/. Accessed August 29, 2010.

265 http://mahdibray.net/2010/06/09/mas-embraces-staten-island-
community-and-rebuffs-attempts-by-islamophobic-propaganda-
to-stop-the-building-of-a-mosque/. Accessed August 29, 2010.

266 http://religion.blogs.cnn.com/2010/07/23/new-york-catholic-
church-rejects-mosque-
plan/?utm_source=twitterfeed&utm_medium=twitter. Accessed
August 29, 2010.

267 *Ibid.*

268 http://bigpeace.com/cbrim/2010/08/29/coming-august-31-direct-access-stimulus-grants-for-the-muslim-brotherhood/. Accessed August 29, 2010.

269 "Backgrounder On the Fiqh Council of North America and the Council on American-Islamic Relations," The Investigative Project on Terrorism, accessed September 9, 2010, http://www.investigativeproject.org/FCNA-CAIR.html

270 "The Muslim Public Affairs Council (MPAC) Dossier," The Investigative Project on Terrorism, accessed September 9, 2010, http://www.investigativeproject.org/profile/181

271 http://www.huffingtonpost.com/salam-al-marayati/five-swirling-questions-a_b_687532.html. Accessed August 29, 2010.

272 American Muslim Task Force's website, http://www.americanmuslimtaskforce.net

273 Organization of The Islamic Conference website, About OIC: http://oic-oci.org/page_detail.asp?p_id=52

274 Speech of His Excellency Prof. Ekmeleddin Ihsanoglu, Secretary General of the Organization of the Islamic Conference, at the Thirty-Fifth Session of the Council of Foreign Ministers of the Organization of the Islamic Conference, Kampala – Republic of Uganda, 18-20 June 2008, OIC/CFM-35/2008/SG-SP. Cited hereafter as "Speech of OIC Sec Gen Ihsanoglu."

275 Organization of The Islamic Conference website, About OIC: http://oic-oci.org/page_detail.asp?p_id=52

276 Article 7, Chapter IV "Islamic Summit," Charter of the Organization of the Islamic Conference.

277 Article 9, Chapter V "Extraordinary Sessions," Charter of the Organization of the Islamic Conference.

278 Article 10, Chapter V "Council of Foreign Ministers," Charter of the Organization of the Islamic Conference.

279 Speech of OIC Sec Gen Ihsanoglu.

280 Final Communiqué of the Eleventh Session of the Islamic Summit
Conference (Session of the Muslim Ummah in the 21st Century),
Dakar – Republic of Senegal, 6-7 Rabiul Awwal 1429 H (13-14
March 2008).

281 OIC Ten Years Programme, http://www.oic-oci.org/ex-
summit/english/10-years-plan.htm accessed September 8, 2010

282 Article 25,
http://www1.umn.edu/humanrts/instree/cairodeclaration.html
accessed September 8, 2010

283 Hui Min Neo, "UN rights body narrowly passes Islamophobia resolution," Agence France-Presse, March 25, 2010, accessed September
8, 2010,
http://www.canada.com/story_print.html?id=2725805&sponsor
=hp-storytoolbox

284 Mohammed Ali Al Taskhiri, *Journal Islam Today*, "Terrorism: Factors
and Countermeasures"
http://www.isesco.org.ma/english/publications/Islamtoday/26/
P2.php, September 8 2010

285 Office of the Secretary of Defense, "Department of Defense Implementation of Recommendations from the Independent Review
Related to Fort Hood," August 18, 2010, accessed September 8,
2010.
http://www.defense.gov/news/d20100820FortHoodFollowon.p
df

286 Text of Mayor Bloomberg's speech "following a vote that clears most
major hurdles for the construction of a mosque near Ground Zero," *The Wall Street Journal*, August 3, 2010.
http://online.wsj.com/article/NA_WSJ_PUB:SB100014240527
4870354560457540767322190 8474.html. Accessed August 29,
2010

287 "Salem al-Mekki: Bin Laden and I ... and the Americans," *The NEFA
Foundation*.

288 Malik, *The Quranic Concept of War*, 54.

289 *Ibid*, 58.

290 "Obama at Odds with Petraeus doctrine on 'Islam'," *The Washington Times*, July 11, 2010.

291 Explanatory Memorandum

292 Constitution of the Islamic Republic of Iran, "The Religious Army" (1989).

293 Imam Khomeini, "Islamic Governance: Governance of the Jurist" (1970).

294 Robert Baer, "Why Sanctions Won't Beat Iran's Revolutionary Guards," *Time*, February 17, 2010, accessed August 31, 2010, http://www.time.com/time/world/article/0,8599,1964509,00.html. In this piece, Baer speaks of a "military takeover" in Iran and quotes U.S. Secretary of State Hillary Clinton, who told a town hall meeting that "The Supreme Leader, the President [and] the parliament is being supplanted, and Iran is moving toward a military dictatorship." See also Abbas Milani, "Is Iran Heading Toward a Military Coup?" *CBS News*, June 18t 2009, accessed August 31, 2010, http://www.cbsnews.com/stories/2009/06/18/opinion/main5095841.shtml

295 Greg Bruno, "Iran's Revolutionary Guards—a Backgrounder," *Council on Foreign Relations*, June 22nd, 2009. See also the Chapter, "The Religious Army" in the 1989 Iranian constitution.

296 Christopher W. Holton, "Iranian Entanglements," *National Review Online*, March 21, 2008, accessed August 4, 2010, http://article.nationalreview.com/352385/iranian-entanglements/christopher-w-holton

297 Kenneth Katzman, "Iran's Activities and Influence in Iraq," *Congressional Research Service*, June 4, 2009.

298 "Hundreds of Taliban Were Trained in Iran: Report," *Daily Times*, March 22, 2010. See also: Miles Amoore, "Iranians Train Taliban to Use Roadside Bombs," *Times Online*, March 21, 2010.

299 Kenneth Timmerman, "Experts Warn of Escalating Chavez Threat," *Newsmax*, April 26, 2010. See also Tim Collie, "Venezuela-Iran Terror Network Growing in Latin America," *Newsmax*, January 29, 2009; Jim Kouri, "Muslim Terrorists in South America Join Forces With Drug Cartels," *Examiner*, February 22, 2010; Sara Carter, "Hezbollah Uses Mexican Drug Routes Into U.S., *Washington Times*, March 27, 2009; Douglas Farah, "Hezbollah's External Support Network in West Africa and Latin America," *International Assessment and Strategy Center*, August 4, 2006, accessed April 28, 2010, http://www.strategycenter.net/research/pubID.118/pub_detail.asp

300 Anthony Cordesman, "Iranian Weapons of Mass Destruction: Doctrine, Policy, and Command," *Center for Strategic and International Studies*," (Working Draft), January 12, 2009, accessed April 28, 2010, http://csis.org/files/media/csis/pubs/090112_iran_wmd_policy.pdf

301 "Qods (Jerusalem) Force, Iranian Revolutionary Guard Corps, (IRGC) Pasdaran-*e Inqilab*," *Global Security*, accessed April 28, 2010,http://www.globalsecurity.org/intell/world/iran/qods.htm

302 Gretchen Peters, *Seeds of Terror: How Heroin is Bankrolling the Taliban and Al Qaeda*, (Thomas Dunne Books, 2009).

303 Thomas Jocelyn, "Petraeus on Iran & al Qaeda," *Weekly Standard*, March 17 , 2010, accessed April 28, 2010, http://www.weeklystandard.com/blogs/petraeus-iran-al-qaeda

304 Thomas Jocelyn, "Petraeus on Iran & al Qaeda," *Weekly Standard*, March 17 , 2010, accessed April 28, 2010, http://www.weeklystandard.com/blogs/petraeus-iran-al-qaeda. See also Dan Darling,, "Iran Amok," *Weekly Standard*, February 26, 2006, accessed April 28, 2010 http://www.weeklystandard.com/Content/Public/Articles/000/000/006/782ppuml.asp

305 Scott Peterson, "How Iran Would Retaliate If It Comes To War," *Christian Science Monitor*, June 20, 2008, accessed April 28, 2010,

http://www.csmonitor.com/World/Middle-East/2008/0620/p07s04-wome.html

306 Anthony Cordesman, "Iran's Revolutionary Guards, the Al Quds Force, and Other Intelligence and Security Forces,"(Rough Working Draft), *Center for Strategic and International Studies*, August 16, 2007, accessed April 28, 2010, http://csis.org/files/media/csis/pubs/070816_cordesman_report.pdf

307 Clare Lopez, "Rise of the Iran Lobby: Tehran's Front Groups Move On—And Into—The Obama Administration," *Center for Security Policy*, February 25, 2009.

308 *Ibid.*

309 *Ibid.*

310 Carl Anthony Wege, "The Hezbollah Security Apparatus," *Perspectives on Terrorism*, Volume II, Issue 7 (April, 2008).

311 Nicholas Blanford, "Hezbollah Says It's Ready For Fresh War With Israel—And Stronger Now," *Christian Science Monitor*, May 7, 2010.

312 "The 'New Hezbollah' Built By Syria Sparks ME Summer War Fears," *DebkaFile*, April 18th, 2010. See also "At a Glance: An Assessment of Hezbollah's Military Capability," *Gulf News*, May 3, 2009, at http://archive.gulfnews.com/articles/06/07/17/10053556.html; and "Despite International Commitments to Prevent Weapons Smuggling, Iran-backed Hezbollah and Hamas Continue to Re-arm," *The Israel Project Newsletter*, February 11, 2010.

313 USCFL, "Everything You Need to Know About Hezbollah and its Terror Network," May 2003, accessed April 28, 2010, http://www.freelebanon.org/articles/a415.htm

314 See Mark Perry, "Red Team: CENTCOM Thinks Outside the Box on Hamas and Hezbollah," *Foreign Policy*, June 30, 2010, accessed July 17, 2010, http://www.foreignpolicy.com/articles/2010/06/29/red_team

315 http://archives.cnn.com/2000/LAW/07/21/charlotte.raids.02/

316 Ronen Bergman, *The Secret War with Iran* (Free Press, 2008), 212.

317 "Hezbollah's Hassan Nasrallah & Top Command Holed up in Hermel," *Debka*, July 17, 2006.

318 Rachel Ehrenfeld, *Funding Evil: How Terrorism is Financed and How to Stop It* (Chicago; Bonus, 2003), 130.

319 Michael Rubin, "The Enduring Iran-Syria-Hezbollah Axis," *AEI Middle East Outlook*, December 2009.

320 Doug Farah, "Hezbollah's External Support Network in West Africa and Latin America," *StrategyCenter.net*, August 4, 2006, accessed July 8, 2010, http://www.strategycenter.net/research/pubID.118/pub_detail.asp

321 *Ibid.*

322 Ehrenfeld, *Funding Evil*, 127.

323 Ronen Bergman, *The Secret War With Iran,Free Press,* September, 2009, 171.

324 "Hezbollah's Hassan Nasrallah & Top Command Holed Up in Hermel," *Debka*, July 17, 2006.

325 Ehrenfeld, *Funding Evil*, 145.

326 Intelligence and Terrorism Information Center at the Center for Special Studies (ITICCS), "Hezbollah," http://www.intelligence.org.il/eng/bu/hizbullah/hezbollah.htm

327 ITICCS http://www.intelligence.org.il/eng/bu/hizbullah/hezbollah.htm

328 Sara Carter, "Hezbollah Uses Mexican Drug Routes Into U.S.," *Washington Times*, March 27, 2009.

329 See the Intelligence and Terrorism Information Center bulletin of August 10, 2009 for an unusual mutual public affirmation of the Hezbollah-Iran relationship. On July 25, 2009, Ali Akbar Velayati, senior advisor to Supreme Leader Ali Khamenei, told *Al-Jazeera* TV that Iran gave both Hamas and Hezbollah full and comprehensive support. Shortly thereafter, on July 30, 2009, Sheikh Naim

Qassem, Hassan Nasrallah's Hezbollah deputy, told the Lebanese daily newspaper *Nahar al-Shabab*, that Hezbollah regards Khamenei as a "guardian jurist," from whom Hezbollah receives its political and religious legitimacy to operate.

330 See the June 30, 2010 *Foreign Policy* article by Mark Perry, titled "Red Team: CENTCOM Thinks Outside the Box on Hamas and Hezbollah" which describes senior U.S. military officers suggestions that outreach by the U.S. could help integrate Hezbollah more completely into the Lebanese political system and effect a reconciliation between Hamas and Fatah that would force Israel to recognize a Palestinian state. The CENTCOM authors fail to recognize the Islamic jihad and *shariah* agenda common to Fatah, Hamas, Hezbollah, and all Islamic organizations.

331 Ami Isseroff, "Hamas History," *Mideast Web*,
http://www.mideastweb.org/Hamashistory.htm

332 Isseroff. Ibid.

333 Often called the Hamas Charter, "Covenant" is actually a more accurate term because it better defines what is, in fact, a pact between Hamas and Allah.

334 Jonathan Schanzer, *Hamas vs Fatah: The Struggle for Palestine*, (Palgrave/Macmillan, 2008), Ch. 3.

335 Matthew Levitt, "The Real Connection between Iran and Hamas," *Counterterrorism Blog*, January 12, 2009. According to Levitt, in March 2007, Khaled Mashaal, HAMAS political bureau chief based in Damascus, visited Iran and stated that Iran had been providing financial support for Hamas since it took office in 2006 and would continue to do so.

336 Weisman, Steven R., "Rice Admits U.S. Underestimated Hamas Strength," *New York Times*, January 30, 2006. Accessed online 31 August 2010 at
http://www.nytimes.com/2006/01/30/international/middleeast/30diplo.html

337 Schanzer, *Hamas vs. Fatah*, (Ch. 8-9)

338 Herzog, Michael, "The Hamas Conundrum," *Foreign Affairs*, February 8, 2010. Accessed online 10 July 10 at http://www.foreignaffairs.com/articles/65952/michael-herzog/the-Hamas-conundrum

339 Such toxic indoctrination by both the ostensibly "moderate" Palestinian Authority – said to be a "partner for peace" for the United States and Israel – and by Hamas is comprehensively monitored by Palestinian Media Watch: http://www.palwatch.org/. Also, as noted elsewhere in this report, the Middle East Media Research Institute (MEMRI) also does an invaluable job collecting and translating materials from these sources, among others: www.memri.org.

340 "Hamas Summer Camps in the Gaza Strip," *Intelligence and Terrorism Information Center*, August 16, 2009.

341 "Masked vandals damage UNRWA summer camp," *Ma'an News Agency* (Gaza), June 28, 2010. Accessed online 10 July 2010 at http://www.maannews.net/eng/ViewDetails.aspx?ID=295158

342 "Hamas 2010 budget mainly 'foreign aid' from Iran," *World Tribune*, January 5, 2010. Accessed online 10 July 2010 at http://www.worldtribune.com/worldtribune/WTARC/2010/me_Hamas0005_01_05.asp

343 Levitt, "The Real Connection between Iran and Hamas".

344 "Egypt's Muslim Brotherhood and Iran, Rapprochement Between Sunnis and Shiites?" *The Global Muslim Brotherhood Daily Report*, April 23, 2009. Accessed online 10 July 2010 at http://globalmbreport.org/?p=1430&print=1. See also Gerecht, Reuel Marc, "Iran's Hamas Strategy," *The Wall Street Journal*, January 7, 2009.

345 "The Muslim Brotherhood, Hamas and Iran—A Complex Picture," *The Global Muslim Brotherhood Daily Report*, January 7, 2009.

346 James Hider, "Al Qaeda has infiltrated Gaza with help of Hamas, says Abbas," *The Sunday Times*, February 28, 2008. Accessed online 10 July 2010 at

http://www.timesonline.co.uk/tol/news/world/middle_east/article3447261.ece

347 *Ibid.*

348 Dore Gold, "Hamas and al Qaeda are the Same," *Arutz 10,* January 6, 2010.

349 Madeleine Gruen, "Why We Should Care About Hizb ut-Tahrir in the United States," *The Investigative Project on Terrorism,* July 14, 2010; Accessed 15 July 2010 online at http://www.investigativeproject.org/2060/why-we-should-care-about-hizb-ut-tahrir-in

350 Jean-Pierre Filiu, "Hizb ut-Tahrir and the fantasy of the caliphate," *Le Monde Diplomatique* (June 2008).

351 Zeyno Baran, "Islam's ideological vanguard," *International Herald Tribune,* October 30, 2005.

352 *Ibid.*

353 Taqiuddin al-Nabhani, *Structure of a Party,* (London, Al-Khalifah Publications, 200), 11.

354 Quoted in Ziauddin Sardar, "The Long History of Violence Behind Hizb ut-Tahrir," *New Statesman,* November 14, 2005.

355 Zeyno Baran, "Fighting the War of Ideas," *Foreign Affairs,* Nov.-Dec. 2005, 68.

356 Evgenii Novikov, "The Recruiting and Organizational Structure of Hizb ut-Tahrir," *Terrorism Monitor,* vol. 2, no. 22, May 9, 2005.

357 John Solomon, "FBI Agent Linked Arab Students Training at Aviation Schools to Radical Group, bin Laden Threat," *Associated Press,* May 22, 2002.

358 *Ibid.*

359 Shiv Malik, "For Allah and the caliphate," *New Statesman,* September 13, 2004.

360 "Radical cleric 'taught' bomb suspects," *BBC,* May 2, 2003.

361 Larry Neumeister, "Syed Hashmi, American Student, Pleads Guilty to Helping Al Qaeda," *Associated Press*, April 27, 2010.

362 Jonathan Wald, "N.Y. Man Admits He Aided Al Qaeda, Set Up Jihad Camp," *CNN*, August 11, 2004.

363 Madeleine Gruen, "Hizb-ut-Tahrir's Activities in the United States," *Terrorism Monitor*, vol. 5, no. 16, August 16, 2007, 8.

364 Diane Macedo, "Islamic supremacist groups holds first U.S. conference," *Fox News*, July 17, 2009.

365 Hoda Osman, "Extremist Islamic conference shut down," *CBS News*, June 25, 2009.

366 Accessed August 28, 2010, http://thehizbuttahrirwatch.wordpress.com/category/news-about-hizb-ut-tahrir/hut-america/2010-conference-canceled

367 Sean O'Neill, "Senior Member of Extreme Islamist Group Hizb ut-Tahrir Teaches at LSE," *The Times*, January 15, 2010.

368 Shiv Malik, "'Guardian' Man Revealed as Hardline Islamist," *The Independent*, July 15, 2005; "Background: The Guardian and Dilpazier Aslam," *The Guardian*, July 22, 2005.

369 Shiv Malik, "How Militant Islamists Are Infiltrating Britain's Top Companies," *The Independent*, September 11, 2005.

370 "Reid to examine extremist claims," *BBC*, November 15, 2006.

371 James Slack and Gordon Rayner, "Extremist at the Home Office Will Keep His Job," *Daily Mail*, November 16, 2006.

372 James Brandon, "The Caliphate: One Nation, Under Allah, with 1.5 Billion Muslims," *Christian Science Monitor*, May 10, 2006.

373 Lisa Myers, "FBI Monitors Islamic Group for Terror Ties," *NBC News*, January 18, 2005.

374 Paul Lewis, "Inside the Islamic Group Accused by MI5 and FBI," *The Guardian*, August 19, 2006.

375 Jane Perlez, "Pakistani Group, Suspected by West of Jihadist Ties, Holds Conclave Despite Ban," *New York Times*, November 19,

2007, accessed September 5, 2010,
http://www.nytimes.com/2007/11/19/world/asia/19jamaat.ht
ml

376 Andrew Gilligan Perlez, "Terror Linked Group to Build London's Biggest Mosque," *Evening Standard*, July 17, 2009.

377 Dominic Whiteman, "Not Bowled Over by Tablighi Jamaat," *Global Politician*, March 22, 2007.

378 Myers, *ibid.*

379 Susan Sachs, "A Muslim Missionary Group Draws New Scrutiny in U.S." *New York Times*, July 14, 2003.

380 *Ibid.*

381 Jerry Zremski, "On Call to Aid Al Qaeda from Unlikely Places," *Buffalo News*, September 18, 2002; Matthew Purdy and Lowell Bergman, "Unclear Danger: Inside the Lackawanna Terror Case," *New York Times*, October 12, 2003

382 "Suspect Mulled Attack on Jews, Attorney Says," *Seattle Post-Intelligencer*, October 12, 2002.

383 Dennis Wagner, "Feds: Arizonan Tied to Terror," *Arizona Republic*, January 19, 2006.

384 Paul Cruickshank, Nic Robertson and Ken Shiffman, "The Radicalization of an All-American Kid," *CNN*, May 13, 2010.

385 Philip Johnston and Peter Foster, "The 'Peaceful' Group Linked to Radical Muslims," *Daily Telegraph*, July 11, 2007.

386 Amardeep Bassey, "London Bomber Linked to Strict Islamic Group," *Sunday Mercury*, July 17, 2005.

387 Andrew Norfolk, "How Bombers' Town is Turning Into an Enclave of Isolationists," *The Times*, October 21, 2006.

388 BBC Monitoring European, March 13, 2007.

389 Victoria Burnett, "Spain Arrests 14 in Plotting Attack," *New York Times*, January 19, 2008.

390 BBC Monitoring Middle East, "Paper Carried Report on Al Qaeda Recruitment, Fundraising in Saudi Arabia," July 16, 2008.

391 Mark Hosenball, "Another Holy War, Waged on American Soil," *Newsweek*, February 28, 1994.

392 Francis Clines, "U.S.-Born Suspect in Bombing Plots: Zealous Causes and Civic Roles," *New York Times*, June 28, 1993.

393 "FBI Searches for Terrorists' Weapons," *New York Daily News*, June 27, 1993.

394 StratFor, "United States: The Jamaat ul-Fuqra Threat," June 3, 2005; Benjamin Weiser, Susan Sachs and David Kocieniewski, "U.S. Sees Brooklyn Link to World Terror Network," *New York Times*, October 22, 1998.

395 U.S. Department of State, Office of the Coordinator for Counter-Terrorism, *Patterns of Global Terrorism: 1994*, 43.

396 Theresa Boyle, "'Cold-blooded' Plot Could Have Killed Thousands," *Toronto Star*, December 22, 1993.

397 Regional Organized Crime Information Center, *Jamaat ul-Fuqra: Gilani Followers Conducting Paramilitary Training in U.S.*, 2006, 2.

398 "Sheikh Gilani," *CBS News*, March 13, 2002.

399 Daren Fonda, "On the Trail of Daniel Pearl," *Time*, September 27, 2003,. accessed September 5, 2010, http://www.time.com/time/arts/article/0,8599,490640,00.html

400 David Kaplan, "Made in the U.S.A.," *U.S. News & World Report*, June 10, 2002.

401 http://www.youtube.com/watch?v=c8_82YGXJe0. Accessed August 28, 2010.

402 The Christian Action Network's website, http://www.christianaction.org

403 Stewart Bell, "Extremists Train at Communes," *National Post*, June 22, 2006.

404 Quoted in Stewart Bell, "The Black Muslim Connection," *National Post*, October 25, 2002.

405 Mary Tabor, "A Trial in Canada is Watched in U.S.," *New York Times*, October 16, 1993.

406 Charlie Brennan, "Ul-Fuqra Tied to Colorado Crimes," *Rocky Mountain News*, February 12, 2002.

407 Colorado Attorney General John Suthers, "Information Regarding Colorado's Investigation and Prosecution of Members of Jamaat Ul Fuqra."

408 Jo Thomas and Ralph Blumenthal, "Rural Muslims Draw New, Unwanted Attention," *New York Times*, January 3, 2002.

409 Howard Pankratz, "Message Spurred Kidnap Arrest Pakistani Sent Communique to Va.," *Denver Post*, February 10, 2002.

410 Harry V. Jaffa, "The American Founding as the Best Regime," *The Claremont Institute*, July 4, 2007, accessed July 14, 2010, http://www.claremont.org/publications/pubid.682/pub_detail.a sp

411 NIV, 1 Peter 2:13

412 NIV, Mark 12:17

413 Accessed July 14, 2010. http://www.vahistorical.org/onthisday/11686.htm

414 Abdul Maududi, *Jihad in Islam*, (Holy Qur'an Publishing House, Beirut, Lebanon, 1980), 5.

415 -*Bukhari, Hadith,* 9:: 84: 57.

416 *The American Annual Register for 1827-28-29*, New York, 1830, published in Chapters X-XIV, 267-402. As cited in "John Quincy Adams Knew Jihad," by Andrew G. Bostom, accessed September 20, 2010, http://archive.frontpagemag.com/readArticle.aspx?ARTID=112 83

417 *Ibid.*

418 al-Misri, *Reliance of the Traveler, op.cit.,* 599.

419 Mark Levin, *Liberty and Tyranny: A Conservative Manifesto,* (Threshold Editions 2009), 28-29: "Islamic law, or *shariah,* dictates the most intricate aspects of daily life, from politics and finance to dating and hygiene. There is not, and never has been, support for a national contract of this sort in America."

420 Bat Ye'or, *Eurabia: The Euro-Arab Axis,* Farleigh Dickinson University Press, 2005, 192

421 *Ibid.,* 192.

422 *Ibid,* 197.

423 *Ibid,* 192.

424 *Ibid,* 197.

425 Ibn Warraq, "Democracy in a Carton," *Islam Watch,* February 4, 2006.

426 *Ibid.*

427 *Ibid.*

428 Stephen Coughlin, "'To Our Great Detriment': Ignoring What Extremists Say About *Jihad,*" unpublished thesis, July 2007, http://www.strategycenter.net/docLib/20080107_Coughlin_Ex tremistJihad.pdf.

429 William Gawthrop, "The Sources and Patterns of Terrorism in Islamic Law," *The Vanguard: Journal of the Military Intelligence Corps Association* 11, no. 4 (2006), 10.

430 J. Michael Waller, LDESP faculty member, letter to Senators Joseph I. Lieberman and Susan Collins, Senate Committee on Homeland Security and Governmental Affairs, September 11, 2010. Waller, who testified before a Senate panel on ISNA's status as a Muslim Brotherhood front in 2003, filed the complaint with the ISNA director and was ultimately suspended from teaching in the LDESP program.

431 Quadrennial Defense Review Report, February 2010, accessed July 17, 2010,

http://www.defense.gov/qdr/images/QDR_as_of_12Feb10_10 00.pdf

432 National Security Strategy, May 2010, accessed July 17, 2010, http://www.whitehouse.gov/sites/default/files/rss_viewer/natio nal_security_strategy.pdf

433 "Terminology to Define the Terrorists: Recommendations from American Muslims," *Department of Homeland Security, Office for Civil Rights and Civil Liberties*, January, 2008, accessed July 17, 2010, http://www.investigativeproject.org/documents/misc/126.pdf

434 "Federal Bureau of Investigation: Counterterrorism Analytical Lexico," accessed July 17, 2010, http://cryptome.org/fbi-ct-lexicon.pdf

435 "Words That Work and Words That Don't: A Guide for Counterterrorism Communication," *National Counterterrorism Center*, Volume 2 Issue 10, March 14, 2008, accessed July 17, 2010, http://www.investigativeproject.org/documents/misc/127.pdf

436 See the "Diversity Guidelines for Countering Racial, Ethnic and Religious Profiling" at the Society of Professional Journalists website, accessed June 28, 2010, http://www.spj.org/divguidelines.asp

437 Patrick Poole, "What's in a Name? 'Jihad' vs 'Hiraba,'" *American Thinker*, September 18, 2007, accessed September 5, 2010, http://www.americanthinker.com/2007/09/whats_in_a_name_ jihad_vs_hirab.html

438 The NCTC document may be found at The Investigative Project on Terrorism, accessed August 31, 2010, http://www.investigativeproject.org/documents/misc/127.pdf

439 http://www.investigativeproject.org/documents/misc/127.pdf

440 See U.S. Code Title 18, Part 1, Chapter 115, Chapter 2382, "Misprision of Treason," *Cornell University Law School.*, accessed July 18, 2010, http://www.law.cornell.edu/uscode/18/2382.html

441 Rule 1.1 Competence, *Aba Model Rules Of Professional Conduct* (2002), Amended February 5th, 2002, American Bar Association

House of Delegates, Philadelphia, Pennsylvania, per Report No. 401, Rule 1.1, accessed June 4th, 2007, http://www.lexis.com/research/retrieve/frames?_m=ffaba7e13d c1219fdf879cff02a072ea&_fmtstr=CUSTOM&docnum=1&_sta rtdoc=1&wchp=dGLbVzW-zSkAb&_md5=926be6625f82 e0319c6aad2190304e5f

442 Video of Brennan's CSIS speech was accessed July 10, 2010, http://www.eyeblast.tv/public/checker.aspx?v=XdqGaGaGaG

443 See http://www.cbsnews.com/8301-503544_162-6190999- 503544.html accessed on July 10, 2010.

444 Video of Brennan's Nixon Center address was accessed July 10, 2010, http://www.youtube.com/watch?v=WHaabrvVTBw&feature=pl ayer_embedded

445 Video of Brennan's address accessed on July 10, 2010,http://www.pipelinenews.org/2010/John-Brennans-Al- Quds-NYU-Address-Providing-Aid.html

446 "Imam's Message Announcing Quds Day", August 7, 1979 (16 Mur- dad 1358 AHS). *Sahifa-yi Nur*, Vol. 8, 229, accessed July 10, 2010, http://www2.irib.ir/worldservice/imam/palestin_E/10.htm

447 *Ibid.*

448 *Ibid.*

449 David Yerushalmi, Esq., "Shariah's "Black Box": Civil Liability and Criminal Exposure Surrounding Shariah-Compliant Finance," *Utah Law Review*, Vol. 2008, No. 3.

450 "Islamic Finance 101", November 6th, 2008, accessed April 24, 2010, http://www.saneworks.us/uploads/news/applications/7.pdf

451 Joy Brighton, "Shariah Finance", YouTube presentation, accessed April 24, 2010, http://www.youtube.com/watch?v=VmRbum9x0nU

452 Jeffrey Immon, "The Treasury, AIG and Sharia-Compliant Finance: It's Your Money," *Right Side News,* November 14, 2008, accessed April 24, 2010,

http://www.rightsidenews.com/200811152617/culture-wars/the-treasury-aig-and-sharia-compliant-financeits-your-money.html

453 David Patten, "Lawsuit: U.S. Controls Unconstitutional AIG 'Islamic Finance' Unit," *Newsmax*, March 28, 2009, accessed April 24, 2010, http://newsmax.com/Newsfront/shariah-finance-aig/2009/03/23/id/329005; See also "Sharia Compliant Product Could Mean Trouble for AIG and Federal Government." *Thomas More Law Center*, May 29, 2009, accessed April 24, 2010, http://www.rightsidenews.com/200905294953/homeland-security/sharia-compliant-product-could-mean-trouble-for-aig-and-federal-government.html

454 Patten; see the CHARTIS Takaful website at http://www.zawya.com/cm/profile.cfm/cid1004663/CHARTIS%20Takaful; See also "Kevin J. Murray, Plaintiff, v. Timothy F. Geithner, in his Official Capacity as Secretary, U.S. Department Of Treasury; Board Of Governors of the Federal Reserve System, Defendants," in the United States District Court for the Eastern District Of Michigan. Case No. 08-CV-15147

455 Patten, *op.cit.*

456 Frank Gaffney, "Shariah Finance, Criminal Wrongdoing in the AIG Takeover: Will the Special Inspector General for the TARP Funds Investigate the Illegal Trust?" *BigGovernment.com*, February 3, 2010, accessed April 24, 2010, http://biggovernment.com/fgaffney/2010/02/03/shariah-finance-criminal-wrongdoing-in-the-aig-takeover-will-the-special-inspector-general-for-the-tarp-funds-investigate-the-illegal-trust

The **Center for Security Policy** is a non-profit, non-partisan national security organization that specializes in identifying policies, actions, and resource needs that are vital to American security and then ensures that such issues are the subject of both focused, principled examination and effective action by recognized policy experts, appropriate officials, opinion leaders, and the general public. The Center was founded in 1988 and has worked to great effect since then in the establishment of successful national security policies through the use of all elements of national power – diplomatic, informational, military, and economic strength.

The philosophy of "Peace through Strength" is not a slogan for military might but a belief that America's national power must be preserved and properly used for it holds a unique global role in maintaining peace and stability. Today's national security threats compel us to ensure we are strong and prepared. We as a nation must also work to undermine the ideological foundations of totalitarianism and Islamist extremism with at least as much skill, discipline and tenacity as President Reagan employed against Communism to prevail in the Cold War.

The role of the Center for Security Policy is to help our government, countrymen and other freedom-loving nations conceptualize, conduct and succeed on this front. The Center's dedicated staff, associates and advisors constitute the Special Forces in this war of ideas – equipped with the experience, imagination, expertise, agility and drive not just to advance strategies for victory, but to get them adopted and implemented.

Find out more at **securefreedom.org**

REPRODUCTION RIGHTS

BULK ORDERS

For bulk orders of *Shariah: The Threat to America,* contact Dave Reaboi, Director of Communications, at dreaboi@securefreedom.org

Made in the USA
Lexington, KY
17 October 2010